ORDERS AND DECORATIONS
OF EUROPE
IN COLOR

The George Medal   (see p 143)

ORDERS AND
DECORATIONS
OF EUROPE
IN COLOR

by

Paul Hieronymussen

and photographed by
Aage Strüwing

THE MACMILLAN COMPANY
NEW YORK

Published in the United States by
The Macmillan Company, New York, 1967.
Library of Congress Catalog Card Number: 67–18403

Originally published in Danish as *Europaeiske Ordner i Farver*
by Politikens Forlag.
Copyright for the World © Politikens Forlag, 1966
Translated into English by Christine Crowley
© Blandford Press, London, 1967.

Text filmset in Malta G.C. by St. Paul's Press Ltd.,
and printed and bound in Denmark.
Color plates printed by
I. Chr. Sørensen & Co., Copenhagen

114616

ACKNOWLEDGMENTS

The Publishers gratefully acknowledge the help and advice of Major General C. H. Colquhoun, C.B., C.V.O., O.B.E., Secretary of the Central Chancery of the Orders of Knighthood, in the preparation of the British sections of this book.

Acknowledgment is due to Peter Parkinson for the photographs of some British insignia (Nos. 70–2, 82–5, 98–102) and to Mrs. V. Goddard for the monochrome drawings on pages 242–251. Also to the Royal Mint for facilities to sketch and photograph some of the British medals and to Collingwood (Jewellers) Ltd. for the loan of the Medal of the Royal Red Cross and First Class Badge as references.

CONTENTS

PREFACE

The Pocket Encyclopaedia of ORDERS AND DECORATIONS OF EUROPE IN COLOR is a reference book of current matters relating to Orders and Decorations. As such it covers the official Orders of all European countries which may today be conferred on the countries' own citizens and also on citizens of other countries. Orders whose conferment has been discontinued, the historic Orders and Orders of a purely national character conferred only on the countries' own citizens therefore fall outside the framework of the book. Periodical Orders, such as wartime Orders of Merit and certain specific Orders from the last World War, have however been included as far as possible.

The book comprises three main sections. First there is a brief *Introduction* with a practical survey of the history of matters pertaining to Orders and Decorations, their organisation and activities. Next there is an *Atlas of Orders* comprising 80 colour plates with reproductions in 7-colour printing of the insignia of 200 current international European Orders. The third section is an *Encyclopaedia of Orders* with detailed information relating to the Orders illustrated. As an appendix to the latter, the book contains a detailed reference to certain official national British medals and decorations of honour, as well as, in a special section, the official regulations applying to the wearing of decorations.

The information given in the book is based on the statutes and other official documents of the respective Orders, supplemented by the most recent literature from each country concerning Orders. The book does not claim to be a scientific work, but is intended to supply the need for a practical and instructive reference book concerning this special subject.

It has been possible to provide the almost complete material, reproduced by colour photography, in this book only with the support and understanding of a great variety of contacts all over Europe. The Meyer Collection of Orders at Holte in Denmark has been the basis. This collection covers more than half the insignia reproduced, and the promptitude and helpfulness of its Founder cannot be too highly appreciated. The Editors also owe a great debt of gratitude to a number of Heads of State, Royal Houses and Chancelleries of Orders all over Europe who, either directly, through their Missions in Denmark, or through Denmark's Missions in the countries concerned, have lent, via the Danish Foreign Office, insignia of Orders for photographing in this country and have made official material available for the preparation of the text. Certain difficulties in this respect have been overcome only by the personal application of the Editors to a number of important personages all over Europe, for example, the former Soviet Premier *Nikita Kruschev*, the former German Federal Chancellor, Dr. *Konrad Adenauer* and the French President, General *Charles de Gaulle*

Messrs. *M. W. Mørch & Søns Eftf.*, Copenhagen, were responsible for mounting the ribands of the Orders reproduced.   *THE EDITORS*

INTRODUCTION: <small>HISTORY</small>

Religious Orders of Chivalry

The origin of Orders and decorations must be sought in the mediaeval organisation of the Catholic Church, whose Religious Orders, the monastic communities, formed the basis. The word "Order" from the Latin "ordo", referred at that time to an association of a limited circle of persons who took upon themselves certain obligations, and who subjected themselves to certain rules. At the time of the Crusades the foundation of Orders in the monastic systems was transferred to Knighthood, and among the crusading knights in the Holy Land a number of Religious Orders of Chivalry were instituted, whose main objects were to fight for the Christian faith and to care for pilgrims and the sick. The best known of these are the *Order of the Knights Templars,* the *Order of Malta* and the *Teutonic Order*, which all exercised considerable power, and at times achieved great political influence.

These Religious Orders of Chivalry were confirmed by the Pope and were directly subordinated to the Holy See, but otherwise they acted independently under the leadership of a Grand Master, elected for life among the knights, assisted by a College of Arms composed of the holders of the highest dignities of the Order.

The Order of the Knights Templars

The Order of the Knights Templars was founded in 1118 by the French knight Hugo de Payns, who became the first Grand Master of the Order. It received its name because it was stationed near the place in Jerusalem where Solomon's temple had stood; the Knights Templars called themselves "Christi milites", Christ's knights. The Order, which was confirmed by Pope Honorius the Second in 1123, was organised according to the Benedictine rule. The members wore a white mantle with a red Cross of St. George as a habit. The main object of the Order was the fight against the infidel. This was later supplemented by hostel and hospital services. Its members were divided into three categories, i.e. knights, who were required to be of noble birth, priests and brother servants. The Knights Templars participated with great bravery in all Crusades and battles against the Mohammedan until the Holy Land was lost in 1291. The Order then moved its headquarters to Cyprus, and later to France. From here it spread over the greater part of Western Europe except Scandinavia. Because of its enormous wealth, the Order became a dangerous power factor and a thorn in the flesh of the worldly rulers. This led to the Order being abolished in 1312 by Pope Clement the Fifth at the instigation of King Philip the Fair of France. The members of the Order were imprisoned, accused of heresy and subjected to torture. Many of them died at the stake, including the Grand Master, Jacques de Molay. The properties of the dissolved Order were given to the Order of Malta, but became confiscated to the Crown in France and in several other West European countries. For the subsequent fate of the Order, see the *Order of Christ* on pages 198–200, 221–3.

The Order of Malta

In contrast to the Order of the Knights Templars, whose main object was the fight against the infidel, the Order of Malta was a hospital Order from its inception. The Order originated from a hospital founded about 1070 in Jerusalem by Italian merchants, whose principal, Gerard, after the conquest of Jerusalem by the Knights Templars in 1099, founded a brotherhood of lay brothers. This was confirmed by Pope Pascal the Second in 1113 as The Hospital Order of St. John of Jerusalem, named after John the Baptist, the patron saint of the hospital. The Order was organised according to the Benedictine rule. The members wore as a habit a black cloak with a white Latin cross, which was later altered to a red cloak with a white Latin cross in times of peace and a black cloak with a white Maltese cross in times of war. In about 1125, the Grand Master at the time, the French knight Raymond de Puy, extended its help to cover not only pilgrims but also military escorts. In this way the Order was converted into a Religious Order of Chivalry, its members being divided into knights for war service, priests for clerical service, and lay brothers for hospital service.

Knights not of noble descent could be admitted into the Order as "knights of grace" in exceptional cases, in contrast to the actual "knights by right" who were required to be of noble birth. Together with the Knights Templars, the Knights of St. John took part in subsequent Crusades and battles against the Mohammedan until the Holy Land was lost in 1291. After a short stay in Cyprus, the Order moved its headquarters to Rhodes in 1310, from which came the name "Knights of Rhodes". Later they moved to Malta, from which is derived the name "Knights of Malta". The Order remained there until General Bonaparte occupied the island and drove them out in 1798. Both Rhodes and Malta were the property of the Order and consequently the Order bore the designation "sovereign", which it still retains today. After a wandering life on the Continent, the Order eventually established its headquarters in Rome in 1834. For the present activities of the Sovereign Military Order of the Knights of Malta, see page 228.

The Teutonic Order

Similarly to the Order of the Knights of St. John, the Teutonic Order was initially a hospital Order. It was founded by the leader of the German crusaders, Duke Frederick of Swabia, during the Siege of Acre in 1190. The Order, which was attached to the German Hospital of Mary in Jerusalem, was confirmed by Pope Clement the Third in 1191 and converted into a Religious Order of Chivalry in 1198. The members were divided into knights, priests and brother servants, organised according to the rules of the Knights Templars and the Knights of St. John respectively. They wore as their habit a white cloak with a large Latin cross. In its early days the Order concentrated its activities in those areas of Eastern Europe which had not yet become Christian. Here it founded the Teutonic State of Order in 1234 which gradually came to include not only Prussia but also Courland, Livonia and Estonia. Another German Order, the Knights of the Sword, was admitted into the Order in 1240. After the loss of the Holy Land, it moved its headquarters in 1309 to Marienburg in West Prussia. Towards the end of the fourteenth century, the decline of the Order began. In the battle of Grünwald (Tannenberg) in

1410, a Polish-Lithuanian army crushingly defeated the Knights of the Teutonic Order, and by the peace at Thorn in 1466 the Order lost West Prussia. The Order was forced to withdraw everywhere, and finally during the Reformation it was pushed back into the Catholic German countries, where it continued its activities until it was dissolved by Napoleon in 1809. The Order was re-established in Austria by Emperor Ferdinand I in 1839. After the First World War, the Grand Master at the time, Archduke Eugene, began the conversion of the Order of Chivalry into a Religious Order, which was confirmed by Pope Pius the Eleventh in 1929. For the present activities of the Order, see the Teutonic Order, pages 176–7.

From Religious to Temporal Orders of Chivalry.

Other Orders were founded apart from the three Religious Orders of Chivalry referred to above. Some of these were founded in the Iberian peninsula, where the centuries' old battle against the Moors inspired the foundation of Orders which had, indeed, the fight against the infidel as their main object. Among these, reference may be made to the Order of Alcantara (1156), the Order of Calatrava (1158), the Order of Aviz (1162), the Order of Sant' Iago (1170) and the Order of Monteza (1316) which all still exist today. As the fight against the Moors was carried on by the rulers of the various kingdoms, these rulers became the natural focal point for the foundation of the Orders. It is true that the Orders were directly subordinated to the Holy See, but over the years, as the Kings gradually took over the offices of Grand Master and made them heritable in their own families, the Orders became more dynastically dependent, although they maintained their religious character. These Orders formed the transition to the next large group, the Royal Knighthoods, also called the Dynastic or Temporal Orders of Chivalry.

Royal Knighthoods

With the change in the structure of society from Church power to Royal power during the fourteenth century, a number of

Temporal Orders of Chivalry were founded all over Europe. Their object was no longer the fight against the infidel, but to strengthen the prestige and power of the Kings. The Kings themselves occupied the offices of Grand Master, but the meetings, the so-called Chapters, were still held in special Chapels of the Orders in churches. Similarly the Orders, like the Religious Orders of Chivalry, generally had a patron saint and sought papal confirmation.

The number of members in these Temporal Orders of Chivalry was limited, and all were equal in one class. Admission was conditional upon noble birth, and initiation was conducted at a solemn ceremony including a vow of fidelity and the receiving of the accolade. The members wore a habit, and the insignia of the Order was often a jewel with a picture of the patron saint of the Order, worn on a chain around the neck. Members who enjoyed these privileges were required to lead a blameless life, to support charity by giving large sums of money, to promote the prestige and power of the king, and always to bear the insignia of the Order, failure to do so being punishable by fines or, if repeated, by expulsion from the Order. Originally, membership of one Order excluded membership of another, at least as regards the Order against whose king one went to war.

Several of these Orders of Chivalry still exist today, for example the British *Order of the Garter* (1348), the Danish *Order of the Elephant* (1462) and the Swedish *Order of the Seraphim* (1748), although their original significance of membership of a society of chivalry has now changed to merely bearing the insignia of membership, the token of Royal favour. People are no longer admitted into an Order, but are awarded one. The development of history has thus made these Temporal Orders of Chivalry dating from the fourteenth century into a form of Order of Merit, although exclusive, as opposed to those emerging around the year 1800 which are decidedly Orders of Merit.

Orders of Merit

Once more a change in the structure of society affected the

development of the Orders. The Commune, which was consolidated by the French Revolution, wished initially to reward the citizen from a military point of view for his services in the fight for freedom, and later from a civilian point of view for his services for the benefit of the new society. Thus arose the Order purely for services, of which the French Legion of Honour (1802), with its division in 1805 into five classes, became the prototype.

In the Legion of Honour, democracy made its entry into the world of chivalry. No longer was it a limited number of men of the most noble birth in the land who could receive favours from their king. The Order of Merit became society's recognition of "acknowledged worthiness of citizenship", which the Head of State personifying society, be he King or President, could bestow on any citizen.

Democratization rapidly swept through all countries, either in the form of dividing existing Orders of one class into several classes – as was the case in 1808 in the Danish Order of the Dannebrog (1671) – or by founding new Orders of several classes. An actual division into classes, however, already existed before the French Revolution in the French Military Order of St. Louis (1693), whose three classes were referred to as the Grand Cross, Commander and Knight. This became the pattern for the democratic Orders, which took over the division into classes as well as the designations.

Military Orders of Merit

Military Orders of Merit can be either purely Military Orders, or mixed Orders which have both military and civil divisions.

Among purely Military Orders which still exist are the Swedish *Order of the Sword* (1522), the Dutch *Military Order of William* (1815) and the Finnish *Order of the Liberty Cross* (1918). The latter is peculiar in that, as with the German *Iron Cross* (1813), it can be awarded only in time of war, and in that it distinguishes between combatants and non-combatants. This also was the case with the Iron Cross before 1939. The greater number of the new Orders founded after the Second World War in Republics having a People's Democracy are solely Military Orders.

Among the mixed Orders still extant are the Belgian *Order of Leopold* (1832) which in addition to a civil and a military division also has a naval division; the Norwegian *Order of St. Olaf* (1847), the British *Order of Merit* (1902) and the Czechoslovak *Order of the White Lion* (1922). The military divisions of the mixed Orders are characteristic in that the otherwise common insignia are provided with crossed swords. The papal *Order of St. Gregory the Great* (1831), however, uses a trophy instead of the crossed swords, and in the *Order of the British Empire* (1917) an extra band in the otherwise common riband indicates the military division. The British *Order of the Bath* (1725) is exceptional in that its classes each have their own insignia.

Civil Orders of Merit

Civil Orders of Merit can be either purely Civil Orders or mixed Orders having both civil and military divisions.

In countries having Civil Orders only, the civil field is often divided into several categories with a separate Order for each. For example, in Sweden the *Order of the Northern Star* (1748) is awarded for the humanities and for official services, and the *Order of Vasa* (1772) for commercial services. In the years just before and just after the Second World War, a marked division took place in France, in that individual Ministries each awarded its own Order. These Ministerial Orders, however, were later absorbed into the new *National Order of Merit* (1964), with one exception.

In countries having several Civil Orders which may be awarded for the same category of services, it is the qualitative side of the question which decides the Order to be awarded. For example, the *Legion of Honour* (1802) is awarded in France for eminent services, and the *National Order of Merit* (1964) for distinguished services. In Finland, a similar distinction is made between the *Order of the White Rose of Finland* (1919) and the *Order of the Lion of Finland*. (1942).

Orders for Science and Art

Several Civil Orders of Merit are also awarded for deserving services to science and art. Special decorations for services in this field were, however, founded quite early on, for example the French Palms in gold and silver (1808) which was extended in 1945 into an Order of three classes. Similar decorations are found in Germany, such as the *Order "Pour le Mérite" for Science and Art* (1842) and in Austria the *Insignia of Honour* and the *Cross of Honour for Science and Art* (1955). When in 1964 the award of Ministerial Orders ceased in France, the *Order of "Arts et Lettres"* (1957) was retained as the exception. Apart from scientific and artistic services, this may also be awarded for literary services.

Personal Orders

Where the Royal Knighthoods, because of the influence of the State in the choice of those to be honoured, gradually took on the character of Orders of State, the Royal Houses often founded special Family Orders, partly as a reward for services rendered to the King personally or to his family, and partly as a sign of mutual alliance when they were conferred on other Sovereigns and their families. Such Family Orders still existing include the British *Royal Victorian Order* (1896), the Dutch *Order of the Family of Orange* (1905) and the Greek *Orders of St. George and St. Constantine* (1936). One and the same Family Order is sometimes conferred by several Sovereigns whose Houses are related, for example, the Luxemburg *Order of the Golden Lion of the House of Nassau* (1859), which can also be conferred by the House of Orange in the Netherlands. Where a Family Order is conferred on the family's own members when they reach a certain age, this should be taken as a token of solidarity of the whole House with the other holders of the Order.

Female Orders

Actual Female Orders were not known until the year 1600, but the number of such Orders has however always been very small. The still extant, newer Female Orders include the Greek *Order for Good Deeds* (1948), which may be conferred for dedicated as well as artistic and scientific services.

The need for Female Orders is, however, dwindling. Equal

rights for men and women in the conferment of an Order is today an accepted fact in most of the newer Orders of Merit. Similarly, a number of the Royal Knighthoods still extant have extended conferment to include women.

Socialistic Orders of State

In about the year 1900, another change in the structure of society affected the development of the system of Orders. First, the Soviet Union, and after the Second World War the new Democratic People's Republics, abolished the existing system of Orders which had been built on the original chivalrous concept. In their place, a number of new Orders of State were founded. It is true that the designation "Order" was maintained, but the division into classes was numbered from 1–5, according to their number. These include, in the Soviet Union the *Order of Lenin* (1930) and the *Order of Honour* (1943); in Rumania the *Order of the Star of the Rumanian People's Republic* (1948); in Bulgaria the *Order of "Georgi Dimitrov"* (1950); and in Hungary the *Order of Merit of the People's Republic of Hungary* (1953).

Only in Poland and Czechoslovakia have a few of the old Orders been maintained in a different form; for example, the *Order "Virtuti Militari"* (1792) in Poland, and in Czechoslovakia the *Order of the White Lion* (1922).

ORGANISATION

Master of the Order or Grand Master

Every Order has statutes or regulations which set out point by point all information concerning the aim, administration, conferment and insignia of the Order. The oldest Orders, the Religious Orders of Chivalry, are from an organisational point of view a pattern for the Royal Knighthoods as well as for the Orders of Merit. The only difference is that the organisation of a Religious Order of Chivalry has practical objectives and classifies its members according to their field of work, the insignia becoming a badge of office. The organisation of Royal Knighthoods and the Orders of Merit, on the other hand, have a reward as an objective, the insignia of the Order becoming a badge of distinction in one or more classes.

In practice, it may be found that the Royal Knighthoods still extant and the true Orders of Merit are identical, but they can differ in their external presentation. The Order can be either the prerogative of The Sovereign, which means that the reigning member of the Royal House rules the institution as Master of the Order, or it can be a State institution, the President of the country, as Grand Master of the State Orders, having the final decision in all questions concerning the Order.

College of Heralds

Both types of Order are administered by a College consisting of the Master or Grand Master of the Order and a number of members chosen from the holders of the highest classes of the Order, supplemented by a number of senior officials of the Order. The assembly of the College is called a *College of Heralds* or *Council of Heralds*, the title now also covering the actual administrative body. The College of Heralds, which may administer one or more Orders of the same country, decides in questions concerning the statutes of the Order, appointments, promotions, exclusions and other administrative matters.

In the case of Orders with Ministerial status, the Minister concerned is generally the President of the Council of Heralds which administers the Order in question, its members being leading personalities within the Ministry covered by the Order.

In Great Britain an Order of Chivalry is administered by the Chancery of the Order.

The Order of the Garter is administered by Garter Principal King of Arms and the Secretary of the Order at the College of Arms in London.

The Order of the Thistle is administered by Lyon King of Arms, who is also Secretary of the Order at the Court of Lord Lyon in Edinburgh.

The Order of the Bath, Royal Victorian Order, the Order of the British Empire, the Orders of Merit and Companion of Honour, and the Imperial Service Order are administered by the Central Chancery of the Orders of Knighthood in London.

The Order of St. Michael and St. George has its Chancery in the Colonial Office.

Insignia for all the Orders given above are provided by the Central Chancery.

Officials of an Order

The Colleges of Heralds of the Royal Knighthoods were originally conducted with pomp and splendour, and the admission into knighthood took place with a great display of ceremonial. Various officials of the Order assisted in the conduct of these Colleges, but as the College festivals fell more and more into disuse, the offices directly engaged in the ceremonial became vacant. Similarly, the heralds and halberdiers or corps of guards originally attached to the Knighthoods have now been abolished.

The officials of the Orders, who are often the holders of high offices of State, are generally divided into superior and subordinate officials, also called senior officers and officers.

The superior officials include the *Chancellor of the Order* and his Deputy, and the *Vice Chancellor of the Order* who is responsible for and supervises the administration of the Order. Further, there are the *Bishop of the Order*, the *Marshal of the Order* and the *Master of Ceremonies of the Order*, all these offices being originally of a ceremonial nature, and consequently are today often vacant. There is also the *Secretary of the Order* and the *Treasurer of the Order* who supervise the daily administration and the finances of the Order respectively.

Among the subordinate officials are the *Secretary of the Chapter*, who is Head of the Chapter Secretariat and in charge of daily transactions, and the *Historiographer of the Order*, whose task it is to assemble all material relating to the history of the Order, and the biographical data of the members.

On ceremonial occasions, the officials of the Order generally wear special insignia of office, also referred to as insignia of rank, as well as the habit of the Order or uniform.

In Great Britain the Officers of the Orders of Chivalry vary in title and numbers, and consist of some of the following:

Prelate	King of Arms	Gentleman Usher
Dean	Secretary	Genealogist
Chancellor	Registrar or Register	

Some examples of Officers of Orders are:

The Officers of the Most Noble Order of the Garter

Prelate	Garter King of Arms
Chancellor	Gentleman Usher of the Black Rod
Register	Secretary

The Officers of the Most Honourable Order of Bath

Dean	Gentleman Usher of the Scarlet Rod
King of Arms	Genealogist
Secretary and	
Registrar	Deputy Secretary

The Officers of the Most Excellent Order of the British Empire

Prelate	Dean
King of Arms	Gentleman Usher of the Purple Rod
Registrar	Prelate Emeritas
Secretary	Sub-Dean

PURPOSE AND CONFERMENT

For Country and Mankind

The reason that Orders are still used in our modern society is because they still represent the best manner in which society, personified by the Head of State, can show its appreciation of a citizen's services to his country and to mankind – a service which, because it is usually of indirect significance as regards value, lies outside the framework of ordinary reward.

The statutes of almost all Orders in different countries consequently usually state in one of the first paragraphs that the object of the Order concerned is to reward an achievement designed to promote the prestige of the country and the good of mankind. The spheres within which an award in the form of an Order can be made are specified more or less precisely as being, for example, of an official, commercial, civil, military, technical or scientific nature.

Conditions of Conferment

An Order may either be an appointment, that is a first conferment, or a promotion, representing a move from a lower to a higher class of the same Order.

Its conferment is not only dependent upon meritorious services; it may also depend on the making of a vow, birth, sex, age, religion, restricted membership or a yearly quota of awards. Admission into the Religious Orders of Chivalry, for instance, necessitates the making of a solemn vow. To enter into the Royal knighthoods, one must take an oath of allegiance, be of noble birth and, if required, be able to prove up to sixteen noble ancestors in both the male and the female line. Sex is also a factor. Many old Orders do not admit women, and this has led to the foundation of special Female Orders. Age is a general condition. The minimum age for becoming a Knight, for instance, is usually 30–40 years. Many Orders of a professional character require seniority of from 5–25 years within the profession concerned.

Religion or creed is a condition which has its root in the Reformation but today it is often ignored in practice. Nationality can be a condition in a double sense – there are Orders which are conferred only on the citizens of the country concerned, and Orders which are given entirely to foreigners.

Admission into Orders can be restricted purely numerically, either as in the Royal Knighthoods where the total number of Knights at any one time may never exceed a number fixed by the statutes, or as in many newer Orders of Merit where there is a fixed annual quota at the disposal of each class.

Conferment or Nomination

In practice, the conferment of an Order is effected on the basis of a reasoned recommendation from circles close to the person concerned from a professional or interested point of view. The recommendation – for an initial conferment and for a promotion – follows the usual official channels, giving an opportunity for comment and commendation, until it is finally considered at a Council of the Order before being submitted to the Master or Grand Master of the Order for final decision. If the recommendation leads to a conferment, an ordinance, decree, or other official document is drawn up and signed by the Master or Grand Master of the Order, and provided with the seal of the Order. This document is sent to the Chancellor of the Order or to an equivalent official, who causes the letter of the Order or the diploma of the Order to be drawn up and signed. Not until then can the appointment be published and the insignia connected with the Order presented, sent or purchased, according to the custom of the country concerned.

The conferment of an Order is normally individual and personal, and is only heritable in exceptional cases. Many newer Orders of Merit, however, also make collective conferment possible, for example to military units and institutions. It is possible for an Order not to be conferred until the person concerned is dead; such an Order is referred to as "posthumous".

The general rule is that whoever requests an Order for himself is prevented from receiving it for ever. (See, however, the Dutch *Military Order of William* which can be applied for by whoever considers himself justified in so doing.)

In Great Britain, The Sovereign personally selects those persons who are to be appointed Knights Companions of the Order of the Garter, Knights of the Thistle and all appointments to the Royal Victorian Order and Order of Merit.

In the case of other awards the procedure is as follows:

1. Recommendations for appointments to the Military Divisions of the Order of the Bath and the Order of the British Empire are submitted for approval direct to The Sovereign by the Secretary of State for Defence.

2. Recommendations for appointments to the Civil Divisions of the Order of the Bath and the Order of the British Empire, to the Order of St. Michael and St. George, to the Order of the Companions of Honour, and to the Imperial Service Order, are submitted for approval to The Sovereign by the Prime Minister's Office.

3. The Ministers of The Queen in other Commonwealth countries overseas are authorized to submit recommendations for honours direct to The Sovereign.

All awards must bear the approval of The Sovereign before they are published in the London Gazette.

To be Granted a Knighthood

In Great Britain, certain rules apply to the conferment of an Order in that a distinction is made here between two forms of conferment: to be granted a Knighthood and to be awarded an Order of Chivalry.

To be appointed to the Order of the Garter, the Order of the Thistle or the two highest classes of the other British Orders of Chivalry automatically entails admission to knighthood and the right to carry the title "Sir". This, however, does not apply to foreigners who can be admitted only as "honorary members".

The names of those who have been awarded honours are given in the London Gazette published on New Year's Day and on The Sovereign's official birthday. In addition to these two main Honours Lists, the London Gazette, which is published frequently, may contain small Honours Lists announcing awards made during military operations overseas, or of awards to military personnel and civilians for brave peace-time actions at home or overseas.

All those people in the Honours Lists on whom the Honour of Knighthood is to be conferred may now use the prefix "Sir" before actually receiving the accolade. They do, however, later on attend an Investiture to receive the accolade from the Queen, or from those persons authorized to hold Investitures and confer knighthood on The Sovereign's behalf, such as the Governors-General of Australia and New Zealand. All who are appointed to an Order of Chivalry are entitled to use after their names the letters of the grade to which they have been appointed. This may be done from the time of the publication of the Gazette in which their names appear. For example, a man appointed to be a Knight Commander of the Order of the British Empire may style himself "Sir——, K.B.E.," and a man appointed to be a Companion of the Civil Division of the Order of the Bath may style himself "——Esq., C.B.,"

All those people who have been appointed to an Order of Chivalry will be presented with their insignia at Investitures held by the Queen at Buckingham Palace or an Investitures overseas held by those entitled to hold them on the Queen's behalf.

Accolade

The accolade, which was formerly bestowed on the Knight-to-be by the Master of the Order during admission into the Order, is not used today, except in Great Britain and a few other countries. For example, in Sweden, according to the statutes of the *Order of the Sword*, he on whom, in time of war, a Knighthood with the Great Cross of the 1st or 2nd Class of this Order is conferred, receives the accolade from the Monarch.

Preferment or Promotion

It is generally the case that a person receiving an Order from his own country starts in the lowest class of the Order, irrespective of his social position at the time. In special cases, however, it is left to the discretion of the Master or the Grand Master of the Order to depart from this rule, but this happens very rarely.

Although it is not emphasized in all statutes of Orders, a certain number of years should always pass between preferments from class to class. On receiving the insignia of the higher class, the insignia of the lower class are discarded. A usual exception to this, however, is wartime Orders of Merit, where all classes conferred upon a person are worn.

The Decoration of Foreigners

As already mentioned, the services of a citizen can be of a national or of an international character, making an Order the natural means by which a country can show its appreciation of any services rendered by a foreigner for its benefit.

Before an Order can be conferred upon a foreigner, however, the Foreign Service will approach the Master or Grand Master of the Order in the country concerned for permission for such a conferment. If there is no objection, the nomination for the Order which it is proposed to confer will be made by the Foreign Service to the Master or Grand Master of the Order concerned.

Whereas a person who is awarded an Order of his own country generally begins in the lowest class of the Order, a foreigner is usually awarded the class suitable for a person of his social position at the time. If the person concerned has already been awarded a decoration by his own country, he is awarded an equivalent Order or, more often than not, one of a higher class.

While the citizens of a country become ordinary members of an Order of their home country, foreigners usually become merely "honorary members".

Foreign decorations cannot be assumed and worn until permission has been obtained from the Master or Grand Master of the Order in the country concerned.

British subjects are not allowed to accept or wear a foreign Order or Decoration or Medal unless permission to do so has been given by The Queen. The foreign governments concerned will make the appropriate recommendation through diplomatic channels to the Secretary of State for Foreign Affairs who advises The Queen accordingly.

The permission granted is of two kinds, viz. "Unrestricted" or "Restricted".

"Unrestricted permission" means that the recipient may wear the insignia of the foreign order on all occasions when British insignia are worn. A warrant is prepared under arrangements made by the Secretary of State for Foreign Affairs which is signed by The Queen, and a notice of the approval is published in the London Gazette.

In the case of "restricted permission", the person concerned receives instructions from the Private Secretary to the Queen that the foreign insignia may only be worn on certain definite occasions. Examples of such occasions are:

1. In the presence of The Sovereign or Head of State to which the decoration belongs.

2. At the *residence* of any Ambassador, Minister or Consular Officer of that country, whether in England or abroad.

3. When attending an official function in that country.

Order Days

Order Days are a generally adopted concept in most Orders. These include, in the first place, the day the Order was founded, which in the case of many new Orders of Merit is also the day on which conferments take place. Conferments on foreigners, however, generally take place all the year round. The Royal Knighthoods often have several Order Days, which may include, as well as foundation day, the birthday of the founder, the day of martyrdom of the patron saint of the Order, dates of decisive events in the history of the Order, not forgetting the birthday of the reigning Monarch. For example, in Great Britain and Holland the birthdays of the reigning Monarchs are the main days of conferment for the Orders of the country.

Among other methods, Order Days are celebrated in those Orders whose insignia include collars by the prescription that they be worn on such days.

International Ranking System

While older Orders, in decorating foreigners, act according to custom, the statutes of the newer Orders establish rules to determine the rank or social position which corresponds to the various classes of an Order.

Where the collar of an Order is not merely worn on special occasions instead of a sash, but has the character of a special class above the other classes of the Order, it is often conferred on foreign Heads of State as a gesture of courtesy. If the collar does not have this function, or if there is no collar appertaining to the Order concerned, the *Class of the Great Cross* is awarded to Heads of State. In this case, it may be divided into several grades. If this does not apply, this class is conferred upon Ambassadors, Prime Ministers, Parliamentary and High Court Presidents, Lieutenant-Generals, Admirals and others of equivalent rank. The *Grand Officer Class*, which in many countries is identical to the first grade of the Commander Class, is conferred on Envoys Extraordinary and Ministers Plenipotentiary, Parliamentary Vice-Presidents, Departmental Ministers, High Court Judges, Major-Generals, Vice-Admirals,

Rear-Admirals and others of equivalent rank. The *Commander Class* is conferred upon Attachés and Consuls of Embassy, First Secretaries of Embassy, Consul-Generals, Members of the Government, Presidents and representatives of scientific institutions, Appeal Court Judges, Colonels, Lieutenant-Colonels, Commodores, Captains and others of equivalent rank. The *Officer Class* is identical to the first grade of the Knight Class and is conferred upon First Secretaries of Legation, Second Secretaries of Embassy, Consuls, Mayors, Commanders, Lieutenant-Commanders and others of equivalent rank. The Knight Classes are conferred upon Second Secretaries of Legation, Third Secretaries of Embassy, Vice-Consuls, Archivists, Lieutenants in Army and Navy and others of equivalent rank.

Privileges

The statutes of most of the newer Orders provide that a person decorated with the Order concerned is entitled to assume and wear the insignia conferred on him and to describe himself as a holder of the Order. No other rights are normally connected with the conferment of an Order. There are, however, Orders which entitle the holder to a military salute when their insignia are visibly worn. There are also Orders which give their holders a military rank. Finally, pension arrangements can be connected with the conferment of an Order. The Royal Knighthoods give their members special honour by the hanging of banners and coats of arms in the Chapels of the Orders and the ringing of bells upon their death.

The right to refer to oneself as the holder of an Order can be exercised, among other ways, by the person concerned adding after his name the official abbreviation of the Order.

Obligations and Exclusions

The Religious Orders of Chivalry require their members to lead a life of poverty, chastity and obedience, and the Royal Knighthoods require their members to lead a blameless life and to carry out acts of charity.

On the other hand, all Orders agree that a penalty incurred

by a member involving the loss of civil rights entails exclusion from the Order with the consequent return of the insignia.

The Return of Insignia in the Event of Promotion or Death

The insignia awarded must be returned in the event of promotion from a lower to a higher class within the same Order. Wartime decorations and special insignia are, however, generally excepted.

In many countries, for example the Scandinavian countries, all insignia must be returned on the death of the holder. In Great Britain the following insignia are returned on the death of the holder:-

1. All the insignia of the Orders of the Garter and Thistle. The Badge and Star of these Orders are normally handed back personally to The Sovereign by the nearest male relative of the deceased Knight. The remainder of the insignia are returned to the Central Chancery of the Orders of Knighthood.

2. Royal Victorian Chain and the Collars of the Order of the Bath, the Royal Victorian Order and the Order of the British Empire are returned to the Central Chancery.

3. The Collars of the Order of St. Michael and St. George are returned to the Chancery of the Order in the Colonial Office. The next-of-kin of Knights Grand Cross who were appointed before the 14th December 1948 are allowed to keep the collar.

4. All insignia and robes held by the officers of the various Orders are returned to the Central Chancery.

All other insignia become the property of the person entitled to receive them under the terms of the deceased holder's will.

Order Fees

In the statutes of the Royal Knighthoods it is prescribed that the members shall pay certain fees on admission. This is also the practice in many of the newer Orders of Merit, but with the limitation that this is only enforced on citizens of the country concerned.

The fees referred to are today purely administration fees.

Classes and Grades

In the Royal Knighthoods which are still extant and have only one class, the member is called "Knight". In the newer Orders of Merit, for example the British *Order of Merit*, the holder is called a "Member". The greater part of the present day Orders of Merit, however, have five classes modelled on the French *Legion of Honour*. Some Orders, it is true, only take into account three classes, but they then divide the 2nd and 3rd classes each into two grades. The division into three classes corresponds to the three manners in which the Badge of the Order is worn; on a riband across the shoulder (sash), a riband around the neck (necklet), and on a riband on the chest (chest riband). The grade divisions of the 2nd Class, where the badge of the Order is worn on a necklet, are marked by wearing a star of the Order or a pectoral cross in addition. In the third class, where the Badge of the Order is worn on a chest riband, the first grade is marked by the Badge of the Order being in gold, in contrast to that of the second grade which is almost always in silver, and in that the riband is usually provided with a rosette.

The designations of the five steps of rank in Orders having five and three classes respectively are given in the table below.

5 classes:	*3 classes:*
1. Grand Cross	1. Grand Cross
2. Grand Officer	2^1 Commander–1st Class
3. Commander	2^2 Commander–with the possible addition "of 2nd Class"
4. Officer	3^1 Knight, 1st Class
5. Knight	3^2 Knight – with the possible addition "of 2nd Class"

One or more badges of honour or medals may also be attached to some Orders.

In addition to the main types with five steps, there are also Orders with three steps, for example the *Order of the Bath* in Great Britain which has the three highest steps only, and in France the *Order "Arts et Lettres"* which has the three lowest steps only. Variations having two or four steps may be considered to be exceptions, but on the other hand the new German and Austrian Orders of Merit with up to eight steps can obviously be explained by the wish to collect in one single Order all possibilities for grading the State's reward requirements.

By way of summary, it must be pointed out that, although the People's Democracies call their decorations "Orders", they merely number the classes instead of employing the normal designations of honour. The number of classes in these Orders varies from one to five, three being the most normal.

In Great Britain, Orders vary in classes from one to five.

The Orders of the Garter and the Thistle have one class, namely Knight Companion and Knight respectively. The Order of Merit and the Order of Companions of Honour have one class, namely Member.

The Distinguished Service Order and Imperial Service Order have one class, namely Companion.

The Order of the Bath and the Order of St. Michael and St. George have three classes, namely:-

Bath	*St. Michael and St. George*
Knight Grand Cross	Knight or Dame Grand Cross
Knight Commander	Knight or Dame Commander
Companion	Companion.

The Royal Victorian Order and the Order of the British Empire have five classes, namely:

Royal Victorian Order	*Order of the British Empire*
Knight or Dame Grand Cross	Knight or Dame Grand Cross
Knight or Dame Commander	Knight or Dame Commander
Commander	Commander
Member – Fourth Class	Officer
Member – Fifth Class	Member

Precedent

A classification of a different nature occurs in countries having several comparable Orders of Merit. If one examines, for example, Sweden's *Order of the Sword*, *Order of the North Star* and *Order of Vasa*, or the Netherlands' *Military Order of William*, the *Civil Order of Merit of the Netherland Lion* and the *Order of Orange Nassau*, which are broadly speaking conferred for military, humanistic and commercial services respectively, it is precisely in the official order of sequence that a classification is to be found. This, the precedence of one Order compared with another, is however only valid for parallel classes. If there is a class distinction between Orders conferred by the same country to the same person, a higher class of an inferior Order will have precedence over a lower class of a superior Order.

Further, each country has a definite order of sequence for the wearing of its Orders, decorations and medals.

Classes and Insignia

The following insignia generally appertain to the various classes of an Order:

The *Grand Cross Class* wears a Badge of the Order, a Grand Cross, on a sash or collar, in addition to a Star of the Order on the right side of the chest. The *Grand Officers Class* wears the same Badge of the Order as the Officer Class on a chest riband with rosette, in addition to a Star of the Order identical with the Star of the Grand Cross on the right side of the chest, or a special Grand Officer Star on the left side of the chest. In some countries, for example Belgium, the latter Star is worn alone. The Commander, First Class, comparable to the Grand Officer, wears the same Badge of the Order as the Commander on a necklet, in addition to a Star of the Order identical with the Grand Officer Star, or a Cross, on the left of the chest. It is true, however, that many countries refer to the class as "Grand Officer", but they employ the same insignia as for a Commander, First Class. The *Commander Class* wears a Badge of the Order, a Commander's Cross, on a necklet. The *Officer Cross* wears a Badge of the Order, an Officer's Cross, on a chest riband with rosette. Knights, First Class, comparable to Officers, wear the same insignia as the Officers, although in some countries without a rosette on the riband. The *Knight Class* wears the same Badge of the Order as the

Officer Class, a Knight's Cross identical with the Officers' Cross, but usually in silver on a chest riband, whereas it is in gold for the other classes.

Decorations and medals appertaining to the Order are worn in the same way as the Badge of the Order of the Knight Class. The wearing of insignia of the various classes of British Orders differs in some respects.

1. *Knights and Dames Grand Cross* wear the Badge of the Order on the collar (on Collar Days) or on a broad riband. They also wear the Star on the *left* side of the coat or dress.

2. *Knights and Dames Commander* wear the Star on the *left* side of the coat or dress. A Knight Commander wears the Badge on a neckband around his neck, and the Dame Commander wears the Badge on the riband made in the form of a bow on the left side of her dress, above the Star.

3. *Commanders or Companions*. A man wears the Badge on a neckband around the neck, and a woman wears the Badge on the riband made in the form of a bow on the left side.

4. *Officers* Wear the Badge together with any decorations or medals mounted on a bar-brooch on the left side of the coat. A woman, if she possesses any other decorations or medals, will wear them in exactly the same way as a man. If she only possesses the one Officer's Badge, she will wear it on the riband made in the form of a bow on the left side of her coat or dress.

5. *Members* Men and women will wear their Badge in exactly the same way as is prescribed for officers above. The insignia of the various classes of British Orders are described on page 133 *et seq*.

The Typology of the Insignia

The word "insignia", which is a plural word, means badges of dignity, and is used as a collective expression for the individual parts belonging to an Order: Badge of the Order, Riband of the Order, Star of the Order, Collar of the Order and Habit of the Order.

The Badge of the Order

The Badge of the Order, which is the main symbol of the Order, may be in the form of a jewel, a cross or a star. As a jewel, it can be a medallion or a modelled figure. As a cross or star, it can have different shapes. The types of cross most employed are the Maltese Cross and the Cross of St. George, and the type of star mostly used is the 5-pointed star. The cross and the star are generally coated with enamel and are provided with a centre medallion bearing a portrait, monogram, device or symbols, often divided between the obverse and the reverse medallion. As a support, the cross often has a crown, a verticil of leaves, or a trophy, a mounting of flags and armour around a cuirass. If the Order has both a civil and a military division, the Badge of the Order for the military division may be distinguished by crossed swords, either located in the angles of the cross or inserted between the cross and the support; a naval division, for example the Belgian *Order of Leopold*, is distinguished by crossed anchors.

The Badge of the Order is normally made of gold or silver. It is usually of silver for the lower classes, and of gold for the other classes. A decoration connected with the Order is often the Badge of the Order in silver without enamel. Appertaining medals may be of gold, silver or bronze.

The Badge of the Order is usually of three sizes; one for the Grand Cross Class, one for the Commander Class and one for the Knight Class, corresponding to the three manners of wearing it; on a sash, on a necklet and on a chest riband. Some Orders, however, have only two sizes, the intermediate size and the Knight's Cross size, and in that case the intermediate size is used for both the Grand Cross and the Commander Classes.

In Great Britain those Orders which have Military and Civil Divisions show the difference between the two Divisions in the following manner:

1. *Order of Merit*

The Badge of the Military Division is distinguished by the addition of two silver swords with gold hilts placed saltirewise between the angles of the cross – the hilts downwards.

2. *Order of the Bath*

The Military and Civil Divisions have their own distinctive Badges.

3. *Order of the British Empire*

The Military Division of the Order is distinguished by narrow pearl-grey stripes down the centre of the rose-pink riband. In those Orders which have three classes, the Badges are the same design but of a different size for each Class.

In those Orders which have five classes, the Badges worn by Knights and Dames Commander and by Commanders or Companions are exactly the same – but smaller than that worn by Knights and Dames Grand Cross.

The Badges of an Officer and Member are the same design but are normally made of silver gilt and silver respectively. In the case of the Royal Victoria Order, however, the Badge of the 4th Class is of white enamel.

The Riband of the Order

The Riband of the Order is a woven silk ribbon, with or without moiré, in one or more colours and of different widths. In addition, there may be anchors, crosses, eagles or other figures woven into the ribbon. The colours are often symbolic, the colours of, for example, countries or Royal Houses often being used. Many colours form patterns of vertical, diagonal or horizontal bands, which are symmetrically or asymmetrically arranged. The Riband of the Order can also be provided with one or more extra bands to mark the various classes of an Order, as is the case in many socialistic Orders of State. And finally the Riband of the Order can be provided with a rosette for marking a certain class in Orders of five and three classes; that is, the Officer Class and the Knight, First Class, respectively.

The Riband of the Order varies in width according to Class. In the Grand Cross sash, the width is about 101 mm for gentlemen and about 55 mm for ladies, the Commander's necklet being 55–37 mm and the Knights' chest riband 37–25 mm.

The Riband was used first by the French *Order of the Holy Ghost* (1578) whose ribbon was pale blue, the symbolic colour of piety.

Mounting the Riband of the Order

The sash of the Grand Cross is worn across the right or left shoulder, according to the statutes of the Order concerned. The sash varies from country to country as concerns the fan which gathers the ends of the riband on the hip. This gathering can be covered by a bow, a rosette or a crimped ribbon, as is the case in Great Britain, France and Luxembourg, or it may be uncovered as in Denmark. The ends of the riband can be fringed, serrated or cut straight or diagonally. Religious Orders usually wear the Badge of the Order for the Grand Cross Class on a Commander's necklet.

The Commander's necklet is worn around the neck, broad necklets being fitted flat as a pleated collar along the edge of the normal collar and narrow necklets being fitted as a ribbon around the actual collar. Although ladies may wear the Riband of the Order for the Commander Class as a necklet, as is the case in Iceland, most Orders prescribe that ladies should wear it as a bow on the left shoulder.

The chest riband of the Knight is worn on the left of the chest. The chest riband varies from country to country in its fitting. It may be fitted in a vertical fashion, as is the case in France, or it may be fitted in a triangular, crossed or trimmed fashion, as is the case in Austria, Denmark and the Netherlands. Even where ladies may also wear the Badge of the Order of the Knight Class on a chest riband fitted in a vertical fashion, as is the case in Finland, most Orders lay down that ladies should wear it as a bow on the left chest.

Ladies' bows for the Commander and Knight Classes are tied in the riband width of the classes concerned.

The Star of the Order

The Star of the Order is usually a 4–12 pointed gold or silver star surmounted by the Badge of the Order. The rays can be facetted, fluted or plain. There are usually two types of Stars of the Order; one for the Grand Cross Class and one for the Grand Officer Class, although the same type of star can also be found in gold and silver respectively to distinguish between the two classes, as in the French *National Order of Merit*. Some Orders have only one type of star. In that case, the Grand

Cross Class wears it on the left of the chest and the Grand Officer Class on the right of the chest. This applies to the French *Legion of Honour*.

Where the Grand Officer Cross has the form of a Cross of the Order without rays, it is called a pectoral cross. Many newer Orders also use, to distinguish the Officer Class, pectoral crosses instead of Badges of the Order on a chest riband with rosette, for example the *Order of Merit of the Federal Republic of Germany*.

The Star of the Orders has its origin in the cross worn by the crusader on his cloak. Initially it was made of cloth, and later of sequins and provided with rays like a star. It was not made of metal until the beginning of the twentieth century.

The Collar of the Order

The Collar of the Order consists of identical or varied links, joined together and made of gold or silver. It is usually provided with a special carrying link for the Badge of the Order. The links are often symbolic.

The Collar of the Order is worn around the neck, resting on both shoulders. In the older Orders, the Collar is worn instead of the Sash on the special Order Days. In many of the newer Orders, the Collar has the character of a special class above the ordinary Grand Cross Class, and in that case it is the privilege of the Head of State, for example the Spanish *Civil Order of Merit*. In Portugal, where on special occasions the Collar may be worn by all classes, a special Grand Collar takes over the function of the special class.

The Habit of the Order

The Habit is no longer used today, except in Great Britain and in the Vatican State where it is still worn on ceremonial occasions. In the Vatican State, however, the habit has more or less the character of a uniform.

Special Insignia

As a special distinction, an Order can be conferred "with diamonds", either the Badge of the Order or the Star of the Order then bearing the stones. If a lower class of the Order has been conferred in this manner, the holder will continue to wear the diamond-set Badge of the Order, even if he is promoted to a higher class. Some Orders confer such special insignia as personal property, whereas with other Orders they must be returned on the holder's death.

While "crossed swords" designate a parallel division of the same Order, a conferment of an Order "with oak leaves" is a special distinction, for example the Finnish *Order of the Cross of Liberty* and the German *Iron Cross*, the latter having varied this even further.

The riband of war decorations is often provided with "palm leaves" or "stars". (For the significance of this, see the French *Croix de Guerre*.)

In Great Britain no Order is conferred "with diamonds", "crossed swords" or "oak leaves", and a riband of war decorations is not provided with "palm leaves" or "stars".

Symbolism and Devices

An Order can express itself symbolically in the form and ornamentation of the Badge of the Order, in the links of the Collar and in the colours of the Riband.

In most of the newer Orders of Merit, the Badge of the Order is in the form of a cross, the symbol of Christianity, while in the Socialist Orders of State it is usually built up around the 5-pointed star of Communism. The two most dominant types of cross are the Maltese Cross and the Cross of St. George, the original cross of the Order of the Knights Templars, which is named after St. George, the patron saint of all Knights. Other types of cross are the St. Andrew's Cross, the Mantic Cross and the Greek and Latin Crosses.

The name of the Order can often be metaphorically expressed on the obverse and reverse medallion, for example by a crown, a lion or a rose, as is found, inter alia, in the Belgian *Order of the Crown*, the Czech *Order of the White Lion* and the Finnish *Order of the White Rose*. The monogram or portrait of the founder can also be reproduced here, or the year and day the Order was founded, or the device of the Order.

Crowns, verticils of leaves, swords, monograms or other

symbols may be found in the angles of the Cross. The crown is the Royal symbol, the laurel leaves are the symbol of honour of the Greeks and Romans, the palm wreath is the symbol of peace and victory and the oak wreath is the symbol of courage and strength. The sword is the military symbol, while a crowned monogram generally indicates the name of the founder.

The carrying link often expresses the origin of the Order. A crown indicates a Royal founder, while the Republican Orders of Merit usually employ a verticil of leaves and the Religious Orders of Chivalry a trophy. There are, however, Orders which in spite of a Royal origin use a verticil of leaves as a carrying link, but the crown then appears in the centre medallion of the Badge of the Order, for example in the Belgian *Order of the Crown*. Mixed Orders with both civil and military divisions can have crossed palm branches and swords inserted between the cross and the carrying link, or located in the carrying wreath itself as symbols of peace and war, for example the Czech *Order of the White Lion*.

In the links of the Collar of the Order, symbolism is used to an even greater extent than in the Badge of the Order.

The symbolism in the colours of the Riband of the Order, however, must be accepted with reservations, partly because the colours need not necessarily be chosen with symbolism in mind, and partly because the colour symbolism can vary from country to country.

An overwhelming number of Royal Knighthoods and early Orders of Merit have a device or motto. If this is not used in the Badge of the Order, it will be found in the Seal of the Order.

Miniature Decorations

Miniature decorations are small editions of the original decorations. The size can vary from country to country. For example in Great Britain half the original size is used, the Scandinavian countries using a 17 mm size and the Netherlands, Belgium and France a 14 mm size, calculated from the diameter of the Badge of the Order. In contrast to earlier times when Stars of the Order were also worn in miniature, only miniatures of the

Badges of the Order are today used. The higher Classes are then designated by placing wings in silver, gold and silver, or gold, *according to class*, below the rosette on the Riband for the Officer Class.

In Great Britain, miniatures are the exact replicas of the Badges they represent, and no additional rosettes or emblems are added to the ribands to denote a particular class.

Certain high Orders are not worn in miniature, for example the *Order of the Garter* and the *Order of the Thistle* in Great Britain.

Ribands of the Order with Civilian Clothes and Uniform

Various types of button-hole ribands are worn with civilian clothes. A decoration or medal is designated by a so-called "Pin of an Order" or by a 2–3 mm-wide Riband of the Order drawn through the button hole of the lapel and outwards around the edge of the lapel. The lapel clip or bow is also used to designate the Knight Class. The Officer Class uses a rosette under which are placed wings in silver, and gold, and gold to designate the Commander, Grand Officer and Grand Classes respectively. Instead of the wing system, bows are used in Germany, and in Italy rosettes in diminutive editions of the respective Badges and Stars of the Order.

In Great Britain there are no types of button-hole ribands with emblems to denote the class of an Order, which are worn with civilian clothes.

Ribands of an Order for uniforms, called the "Brooch of an Order", consist of Ribands of the Orders corresponding to the holder's decorations in the riband width employed for their classes mounted next to one another around a piece of 10 mm rigid material in one or more rows as required. Decorations and medals, as well as the Knight Class, are designated by the riband colour alone, while the higher classes in most countries are designated by the rosette and wing system referred to above.

In Great Britain rosettes and emblems are not worn on ribands to denote a class. The ribands of Orders, decorations and medals are mounted on a bar in the correct order and worn on the left side of the uniform coat.

NOTES ON THE PLATES

The following 80 plates in modern 7-colour printing provide a number of reproductions of the insignia of all extant *international* European Orders; that is to say Orders which are not reserved for a country's own citizens, but which may also be conferred on foreigners. The insignia are reproduced at three-fifth of their actual size, and are illustrated to the extent necessary, in line with the information in the following dictionary of Orders, to make clear the insignia worn by the various classes or degrees of the Orders concerned.

The colour plates are designed along the following general lines:

Badges of an Order are generally shown in several of the sizes for each Order, but for reasons of space they may be shown exceptionally in one size only. Stars of the Order are almost always shown in both the normal sizes or designs. If an Order has both civilian and military divisions, the Badge of the Order is generally shown in both forms. Decorations and medals are usually shown only in so far as they are attached to the Order. Collars are illustrated by a section large enough for all the symbolic links of the Collar to be represented. The captions give the actual class of the insignia illustrated, and the insignia are shown on the riband mounting corresponding to the classes. For reasons of space or symmetry, however, departures from the correct mounting may have been made in individual cases, but in this event it is made clear in the captions. For the sash of the Grand Cross Class, the fan which gathers the ends of the riband on the hip is shown with the Badge of the Order, the fan being mounted in the fashion customary in the country concerned. The width of the riband is that generally employed by gentlemen. For the necklet of the Commander Class, the fold of the riband formed by the mounting bar of the Badge of the Order is shown. The

ladies' bow of the Commander Class is also shown in a few cases. The chest riband of the Knight's Class or Officer's Class is shown in full, the riband being mounted in a vertical, crossed or triangular fashion, more rarely in the form of a bow for ladies, according to the customs of the country concerned. It is also shown with or without rosette or on a bar as prescribed in the Statutes of the Order. Ribands mounted on bars are shown only to the extent that the riband colours of the Order are not in any other way apparent from the insignia. The numbers beneath, above or beside the individual insignia correspond to the numbers in front of the article on the Order concerned in the following dictionary of Orders. They refer to the number references given in the article where reference is made to the class division of the Orders. For all insignia illustrated, the obverse side only is shown on the colour plates, the reverse side being described in the text.

New insignia, or those altered during the preparation of this book, examples of which have not as yet been made, are not reproduced on the colour plates but are shown by a line drawing attached to the text.

The precedence of the insignia

On the colour plates, the insignia are reproduced in geographical order, the insignia of each country following the official precedence valid in the country concerned. Where this has been departed from for technical reasons, there is a note to this effect in the article concerned in the dictionary of the Orders.

All European countries except four are represented in the colour plates. Albania did *not* wish to make her Orders available for photography, but the insignia of these are shown by a line drawing attached to the text. Andorra and Switzerland have *no* decorations, and Ireland has no *international* decorations.

ICELAND

The Icelandic Order of the Falcon: 1. Badge of the Order, Grand Cross. - 2. Collar of the Order. - 3. Star of the Order, Grand Cross. - 4. Star of the Order, Grand Knight with Star. - 5. Badge of the Order, Knight. - 6. **The Icelandic Life-Saving Medal.** - 7. **The President of Iceland's Medal.**

NORWAY

The Order of Saint Olaf: 8. Badge of the Order, Military, Grand Cross. - 9. Collar of the Order.
- 10. Star of the Order, Grand Cross. - 11. Star of the Order, Commander with Star.

NORWAY

12. Badge of the Order, Commander with Star and Commander. - 13. Badge of the Order, Knight, 1st Class. - 14. Badge of the Order, Military, Knight. - 15. **The Medal of Saint Olaf.** - 16. **The War Cross.** - 17. **King Haakon VII's Liberty Medal.**

SWEDEN

The Most Noble Order of the Seraphim: 18. Badge of the Order. - 19. Collar of the Order. - 20. Star of the Order, old model.

SWEDEN

The Royal Order of the Sword: 21. Badge of the Order, Commander Grand Cross. - 22. Collar of the Order. - 23. Star of the Order, Commander Grand Cross. - 24. Badge of the Order, Knight, 1st Class. - 25. Badge of the Order, Knight. - 26. The Badge of the Sword. - 27. The Medal of the Sword.

SWEDEN

The Royal Order of the Northern Star: 28. Badge of the Order, Commander Grand Cross. - 29. Collar of the Order. - 30. Star of the Order, Commander Grand Cross. - 31. Star of the Order, Commander 1st Class. - 32. Badge of the Order, Knight.

SWEDEN

The Royal Order of Vasa: 33. Badge of the Order, Commander Grand Cross. - 34. Collar of the Order. - 35. Star of the Order, Commander Grand Cross. - 36. The Royal Badge of Vasa. - 37. The Royal Medal of Vasa.

FINLAND

The Order of the Cross of Liberty: 38. Star of the Order, Grand Cross. - 39. Badge of the Order, 1st Class with Star and 1st Class. - 40. Badge of the Order, 3rd Class. - 41. Badge of the Order, Civil, 4th Class. - **The Mannerheim Cross of the Cross of Liberty:** 42. Badge of the Order, 1st Class. - 43. Badge of the Order, 2nd Class. - **The Medal of Liberty:** 44. 1st Class. - 45. 2nd Class. - 46. The Medal of Merit of the Cross of Liberty.

FINLAND

Finland's Order of the White Rose: 47. Badge of the Order, Commander Grand Cross. - 48. Collar of the Order, older model. - 49. Star of the Order, Commander Grand Cross. - 50. Star of the Order, Military, Commander 1st Class. - 51. Badge of the Order, Military, Commander 1st Class and Commander. - 52. Badge of the Order, Knight 1st Class. - 53-54. Finland's Badge and Medal of the White Rose.

FINLAND:

The Order of the Lion of Finland: 55. Badge of the Order, Commander Grand Cross. - 56. Star of the Order, Commander Grand Cross. - 57. Badge of the Order, Military, Commander 1st Class and Commander. - 58. The Cross of Merit of the Order of the Finnish Lion. - 59. The Pro Finlandia Medal.

FINLAND

The Order of the Holy Lamb: 60. Badge of the Order; Commander 1st and 2nd Class. - 61. Star of the Order, Commander 1st Class. - 62. The Medal of the Holy Lamb. - **Finland's Olympic Cross of Merit:** 63. 1st Class. - **Finland's Cross of Merit for Athletics:** 64. 2nd Class.

GREAT BRITAIN

The Most Noble Order of the Garter: 65. Badge of the Order, 'The George'. - 66. Collar of the Order.

GREAT BRITAIN

67. Star of the Order. - 68. Badge of the Order, 'The Lesser George'. - 69. Garter.

GREAT BRITAIN

The Most Noble and Most Ancient Order of the Thistle: 70. Badge of the Order. - 71. Collar
of the Order. - 72. Star of the Order.

GREAT BRITAIN

The Most Honourable Order of the Bath: 73. Badge of the Order, Civil, Knight Grand Cross. - 74. Collar of the Order. - 75. Star of the Order, Civil, Knight Grand Cross. - 76. Star of the Order, Military, Knight Commander. - 77. Badge of the Order, Military, Knight Commander and Companion.

GREAT BRITAIN

The Most Distinguished Order of Saint Michael and Saint George: 78. Badge of the Order, Knight Grand Cross. - 79. Collar of the Order. - 80. Star of the Order, Knight Grand Cross. - 81. Star of the Order, Knight Commander.

GREAT BRITAIN

The Order of Merit: 82. Badge of the Order, Military. - **The Order of the Companions of Honour:** 83. Badge of the Order. - 84-85. **The Royal Victorian Chain, with Badge.**

GREAT BRITAIN

The Royal Victorian Order: 86. Badge of the Order, Knight Grand Cross. - 87. Collar of the Order. - 88. Star of the Order, Knight Grand Cross. - 89. Star of the Order, Knight Commander. - 90. Badge of the Order, Member of 5th Class. - 91. The Royal Victorian Medal, Silver (Honorary).

GREAT BRITAIN

The Most Excellent Order of the British Empire: 92. Badge of the Order, Knight Grand Cross, on Civil Division Riband. - 93. Star of the Order, Knight Grand Cross. - 94. Badge of the Order, Knight Commander and Commander. - 95. Star of the Order, Knight Commander. - 96. Badge of the Order, Officer, Military Division. - 97. The British Empire Medal, Civil.

GREAT BRITAIN

98. The Victoria Cross. - 99. The George Cross. - 100. The Distinguished Service Order.
- 101. The Distinguished Service Cross. - 102. The Military Cross. - 103. The Distinguished
Flying Cross.

DENMARK

The Order of the Elephant: 104-105. Badges of the Order. - 106. Collar of the Order. - 107. Star of the Order.

DENMARK

The Order of the Dannebrog: 108. Badge of the Order, Grand Commander, Ladies' Bow. - 109. Badge of the Order, Grand Cross. - 110. Collar of the Order. - 111. Star of the Order, Grand Cross 'with diamonds'. - 112. Star of the Order, Grand Commander and Grand Cross.

DENMARK

113. Badge of the Order, Commander, 1st Degree and Commander. - 114. Breast Cross, Commander, 1st Degree. - 115. Badge of the Order, Knight, 1st Degree, Ladies' Bow. - 116. Badge of the Order, Knight. - 117. The Silver Cross of the Order of the Dannebrog.

THE NETHERLANDS

The Military Order of William: 118. Badge of the Order, Grand Cross. - 119. Star of the Order, Grand Cross. - 120. Badge of the Order, Knight, 3rd Class. - 121. Badge of the Order, Knight, 4th Class.

THE NETHERLANDS

The Civil Order of Merit of the Netherlands Lion: 122. Badge of the Order, Grand Cross. -
123. Star of the Order, Grand Cross. - 124. **The Bronze Lion Decoration.** - 125. **The Airman's
Cross.** - 126. **The Bronze Cross.** - 127. **The Cross of Merit.**

THE NETHERLANDS

The Order of Orange-Nassau: 128. Star of the Order, Military, Grand Cross. - 129. Star of the Order, Grand Cross. - 130. Star of the Order, Military, Grand Officer. - 131. Badge of the Order, Officer. - 132. Badge of the Order, Military, Knight. - 133. The Honorary Medal.

THE NETHERLANDS

The Family Order of Orange: 134. Badge of the Order, Grand Cross. - 135. Star of the Order, Grand Cross. - 136. Star of the Order, Grand Officer. - 137. Badge of the Order, Officer - 138. The Cross of Merit. - 139. The Honorary Medal.

BELGIUM

The Order of Leopold: 140. Badge of the Order, Grand Cross. - 141. Collar of the Order. - 142. Star of the Order, Grand Cross. - 143. Badge of the Order, Officer. - 144. Badge of the Order, Knight.

BELGIUM

145. Badge of the Order, Military, Officer. - 146. Badge of the Order, Maritime, Officer. - 147. Star of the Order, Maritime, Grand Cross. - 148. Star of the Order, Military, Grand Officer. - 149. Star of the Order, Maritime, Grand Officer.

BELGIUM

The Order of the Crown: 150. Badge of the Order, Commander. - 151. Star of the Order, Grand Cross. - 152. Star of the Order, Grand Officer. - 153. Badge of the Order, Officer. - 154. Palms. - 155. Medal.

BELGIUM

The Order of Leopold II: 156. Badge of the Order, Grand Cross. - 157. Star of the Order, Grand Cross. - 158. Badge of the Order, Knight. - 159. Medal.

BELGIUM

The Military Decoration of Merit: 160. 1st Class. - 161. 2nd Class. - **The Military Cross:** 162. 1st Class. - 163. 2nd Class. - 164. **The War Cross, 1940.** - **The Order of the Lion:** 165. Badge of the Order, Officer. - **The Order of the Star of Africa:** 166. Badge of the Order, Officer.

LUXEMBOURG

The Order of the Golden Lion of the House of Nassau: 167. Badge of the Order. - 168. Star of the Order. - **The Civil and Military Order of Merit of Adolph of Nassau:** 169. Star of the Order, Grand Cross. - 170. Star of the Order, Grand Officer. - 171. Badge of the Order, Commander, with Crown. - 172. The Cross of Merit. - 173. Palm, 1940-1945.

LUXEMBOURG

The Order of the Oaken Crown: 174. Badge of the Order, Grand Cross. - 175. Star of the Order, Grand Cross. - 176. Star of the Order, Grand Officer. - 177. Badge of the Order, Knight. - 178–179. Medal of Merit.

LUXEMBOURG

The Order of Merit: 180. Star of the Order, Grand Cross. - 181. Star of the Order, Grand Officer. - 182. Badge of the Order, Grand Officer and Commander. - 183. Badge of the Order, Officer. - 184. The Order of Merit. - 185. **The War Cross, 1940–1945.**

FRANCE

The Legion of Honour: 186. Badge of the Order, Grand Cross. - 187. Star of the Order, Grand Cross and Grand Officer. - 188. Badge of the Order, Grand Officer and Officer. - 189. Badge of the Order, Knight.

FRANCE

The National Order of Merit: 190. Badge of the Order, Grand Cross. - 191. Star of the Order, Grand Cross. - 192. Badge of the Order, Grand Officer and Officer. - 193. Badge of the Order, Knight.

FRANCE

194. **The Order of Liberation.** - 195. **The Military Medal.** - 196. **The War Cross, 1939-1945.**
- 197. **The War Cross, T.O.E.** - **The Order of the Black Star:** 198. Badge of the Order, Officer.
- **The Order of the Anjouan Star:** 199. Badge of the Order, Officer. - **The Order of Nichan-el-Anouar:** 200. Badge of the Order, Officer.

FRANCE

The Order of the 'Palmes Académiques': 201. Badge of the Order, Commander. - 202. Badge of the Order, Officer. - **The Order of 'Mérite Agricole':** 203. Badge of the Order, Officer. - **The Order of 'Mérite Maritime':** 204. Badge of the Order, Officer. - **The Order of 'Mérite Social':** 205. Badge of the Order, Commander. - 206. Badge of the Order, Officer.

FRANCE

207. The Order of 'Santé Publique'. - 208. The Order of 'Mérite Commercial'. - 209. The Order of 'Mérite Touristique'. - 210. The Order of 'Mérite Artisanal'. - 211. The Order of 'Mérite Combattant'. - 207-211. Badge of the Order, Officer. - **The Order of 'Mérite Postal'.** 212. Badge of the Order, Commander. - 213. Badge of the Order, Knight.

FRANCE

The Order of 'Economie Nationale': 214. Badge of the Order, Officer. - **The Order of 'Mérite Sportif':** 215. Badge of the Order, Commander. - 216. Badge of the Order, Officer. - **The Order of 'Mérite du Travail':** 217. Badge of the Order, Officer. - **The Order of 'Mérite Militaire':** 218. Badge of the Order, Commander. - 219. Badge of the Order, Officer.

FRANCE

The Order of 'Mérite Civil': 220. Badge of the Order, Commander. - 221. Badge of the Order, Knight. - **The Order of 'Mérite Saharien':** 222. Badge of the Order, Commander. - 223. Badge of the Order, Officer. - **The Order of 'Arts et Lettres':** 224. Badge of the Order, Commander.

MONACO

The Order of Charles the Holy: 225. Badge of the Order, Grand Cross. - **The Order of the Crown:** 226. Star of the Order, Grand Cross and Grand Officer. - 227. Badge of the Order, Officer. - **The Order of Grimaldi:** 228. Star of the Order, Grand Cross and Grand Officer. - 229. Badge of the Order, Officer. - **The Order of 'Mérite Culturel':** 230. Badge of the Order, Officer.

WESTERN GERMANY

The Order of Merit of the Federal Republic of Germany: 231. Badge of the Order, Grand Cross. - 232. Star of the Order, Grand Cross, Special Class. - 233. Star of the Order, Grand Cross. - 234. Star of the Order, Grand Cross of Merit with Star and Sash.

WESTERN GERMANY

235. Badge of the Order, Grand Cross of Merit with Star and Grand Cross of Merit on Ladies' Bow. - 236. Star of the Order, Grand Cross of Merit with Star. - 237. Badge of the Order, Cross of Merit, 1st Class. - 238. Badge of the Order, Cross of Merit with Riband. - 239. The Medal of Merit.

WESTERN GERMANY

The Order 'Pour le Mérite' for Science and the Arts: 240. Badge of the Order. - **The Iron Cross:** 241. Badge of the Order, Knight's Cross with Oak Leaves and Swords. - 242–243. Badge of the Order, 1st and 2nd Class. - **The War Cross of Merit:** 244. Badge of the Order, 1st Class with Swords. - 245. Badge of the Order, 2nd Class. - 246. **The War Medal of Merit.** - **The German Cross:** 247. Badge of the Order, 1st Class. - 248. Badge of the Order, 2nd Class.

EASTERN GERMANY

The Order of Karl Marx: 249. Badge of the Order. - **The Order of Merit of the Fatherland:** 250. Badge of the Order. - **The Order of the 'Star of Friendship between Peoples':** 251. Badge of the Order. - **The Order of the Banner of Work:** 252. Badge of the Order.

253

254

AUSTRIA

The Decoration of Honour for Merit: 253. Badge of the Order, Grand Star and Grand Decoration of Honour in Gold with Sash. - 254. Star of the Order, Grand Decoration of Honour in Gold with Sash. - 255. Badge of the Order, Grand Decoration of Honour in Gold with Star and Grand

AUSTRIA

Decoration of Honour in Gold. - 256. Badge of the Order, Grand Decoration of Honour. - 257.
Badge of the Order, Grand Decoration of Honour in Silver. - 258. The Decoration of Merit. -
259. The Medal of Merit.

AUSTRIA

The Decoration of Honour for Science and the Arts: 260. Badge of Honour. - 261. Cross of Honour, 1st Class. - 262. Cross of Honour. - **The Teutonic Order:** 263. Badge of the Order, Honorary Knight. - 264. Badge of the Order, Marian Knights until 1929. - **The Order of St. John and of Malta:** 265. Profess Cross. - 266. Badge of the Order. - 267. Cross of Merit until 1928.

LIECHTENSTEIN

The Order of Merit of the Principality of Liechtenstein: 268. Badge of the Order, Grand Star and Grand Cross. - 269. Star of the Order, Grand Cross.

CZECHOSLOVAKIA

The Order of the White Lion: 270. Badge of the Order, Military, 1st Class. - 271. Collar of the Order. - 272. Star of the Order, 1st and 2nd Class. - 273. Badge of the Order, Military, 2nd and 3rd Class. - 274. Badge of the Order, Civil, 2nd and 3rd Class.

CZECHOSLOVAKIA

The Military Order of the White Lion: 275. Star, 1st Class. - 276. Cross of the Order. - 277. Gold Medal. - **The Military Order 'For Liberty':** 278. Gold Star. - 279. Silver Medal. - 280. Bronze Medal. - **The Officers' Order of Jan Zizka of Trochnova:** 281. Gold Star. - 282. Silver Star. - 283. Medal.

HUNGARY

The Order of Merit of the People's Republic of Hungary: 284. Badge of the Order. - **The Order of the Flag of the People's Republic of Hungary:** 285. Star of the Order, 1st Degree. - 286. **The Order of Merit of the Red Flag of Work.** - 287. **The Order of the Red Flag.** - 288. **The Order of Merit of Work.** - 289. **The Order of the Red Star.** - 290. **The Order of Merit for Special Services.** - 291. **The Official Order of Merit.** - 286–291. Badges of the Orders.

RUMANIA

The Order of the Star of the Rumanian People's Republic: 292–293. Badges of the Order, 1st and 3rd Class. - **The Order of '23rd August':** 294–295. Badges of the Order, 1st and 3rd Class. - **The Order of 'The Defence of the Fatherland':** 296–297. Badges of the Order, 2nd and 3rd Class. - **The Order of Work:** 298–299. Badges of the Order, 1st and 2nd Class. - 300. The Medal of Work.

BULGARIA

The Hero of Socialistic Work: 301. Badge of Distinction. - **The Order of Georgi Dimitrov:** 302. Badge of the Order. - 303. **The Order 'The People's Republic of Bulgaria'.** - 304. **The Order of '9th September 1944'.** - 305. **The Order 'For the Liberation of the People, 1941–1944'.** - 303 and 305. Badges of the Order, 1st Degree. - 304. Badge of the Order, 2nd Degree. - **The Order 'The Red Flag of Work':** 306. Badge of the Order.

POLAND

The Order 'Polonia Restituta': 307. Star of the Order, Grand Cross and Commander with Star. - 308. Badge of the Order, Officer. - **The Order 'Virtuti Militari':** 309. Star of the Order, Grand Cross. - 310. Badge of the Order, 4th Class. - **The Cross of Merit:** 311. Badge of the Order, 2nd Class. - 312. **The War Cross, 1944.** - 313. **The Partisan Cross.**

THE SOVIET UNION

The Medal 'The Golden Star': 314. Badge of Distinction. - **The Gold Medal 'The Hammer and Sickle':** 315. Badge of Distinction. - **The Order of Lenin:** 316. Badge of the Order. - **The Order of Victory:** 317. Badge of the Order. - **The Order of the Red Flag:** 318. Badge of the Order. - **The Order of the Red Flag of Work:** 319. Badge of the Order.

THE SOVIET UNION

320. **The Order of Suvorov.** - 321. **The Order of Usjakov.** - 322. **The Order of Kutuzov.** - 323. **The Order of Nakhimov.** - 324. **The Order of Bogdan Khemlnitskij.** - 320–324. Badges of the Orders, 1st Degree. - **The Order of Alexander Nevskij:** 325. Badge of the Order. - **The Order of the Patriotic War:** 326. Badge of the Order, 1st Degree. - **The Order of Honour:** 327. Badge of the Order, 2nd Degree. - **The Order of the Red Star:** 328. Badge of the Order.

PORTUGAL

The Order of the Tower and the Sword: 329. Badge of the Order, Grand Collar and Grand Cross. - 330. Collar of the Order. - 331. Badge of the Order, Knight, old model. - **The Order of Christ:** 332. Star of the Order, Grand Cross and Grand Officer. - 333. Badge of the Order, Officer. - **The Order of Aviz:** 334. Star of the Order, Grand Cross and Grand Officer. - 335. Badge of the Order, Grand Cross, Grand Officer and Commander, shown here on breast riband.

PORTUGAL

The Order of Sant' Iago: 336. Collar of the Order. - 337. Badge of the Order. - 338. Star of the Order, Commander. - 339. Badge of the Order, Knight. - **The Order of Infante Dom Henrique:** 340. Grand Collar. - 341. Badge of the Order, Grand Collar. - 342. Star of the Order, Grand Collar, Grand Cross, and Grand Officer. - 343. The Infante Dom Henrique Medal.

PORTUGAL

The Imperial Order: 344. Badge of the Order, Knight. - **The Order of Merit:** 345. Breast Cross, Commander. - 346. Badge of the Order, Officer. - **The Order 'Instruçao Publica':** 347. Star of the Order, Commander. - 348. Badge of the Order, 5th Class. - **The Order of 'Mérito Agricola e Industrial':** 349-350. Badges of the Order, Commander.

SPAIN

The Order of Charles III: 351. Badge of the Order, Grand Cross with Collar and Commander, here shown on a sash. - 352. Star of the Order, Grand Cross. - 353. Star of the Order, Commander by Number. - 354. Badge of the Order, Knight.

355

357

356

358

SPAIN

The Order of Isabella the Catholic: 355. Badge of the Order, Grand Cross. - 356. Star of the Order, Grand Cross with Collar and Grand Cross. - 357. The Silver Cross. - 358. The Medal of Isabella the Catholic.

SPAIN

The Civil Order of Mercy: 359-360. Badge of the Order, 4th Class. - 361. Star of the Order, Grand Cross and 2nd Class. - **The Order 'Mérito Agricola':** 362. Badge of the Order, Grand Cross, here shown on a breast riband. - **The Order of Africa:** 363. Badge of the Order, Commander. - **The Civil Order of Merit:** 364. Badge of the Order, Commander. - 365. Star of the Order, Grand Cross.

SPAIN

The 'Yoke and Arrows' Order: 366. Badge of the Order, 2nd to 4th Class, here shown on a breast riband. - **The Order of Alfonso X, the Wise:** 367. Badge of the Order, 3rd Class. - 368. Medal. - **The Civil Order of Health:** 369. Badge of the Order, 3rd Class. - **The Order of San Raimundo de Penafort:** 370. Badge of the Order, 1st and 2nd Class. - 371. Collar of the Order, 2nd Class. - 372. Star of the Order, 2nd Class. - 373. Badge of the Order, 3rd and 4th Class.

SPAIN

The Military Order of Merit: 374. Star of the Order, 2nd Class. - 375. Star of the Order, 3rd Class. - 376-377. Badges of the Order, 1st Class. - **The Naval Order of Merit:** 378. Star of the Order, 2nd Class. - 379-380. Badge of the Order, 1st Class. - **The Air Force Order of Merit:** 381-382. Badges of the Order, 1st Class.

ITALY

The Order of Merit: 383. Badge of the Order, Grand Cross with Collar. - 384. Collar of the Order. - 385. Star of the Order, Grand Cross. - 386. Badge of the Order, Officer. - 387. Badge of the Order, Knight.

ITALY

The Military Order of Italy: 388. Star of the Order, Grand Cross. - 389. Badge of the Order, Grand Officer and Commander. - 390. Badge of the Order, Officer. - 391. **The War Cross. - The Order 'Stella della Solidarietà Italiana':** 392. Star of the Order, 1st Class. - 393. Badge of the Order, 2nd Class. - 394. Badge of the Order, 3rd Class.

THE VATICAN STATE

The Order of the Golden Spur: 395. Badge of the Order. - 396. Collar of the Order. - 397. Star of the Order.

THE VATICAN STATE

The Order of Pius: 398. Badge of the Order, Commander with Star and Commander. - 399. Star of the Order, Grand Cross. - 400. Star of the Order, Commander with Star. - 401. Badge of the Order, Knight. - **The Order of Saint Gregory the Great:** 402. Star of the Order, Grand Cross. - 403. Badge of the Order, Military, Knight. - 404. Badge of the Order, Civil, Knight.

THE VATICAN STATE

The Order of Saint Sylvester: 405. Badge of the Order, Commander with Star and Commander, here shown on the Collar. - 406. Collar of the Order until 1905. - 407. Star of the Order, Grand Cross. - 408. Badge of the Order, Knight. - 409. **The Papal Lateran Cross.** - 410. **The Cross of Honour 'Pro Ecclesia et Pontifice'.**

THE VATICAN STATE

The Cross of Merit of the Sovereign Military Order of Malta: 411. Badge of the Order, Grand Cross of Merit with Star and Sash. - 412. Star of the Order, Collar of Merit, Grand Cross of Merit with Star and Sash, and Grand Cross of Merit with Star. - **The Sovereign Military Order of Malta:** 413-414. Badges of the Order. - 415. Profess Cross.

JUGOSLAVIA

The Jugoslavian Grand Star: 416. Badge of the Order. - 417. Star of the Order. - **The Order of the Jugoslav Star:** 418. Badge of the Order, 2nd and 3rd Class. - 419. Star of the Order, 2nd Class.

JUGOSLAVIA

The Order of the Jugoslav Flag: 420. Badge of the Order, 1st Class. - 421. Star of the Order, 1st Class. - 422. Badge of the Order, 2nd and 3rd Class. - 423. Badge of the Order, 4th Class.

SAN MARINO

The Order of Saint Marinus: 424. Star of the Order, Grand Cross. - 425. Badge of the Order, Grand Officer and Commander. - 426. Badge of the Order, Officer. - **The Order of Saint Agatha:** 427. Star of the Order, Grand Cross. - 428. Badge of the Order, Knight.

GREECE

The Order of the Saviour: 429. Badge of the Order, Grand Cross. - 430. Star of the Order, Grand Cross. - 431. Badge of the Order, 4th Class. - 432. Badge of the Order, 5th Class.

GREECE

The Order of Saint George and Saint Constantine: 433. Badge of the Order, Civil, Collar. - 434. Collar of the Order. - 435. Breast Cross, Civil, Collar. - **The Order of Saint Olga and Saint Sophia:** 436. Badge of the Order, 1st Class. - 437. Star of the Order, 1st and 2nd Class.

GREECE

The Order of George I: 438. Badge of the Order, Military, Grand Cross. - 439. Star of the Order, Military, Grand Cross. - 440. Star of the Order, Civil, Grand Commander, here gilded. - 441. Badge of the Order, Civil, 4th Class. - 442. The Memorial Medal.

GREECE

The Order of the Phoenix: 443. Badge of the Order, Grand Cross. - 444. Star of the Order, Grand Cross and Grand Commander. - 445. Badge of the Order, 4th Class. - 446. Badge of the Order, Military, 5th Class. - **The Hundredth Anniversary Memorial Medal of the Greek Royal House:** 447. Gentleman's Medal. - 448. Lady's Medal. - 449. **The War Cross, 1940.** - **The Order for Good Deeds:** 450. Badge of the Order, 4th Class.

DESCRIPTIONS

This encyclopaedia of Orders gives on the following pages some information concerning all present-day *international* European Orders, that is to say Orders which are not merely reserved for the nationals of a country but which may also be conferred on foreigners. The descriptions follow the same geographical order of sequence as the insignia of Orders reproduced in the colour plates, as well as the official order of sequence applicable to the Orders concerned in each country, and have been prepared on the basis of the statutes of the respective Orders and other official announcements, supplemented by the latest literature concerning Orders from each country.

The descriptions have been constructed on the following lines:

First, the official English name of the Order is given, where this exists; otherwise a translation of the name of the Order in the original language, which follows in brackets, is given. Then follow the date of institution of the Order and the name of the founder, together with information concerning any historical cause for the institution, in addition to a brief reference to red-letter days in the history of the Order. In a discussion of the field of conferment of the Orders, an explanation is given of the services for which and to whom the Order may be conferred, including whether it may be conferred on civilians or military, whether it is reserved for Heads of State or is subject to limitations such as rank, age, religion or a fixed annual quota of conferment and

if it may perhaps be conferred posthumously. A reference to the organisation of the Order gives information concerning the Master of the Order, Grand Master, College of Heralds or Council, as well as Days of the Order and of investiture. Then follows a detailed exposition of the division of the Order into sections and classes, giving the insignia of the Order appertaining to each class or degree, and with a number referring to the reproductions of the insignia concerned in the colour plates. This is rounded off with a brief description of the insignia of the Order, with an explanation of any symbolism and a translation of any inscriptions; the designations "gold" and "silver" in these descriptions may equally cover "gilt" or "silver plate" and any sash appertaining to the Order is always worn across the *right* shoulder and Badges of the Order and Stars of the Order on the *left* side of the breast where nothing to the contrary is stated. Finally where there is an obligation to surrender the Order in the event of death, this is stated.

The numbers preceding the individual articles refer to the numbers on the colour plates for the insignia appertaining to the Order concerned. If an article is not numbered, the insignia of the Order concerned are not reproduced in the colour plates, but are shown in a line drawing in connection with the text. The latter also applies to insignia which differ only to a small extent from those already reproduced.

ICELAND

1–5. The Icelandic Order of the Falcon *(Hin Islenzka Falkaorda)* was instituted on 3rd July 1921 by King Christian X of Denmark and Iceland. The Order received new statutes on 11th July 1944 when Iceland was declared a Republic. The Order may be awarded to Icelanders and to foreigners for services to the country and to mankind. The President of Iceland is the Grand Master of the Order. The Order is conferred after nomination by a council of five, but in special cases on the President's own initiative.

The Order has three classes, the 2nd Class being divided into two grades:

1. *Grand Cross*, which wears the Badge of the Order (1) on a sash or collar (2) and Star of the Order (3).

2. (i) *Grand Knight with Star* which wears the Badge of the Order (1) on necklet and the Star of the Order (4).

(ii) *Grand Knight*, which wears the Badge of the Order (1) on a necklet.

3. *Knight* which wears the Badge of the Order (5) on a chest riband.

The Collar of the Order is reserved for the Grand Master and foreign Heads of State.

The Badge of the Order is a white-enamelled Latin Cross in gold with arms widened out. The obverse medallion bears a falcon, the national bird of Iceland, on a blue background. The reverse medallion bears the inscription "Seytjandi juni 1944" (seventeenth June, 1944), the date of the declaration of the Republic, in an oval scroll. The original Royal Crown above the cross has now been replaced by a stylized lily.

The Stars of the Order, which vary in size according to class, are silver with 8 points and with faceted rays. The Grand Cross Star bears a Badge of the Order, and the Star of the 2nd Class a medallion with a falcon on a blue background.

The Collar of the Order, which is in gold, consists of 25 medallions with a falcon on a blue background and 25 medallions with the coat of arms of the Icelandic State.

The Riband of the Order is blue with white-edged red border stripes, the national colours of Iceland. It is worn across the *left shoulder* or around the neck, also by ladies. When worn as a chest riband, it is mounted in crossed form.

All insignia must be returned on the death of the holder.

6. The Icelandic Life-saving Medal was instituted on 9th October 1950. The Medal may be awarded to Icelanders and foreigners who have saved the lives of Icelanders while endangering their own.

The Medal has two classes, *gold and silver*, and is worn on an ultramarine chest riband. The subject on the obverse is the Mountain Queen with the legend "Afreksmerki hins isslenzka lydveldis" (The Icelandic Life-saving Medal), and the reverse bears the coat of arms of the Icelandic State.

7. The President of Iceland's Medal was instituted in 1954. The Medal may be awarded to Icelanders and to foreigners for services to the President during his tenure of office.

The Medal has one class, *silver*, and is worn on an ultramarine vertically mounted chest riband. The subject of the obverse is Ingolfr Arnarson, Iceland's first settler, in the bow of a Viking boat with the legend "Heidurspenningur forseta Islands" (The President of Iceland's Medal), and the reverse bears the coat of arms of the Icelandic State.

NORWAY

8–14. The Order of Saint Olaf *(Sanct Olavs Orden)* was instituted on 21st August 1847 by King Oscar I and revived on 9th June 1906 by King Haakon VII. Its present statutes date from 15th March 1928. The Order is named after Olaf the Holy, the patron saint of Norway, who was killed in the battle of Stiklestad in 1030. The Order may be conferred upon Norwegians and foreigners for services to the country and to mankind. The ruling Monarch is the Master of the Order.

The Order has three classes, the 2nd and 3rd Class each being divided into two grades:

1. *Grand Cross*, which wears the Badge of the Order (8) on a sash or collar (9) and the Star of the Order (10).

2. (i) *Commander with Star*, which wears the Badge of the Order (12) on a necklet and the Star of the Order (11).

(ii) *Commander*, which wears the Badge of the Order (12) on a necklet.

3. (i) *Knight 1st Class*, which wears the Badge of the Order (13) on a chest riband.

(ii) *Knight*, which wears the Badge of the Order (14) on a chest riband.

In special cases, the Collar of the Order may be awarded to holders of the 1st Class. Similarly, all classes of the Order, as a special distinction, may be awarded the Order "with diamonds". In this event they are worn even after conferment of a higher class of the Order. A military person on whom the Order is conferred receives the Badge of the Order with crossed swords beneath the crown (8).

The *Badge of the Order* is a white-enamelled Maltese Cross in gold (in silver for knights) pendant on the Norwegian Royal Crown. The obverse medallion bears the Norwegian lion on a red background, and the reverse medallion the motto of the founder "Justice and Truth". There is a crowned "O" for "Olaf" between the arms of the cross. Until 1937 the Royal Crown bore a lion above the orb.

The *Stars of the Order* for 1st and 2nd Classes are an 8-pointed faceted silver star and a faceted Maltese Cross in silver respectively. The Grand Cross Star bears a Badge of the Order without the crown, and the Star 2nd Class a medallion with the Norwegian lion on a red background and crowned "O"s between the arms of the cross.

The *Collar of the Order*, which is in gold, consists of 6 crowned "O"s and 6 State coats of arms with 12 old Trondheim archiepiscopal insignia: a gold cross with trefoil ends and silver axes with gold shafts.

The *Riband of the Order* is red with white-edged blue border stripes, the national colours of Norway. Clergy wear the Grand Cross Riband around the neck with vestments, and ladies wear the Badge of the Order for 2nd and 3rd Classes on a bow.

All insignia must be returned on the death of the holder. This, however, does not apply to insignia awarded "with diamonds".

15. The Medal of Saint Olaf was instituted on 17th March 1939. The Medal may be awarded to Norwegians and to foreigners for the meritorious spreading of knowledge concerning Norway abroad and, in time of war, for personal services to the Norwegian cause. In the latter case, it is awarded with an oak branch in silver on the riband. It may also be awarded posthumously.

The Medal has one class, *silver*, and is worn on a vertically mounted red chest riband with white-edged blue border stripes, as for that of the *Order of Saint Olaf* (8–14). The obverse bears the portrait and motto of the reigning Monarch; the reverse the Trondheim archiepiscopal insignia. At the top, the Medal bears the monogram of the reigning Monarch.

The Medal is personal property and is not returned on the death of the holder.

16. The War Cross was instituted on 21st May 1941 by King Haakon VII in exile in London. The decoration may be awarded to civilians and to the military, to Norwegians and to foreigners, who have in war time distinguished themselves in a particularly outstanding manner by showing personal bravery or by leading military units in the Army, Navy or Air Force. It may also be awarded posthumously. The War Cross is worn by Norwegians before all other decorations.

The Cross is a trefoil cross, also called an Olaf Cross, in bronze with the coat of arms of the Norwegian State on a shield in the centre. It is worn on a vertically mounted red chest riband with a white-edged blue centre stripe and an added sword.

The Cross is personal property and is not returned on the death of the holder.

The *War Medal* was instituted at the same time as the War Cross.

17. King Haakon VII's Cross of Liberty was instituted on 18th March 1945. The decoration may be awarded to civilians and to the military, to Norwegians and to foreigners, who have acquired great merit for the Norwegian cause by outstanding civil or military action in time of war. It may also be awarded posthumously.

The Cross is a white-enamelled, so-called "George Cross" in gold with trefoil ends. The centre medallion bears the monogram of the founder above a "V" for the Latin word "Victoria" (victory) on a red background, and the plain back of the Cross bears his motto "Alt for Norge", (Everything for Norway) and the date "7th June, 1945". The Cross is worn on a vertically mounted blue chest riband with white-edged stripes.

The Cross is personal property and

is not returned on the death of the holder.

King Haakon VII's Liberty Medal was instituted at the same time as King Haakon VII's Cross of Liberty.

SWEDEN

18–20. The Most Noble Order of the Seraphim *(Kungliga Serafimerorden)* was instituted on 23rd February 1748 by King Frederik I as – it is said – a revival of an older Order of the Seraphim dating from the second half of the sixteenth century. The present statutes of the Order date from 22nd March 1952. Swedish Princes are born Knights of the Order of the Seraphim, while others must be Knights Grand Cross of another Swedish Order to become a Knight of the Order of the Seraphim. The number of Swedish Knights of the Order of the Seraphim is restricted to 32. The Order may only be conferred on Swedes for the very highest services to Monarch and country which have rendered the person concerned worthy of the highest Offices in the land. It may also be conferred upon foreign Princes and Heads of State, and upon other foreigners for special services. The reigning Monarch is the Master of the Order. At

The Order of the Seraphim: Star of the Order, new model

the death of a Knight of the Order of the Seraphim, the bells are rung at the *Riddarholmskyrkan* in *Stockholm*, and his coat of arms is set up in the church.

The Order has one class, *Knight* and *Commander* (for clergy and ladies, *Member* and *Commander*) of his *Royal Majesty's Order*, which wears the Badge of the Order (18) on a sash or on a collar (19) and the Star of the Order (20).

The *Badge of the Order* is a white-enamelled Maltese Cross in gold pendant on the Swedish Royal Crown. The obverse medallion bears the monogram of Christ "IHS" for "Iesus Hominum Salvator" (Jesus, Saviour of Mankind) surrounded by Sweden's three golden crowns, together with a Latin Cross and three Nails of the Cross on a blue background. The reverse medallion bears the monogram of the institutor, "FRS" for "Fridericus Rex Sueciæ". There are patriarchal crosses on the arms of the cross, and seraphs in the angles of the cross.

The *Star of the Order* is a Maltese Cross in silver with the same ornamentation as the Badge of the Order.

The *Collar of the Order*, which is in gold, consists of 11 blue-enamelled patriarchal crosses and 11 seraphs.

The *Riband of the Order* is plain, pale blue.

The *Seraphim Medal* is associated with the Order. It may be awarded to people who have carried out specially deserving work in the care of the poor and the sick.

21–27. The Royal Order of the Sword was instituted on 23rd February 1748 by King Frederik I as, it is said, a revival of the Livonian Order of the Knights of the Sword dating from the first half of the thirteenth century, which was later adopted into the *Teutonic Order* (see page 176). Its present statutes date from 22nd March 1952. The Order may be awarded to Swedish officers for long and efficient service in the Forces in times of war and of peace. It may also be awarded to foreigners. The reigning Monarch is the Master of the order.

The Order has three classes, the 2nd and 3rd Classes each being divided into two grades:

1. *Commander Grand Cross* which wears the Badge of the Order (21) on a sash or on a collar (22) and the Star of the Order (23).

2. (i) *Commander 1st Class*, which wears the Badge of the Order (21) on a necklet and the Star of the Order (23) without the angles of the cross filled in.

(ii) *Commander*, which wears the Badge of the Order (21) on a necklet.

3. (i) *Knight* (for clergy and ladies, *Member*), 1st Class, which wears the Badge of the Order (24) on a chest riband.

(ii) *Knight* (for clergy and ladies, *Member*), which wears the Badge of the Order (25) on a chest riband.

The Collar of the Order is worn by Swedes on special command. It may be awarded to foreigners as a special distinction. Insignia awarded "with diamonds" or for war services are worn even after the conferment of a higher class of the Order.

The *Badge of the Order* is a diagonal white-enamelled Maltese Cross in gold (in silver for Knights) pendant on the Swedish Royal Crown. The obverse medallion bears Sweden's three golden crowns around an upright sword on a blue background, and the reverse medallion an upright sword with a laurel wreath around the point and the legend "Pro Patria" (For Homeland). There are golden crowns in the angles of the cross. The Badge of the Order has crossed swords with blades turned downwards beneath the crown, and for 1st and 2nd class also swords pointing downwards at the sides and crossed swords beneath the cross.

The *Stars of the Order* are each a Maltese Cross in silver with the same obverse medallion as the Badge of the Order. The Grand Cross Star has golden crowns in the angles of the cross, whereas the Star, 2nd Class, is without filled-in angles of the cross.

The Collar of the Order, which is in gold, consists of 11 swords in blue-enamelled scabbards with sword-belt and 11 shields with blue-enamelled helmets.

The *Riband of the Order* is yellow with blue-edged stripes, Sweden's national colours.

Associated with the Order are the *Badge of the Sword* (26) and the *Medal of the Sword* (27), both instituted on 26th June 1850, which may be awarded to non-commissioned officers and men respectively for at least 16 years' service.

Further, the Order has the following ranks which are only awarded when Sweden is at war:

The Order of the Sword: War Cross

Knight of the Grand Cross of the Order of the Sword 1st Class, which wears a Knight's Cross (24) of the same size as the Grand Cross (21) on a necklet and an upright silver sword on the left side of the chest.

Knight of the Grand Cross of the Order of the Sword, which wears a Knight's Cross (24) of the same size as the Grand Cross (21) on a necklet and a set of crossed silver swords with up-turned blades on the left side of the chest.

The War Cross of the Order of the Sword, which has three classes, *gold*, *silver* and *bronze*, is worn on the chest riband of the Order and is provided

with an upright sword of the same metal as the cross.

The first two decorations were instituted in 1788, and the last in 1952.

28–32. The Royal Order of the Northern Star *(Kungliga Nordstjärneorden)* was instituted on 23rd June 1748 by King Frederik I. Its present statutes date from 22nd March 1952. The Order may be awarded to Swedes and to foreigners for civilian services, official and Civil Service activities, scientific services, literary, scholastic and beneficial work, as well as for advantageous innovations. The reigning Monarch is the Master of the Order.

The Order has three classes, the 2nd Class being divided into two grades:

1. *Commander Grand Cross*, which wears the Badge of the Order (28) on a sash or on a collar (29) and the Star of the Order (30).

2. (i) *Commander 1st Class*, which wears the Badge of the Order (28) on a necklet and the Star of the Order (31).

   (ii) *Commander*, which wears the Badge of the Order (28) on a necklet.

3. *Knight*, (for clergy and ladies, *Member*), which wears the Badge of the Order (32) on a chest riband.

The Collar of the Order is worn by Swedes on special command. It may be awarded to foreigners as a special distinction. Insignia awarded "with diamonds" are worn even after the conferment of a higher class of the Order.

The *Badge of the Order* is a white-enamelled Maltese Cross in gold, pendant on the Swedish Royal Crown. The obverse medallion bears a white Northern Star with the legend "Nescit Occasum" (It knows no decline) on a blue background, and the reverse medallion is the same. There are golden crowns in the angles of the cross.

The *Stars of the Order* are both a Maltese Cross in silver with a Northern Star in the centre. The Grand Cross Star has pencils of rays in the angles of the cross, and in the Star 2nd Class the angles of the cross are not filled in.

The *Collar of the Order*, which is in gold, consists of 11 pairs of blue-enamelled, back-to-back, crowned "F"s for "Frederik" interlinked with 12 white Northern Stars.

The *Riband of the Order* is plain black, perhaps modelled on the French *Order of St. Michael* of 1469.

33–37. The Royal Order of Vasa *(Kungliga Vasaorden)* was instituted on 29th May 1772 by King Gustav III. Its present statutes date from 22nd March 1952. The Order may be conferred on Swedes and on foreigners for meritorious services in the fields of agriculture, mining, trade, crafts, industry, art and education, as well as in public office and public representation. The reigning Monarch is the Master of the Order.

The Order has three classes, the 2nd and 3rd Classes each being divided into two grades:

1. *Commander Grand Cross*, which wears the Badge of the Order (33) on a sash or on a collar (34) and the Star of the Order (35).

2. (i) *Commander 1st Class*, which wears the Badge of the Order (33) on a necklet and the Star of the Order (35) without the angles of the cross being filled in.

(ii) *Commander*, which wears the Badge of the Order (33) on a necklet.

3. (i) *Knight* (for clergy and ladies, *Member*), *1st Class*, which wears the Badge of the Order (33) in the same size as the Knight's Cross (36) on a chest riband.

(ii) *Knight* (for clergy and ladies, *Member*), which wears the Badge of the Order (33) in silver with a gold medallion, in the same size as the Knight's Cross (36), on a chest riband.

The *Collar of the Order* is worn by Swedes on special command; it may be conferred on foreigners as a special distinction. Insignia conferred "with diamonds" are worn even after conferment of a higher class of the Order.

The *Badge of the Order* is a white-enamelled Maltese Cross in gold (for Knights in silver) pendant on the Swedish Royal Crown. The obverse medallion bears a sheaf and a vase, Gustav Vasa's coat of arms, with the legend "Gustav 3. Instiktare 1772" (Gustav III, instituted 1772) on a red background, and the reverse medallion is the same. There are gold crowns in the angles of the cross.

The *Stars of the Order* are both a Maltese Cross in silver with a sheaf in the centre. The Star Grand Cross bears a nettle leaf, (the coat of arms of Holstein) in the angles of the cross, which indicates that the founder's father, King Adolf Frederik, came from Holstein. The Star 2nd Class has the angles of the cross not filled in.

The *Collar of the Order*, which is in gold, consists of 4 sheaves and 4 nettle leaves interlinked with 12 crowned shields with Sweden's three golden crowns on a blue background. Each shield is equipped with two caduceuses and two cornucopias, symbolizing trade and agriculture.

The *Riband of the Order* is plain green, probably symbolizing agriculture.

The Royal Badge of Vasa (36) and the *Royal Medal of Vasa* (37) belong to the Order. The latter of these has three grades, *gold*, *silver-gilt* and *silver*, and is struck in two sizes, 8th and 5th size. The Royal Crown above the medal is now replaced by a Vasa crown, as with the *Medal of the Sword* (27).

FINLAND
38–46. The Order of the Cross of Liberty *(Vapaudenristin ritarikunta)* has its origin in the *Cross of Liberty*, which, on the recommendation of the Finnish Commander-in-Chief at the time, Baron Carl Gustav Mannerheim, was instituted on 4th March 1918 for the War of Freedom and revived for the Winter War on 8th December 1939. It was converted into a permanent Order for time of war and time of peace on 16th December 1940. The present statutes of the Order date from 18th August 1944. The Order may

be conferred on officers, non-commissioned officers and men in the Finnish Defence Forces for military service, and to civilians for meritorious services for the benefit of defence. It may also be conferred on foreigners. Apart from individuals, the Order may be conferred on military units and organisations in Finland in time of war. The Commander-in-Chief of the Finnish Defence Forces is the Grand Master of the Order. The festival day of the Order is 4th June, the birthday of Marshal Mannerheim. The conferment of the Order in peace time has been suspended for the present.

The Order has a *Military* and a *Civil* Division, whose insignia are conferred with and without sword respectively. Each Division has a Grand Cross and four classes, the 1st Class being divided into two grades.

Classes and insignia for the *Military* Division are:

1.* *The Grand Cross of the Cross of Liberty*, which wears the Badge of the Order (39) in the same size as the Grand Cross (47) without oak leaves on a sash and the Star of the Order (38) in a size (49) corresponding to the Grand Cross Class.

1. (i) *The Cross of Liberty 1st Class with Star*, which wears the Badge of the Order (39) but with oak leaves only if conferred, on a necklet and the Star of the Order (38).

(ii) *The Cross of Liberty 1st Class*, which wears the Badge of the Order (39) on a necklet, but with oak leaves only if conferred.

2. *The Cross of Liberty 2nd Class*, which wears the Badge of the Order (39) on a chest riband, but with oak leaves only if conferred, and in a size corresponding to 2nd Class (40).

3. *The Cross of Liberty 3rd Class*, which wears the Badge of the Order (40) on a chest riband.

4. *The Cross of Liberty 4th Class*, which wears the Badge of the Order (40) in silver on a chest riband.

As a special distinction, the Grand Cross may be conferred "with diamonds", and similarly the four classes with swords may be conferred "with oak leaves" for special services at the Front or in command in time of war.

The insignia for the *Civil* Division of the Order are conferred without sword, the Riband of the Order being of a different colour, (yellow with red border or centre stripes). The Badge of the Order for 3rd and 4th Classes is in blue enamel (41).

According to the class, the *Badge of the Order* is an enamelled white, black or blue Cross of St. George surmounted by swastikas in gold or silver. The centre medallion bears a heraldic rose symbolizing the coat of arms of the Finnish State, nine roses for Finland's nine provinces. The cross has a laurel wreath as a mounting. For the *Military* Division, this is provided with swords, the two arms in armour with sword and scimitar of the Karelian coat of arms, symbolizing the eternal battle between East and West. Badges of the Order conferred in time of war bear the year of the outbreak of the war on the reverse.

The *Stars of the Order*, which vary in size according to class, are 5-pointed silver stars, provided with crossed swords for the *Military* Division. The centre medallion bears an heraldic rose on a background of a swastika on a black background with the legend "Isänmaan puolesta" (For the Fatherland) on a red background.

The *Riband of the Order* for the *Military* Division is red with white stripes, and for the *Civil* Division yellow with red stripes. The Grand Cross Riband and the Riband for the 1st and 2nd Classes have border stripes and the Riband for the 3rd and 4th Classes has centre stripes. The chest riband of the *Military* Division also bears a rosette (bow) behind the wreath of the Badge of the Order. Badges of the Order conferred "with oak leaves" have the oak leaves fixed to the wreath for 1st Class, and for the other classes they are sewn on to the Riband close above the wreath.

For outstanding bravery and meritorious military operations in time of war, the military irrespective of rank can be appointed Knights of the *Mannerheim Cross of the Cross of Liberty*, which has two classes:

1. *1st Class*, which wears the Badge of the Order (42) on a necklet.

2. *2nd Class*, which wears the Badge of the Order (43) without riband.

For a second award of 2nd Class, a set of crossed Field-Marshal's batons (43) are also worn.

The military may also be awarded the *Medal of Liberty*, which has two classes:

1. *1st Class*, which wears a medal in silver (44) on a chest riband with white border stripes.

2. *2nd Class*, which wears a medal in bronze (45) on a red chest riband with yellow border stripes.

The 1st Class may be conferred with a rosette as the highest military decoration.

Medals awarded in time of war bear on the obverse the Finnish lion with the legend "Urheudesta – För Tapperhet" (From the People of Finland – For Bravery) and the year of the outbreak of the war. Medals conferred in peace time have the same obverse and reverse subject as the *Medal of Merit of the Cross of Liberty*.

Medical personnel may be awarded:

The Cross of Liberty 3rd Class with Red Cross, which wears the Badge of the Order (40) with a Geneva Cross in the rose of the centre medallion.

The Cross of Liberty 4th Class with Red Cross, which wears the Badge of the Order (40) in silver with a Geneva Cross in the rose of the centre medallion.

According to whether the award is made in time of war or of peace, the Badge of the Order is worn on the Military Division's red chest Riband (40), but without the rosette, or on the Civil Division's yellow chest Riband (41).

Civilians may be awarded the *Medal of Merit of the Cross of Liberty*, which has two classes:

1. *1st Class*, which wears a medal (46) in silver on a green chest riband with red border stripes and black centre stripe.

2. *2nd Class*, which wears a medal (46) in bronze on the same riband as for 1st Class.

The medal may be conferred in gold (46) for special services.

On the obverse the medal bears the Finnish lion with the legend (Isänmaan puolesta" – (For the Fatherland) and on the reverse the inscription "Suomen kansalta" (From the people of Finland) without date.

Surviving relatives of the fallen may be awarded *The Cross of Mourning of the Cross of Liberty*. This is a Badge of the Order (40) in silver on a black chest riband with a rosette. Surviving relatives of others who perish in war may be awarded the *Medal of Mourning of the Cross of Liberty*. This is a medal (46) in silver on a black chest riband.

In all, the Order, in its various forms, may be awarded in 41 different ways. If more than one of the decorations of the Order are conferred on a person in time of war, they are all worn. Only the highest of decorations for services in peace time is worn. Decorations conferred on foreigners in peace time must be returned on the death of the holder.

47–54. Finland's Order of the White Rose (*Suomen Valkoisen Ruusun ritarikunta*) was instituted on 28th January 1919 by the Regent at the time, Baron Carl Gustav Mannerheim. Its present statutes date from 16th May 1919. The Order may be conferred on Finns for civilian services and on foreigners for services to Finland. In time of war it may also be awarded for bravery in the Field. The President of Finland is the Grand Master of the Order, and 6th December, Finland's Day of Independence, is the festival day of the Order.

The Order has five classes:

1. *Commander Grand Cross*, which wears the Badge of the Order (47) on a sash or on a collar (48) and the Star of the Order (49).

2. *Commander 1st Class,* which wears the Badge of the Order (51) on a necklet and the Star of the Order (50), both, however, with sword only when

conferred.

3. *Commander*, which wears the Badge of the Order (51) only, on a necklet.

4. *Knight* or *Member 1st Class*, which wears the Badge of the Order (52) on a chest riband with rosette.

5. *Knight* or *Member*, which wears the Badge of the Order (52) in silver on a chest riband with rosette.

The *Collar of the Order* is reserved for the Grand Master, but as a gesture of courtesy it may be conferred on foreign Heads of State. Similarly all classes of the Order may be conferred "with diamonds". Insignia awarded for bravery in war are provided with crossed swords (50–51).

The *Badge of the Order* is a white-enamelled Cross of St. George in gold (for Knights in silver), with the Finnish lion in the angles of the cross. The centre medallion bears a white heraldic rose on a blue background; the reverse is without the medallion.

The *Stars of the Order* are 5-pointed silver stars. The Star of the Grand Cross has partially-gilded rays. The centre medallion bears a white heraldic rose on a blue background with the legend "Isänmaan hyväksi" (For the Good of the Fatherland) on a black background.

The *Collar of the Order*, which is in gold, consists of 9 white heraldic roses symbolizing Finland's nine provinces and 6 stylized spruce branches. The original swastikas (48) were replaced by spruce branches in 1963.

The *Riband of the Order* is plain navy blue. The clergy wear the Grand Cross around the neck with vestments.

If the Order is conferred "with diamonds", they are fitted in the rose on the Badge of the Order, and on the Star of the Order also around the inscription.

Associated with the Order are: *Finland's Badge of the White Rose* (53) which has one class, silver. This is only conferred on ladies and is worn on the chest riband of the Knight's Cross. In time of war, the decoration may be conferred in *bronze with swords* as a parallel to the British *Victoria Cross* (98).

Finland's Medal of the White Rose (54), which has three classes: *1st Class with Gold Cross*, silver with gold cross; *1st Class*, silver; and *2nd Class*, bronze. They are worn on the chest riband of the Knight's Cross.

55–59. The Order of the Lion of Finland

(Suomen Leijonan ritarikunta) was instituted on 11th September 1942. The Order may be conferred on both Finns and foreigners for general civic achievement; in time of war it may also be conferred for military services. The President of Finland is the Grand Master of the Order and the 6th December, Finland's Day of Independence, is the festival day of the Order.

The Order has 5 classes:

1. *Commander Grand Cross*, which wears the Badge of the Order (55) on a sash and the Star of the Order (56).

2. *Commander 1st Class*, which wears the Badge of the Order (57), but with swords only when specially conferred, on a necklet, and the Star of the Order (56) in a size corresponding to the 2nd Class (50) but without silver-gilt rays.

3. *Commander*, which wears the Badge of the Order (57) on a necklet, but with swords only when conferred.

4. *Knight 1st Class*, which wears the Badge of the Order (57) in the same size as the Knight's Cross (58), but with swords only when conferred, on a chest riband with rosette.

5. *Knight*, which wears the Badge of the Order (57) in silver and in the same size as the Knight's Cross (58), but with swords only when conferred, on a chest riband without rosette. Insignia conferred for military services are provided with crossed swords (57).

The *Badge of the Order* is a white-enamelled Cross of St. George in gold, and in silver for Knights. The centre medallion bears the Finnish lion on a red background. The reverse is without a medallion.

Finland's Order of the White Rose: Collar of the Order, new model, with Badge of the Order, Commander, Grand Cross

The *Stars of the Order* vary in size according to class and are 5-pointed silver stars. The Star Grand Cross has rays partly silver-gilt, and the same centre medallion as the Badge of the Order.

The *Riband of the Order* is plain dark red.

Associated with the Order are:

The Cross of Merit of the Order of the Finnish Lion (58), which may be awarded to civilians and non-commissioned officers. The Cross is a silver cross with the same centre medallion as the Knight's Cross, and is worn on its chest riband.

The Pro Finlandia Medal (59), which was instituted on 10th December 1943 and may be awarded to authors and artists. The Medal ranks after Commander.

The Medal is of silver-gilt and is worn on the chest riband of the Knight's Cross. The obverse bears the Finnish lion and the reverse the inscription "Pro Finlandia" (For Finland) and the name of the holder.

60–62. The Order of the Holy Lamb (*Pyhän Karitsab ritarikunta*) was instituted on 20th June 1935 by the Greek Orthodox Catholic Church of Finland as a reward for services to it. It may be conferred on persons irrespective of confession or nationality. Finland's Greek Orthodox Archbishop is the Grand Master of the Order.

The Order has 5 classes:

1. *Commander Grand Cross*, which wears the Badge of the Order (60) in the same size as the Grand Cross (55) on a sash and the Star of the Order (61) with the seraphims at the angles of the cross in gold.

2. *Commander 1st Class*, which wears the Badge of the Order (60) on a necklet and the Star of the Order (61).

3. *Commander 2nd Class*, which wears the Badge of the Order (60) on a necklet.

4. *Knight* or *Member 1st Class*, which wears the Badge of the Order (60) in the same size as the Knight's Cross (58) on a chest riband.

5. *Knight* or *Member 2nd Class*, which wears the Badge of the Order (60) in silver and in the same size as the Knight's Cross (58) on a chest riband.

The *Badge of the Order* is a blue-enamelled bar cross in gold, and for Knights 2nd Class in silver. The centre medallion bears the Agnus Dei (Lamb of God) badge on a white background. There are seraphims at the angles of the cross.

The *Stars of the Order* are Badges of the Order in an extended form, the Star Grand Cross with the seraphims at the angles of the cross in gold, and the Star 2nd Class with the seraphims at the angles of the cross in silver. Further, the centre medallion bears the Agnus Dei badge on a white background with the legend "Kirkon hyväksi" (For the benefit of the Church) on a black background.

The *Riband of the Order* is pale blue with white edge stripes.

All insignia conferred on foreigners must be returned on the death of the holder.

Associated with the Order is *The Medal of the Holy Lamb* (62) which has two grades, *gold* and *silver*, and is worn on the chest riband of the Order.

63. Finland's Olympic Cross of Merit (*Suomens Olympialainen*) was instituted in 1952 as a reward for achievement on the occasion of the 15th Olympiad in Finland.

The decoration has two classes:

1. *1st Class*, which wears the Badge of the Order (63) on a necklet.

2. *2nd Class*, which wears the Badge of the Order (63) in a size corresponding to that of the 2nd Class (64) on a chest riband.

The *Badge of the Order* is a 5-armed white-enamelled star in gold with the five Olympic rings in the centre. In the four upper spaces between the arms of the cross there is a stylized spruce branch, and in the lower the Finnish lion. The Star is crowned by a sacrificial bowl with the Olympic flame.

The *Riband of the Order* is blue with five white stripes, one along each border of the riband and three in the centre, Finland's national colours.

Finland's Olympic Medal of Merit was instituted at the same time as Finland's Olympic Cross of Merit.

64. Finland's Cross of Merit for Athletics (*Suomen Urheilun ansioristi*) was instituted on 1st March 1945. The decoration may be conferred on Finns and on foreigners, although the highest class is for Finns only with a maximum of 12, for outstanding achievement in Finnish athletics and in the field of physical education in general. It is conferred by the Ministry of Education, and is awarded on 26th February, the birthday of the Finnish Director of Sport, Professor Ivar Wilskman.

The decoration has three classes:

1. *The Grand Cross of Merit*, which wears the Badge of the Order (64) in a size corresponding to 1st Class (63) on a necklet.

2. *The Cross of Merit* in *gold*, which

wears the Badge of the Order (64) on a chest riband.

3. *The Cross of Merit* in *silver*, which wears the Badge of the Order (64) in silver on a chest riband.

The *Badge of the Order* is a white-rimmed blue-enamelled Cross of St. George in gold, and for 3rd Class in silver. The subject of the obverse medallion is a ball between two hands surrounded by a stylized laurel wreath, and the reverse medallion is an heraldic rose with the legend "Urheilu – Isänmaa" (Athletics – Fatherland). The cross has a stylized laurel wreath as a mounting.

The *Riband of the Order* is in a blue and white ladder pattern, the national colours of Finland.

Finland's Medal of Merit for Athletics was instituted at the same time as Finland's Cross of Merit for Athletics.

GREAT BRITAIN

65–69. The Most Noble Order of the Garter was founded in 1348 by King Edward III as a noble fraternity consisting of the King and 25 Knights Companions. Members of the Royal Family are known as "Royal Knights Companions" and foreigners are considered as "Extra Knights". In the course of time more than 100 commoners have become Knights of the Garter, but non-Christians cannot become members of the Order. There are several versions of the origin of the Order. The most picturesque is the anecdote concerning King Edward at a Court ball, where a lady, maybe the Countess of Salisbury, lost one of her garters. Bending down and picking it up, the lady blushing and those present laughing, he tied it around his own leg with the remark, "Honi soit qui mal y pense. I shall turn it into the most honoured garter ever worn". (Dishonoured be he who thinks evil of it.) The Order is considered to be the highest British civil and military honour obtainable. The conferment of the Order entails adoption into knighthood and the right to use the title "Sir".

Further, holders of the Order are entitled to add the letters "K.G.", (Knight of the Garter) after their name. The banners and coats of arms of the Knights are hung in the Chapel of the Order, St. George's Chapel at Windsor. The reigning Monarch is The Sovereign of the Order, and 23rd April, St. George's Day, is the Day of the Order. A fee is paid to cover the cost of the Knight's Banner, Crest and Stall plate in St. George's Chapel.

The insignia consist of the Collar (66) and Badge Appendant known as the George (65), the Star (67), the Garter (69) and the Sash with the Investment Badge, called the Lesser George (68). The Collar with the George is only worn on Collar Days or on special occasions commanded by The Sovereign. At ceremonies in St. George's Chapel the Knights Companion wear the Mantle and Hat of the Order. The Collar with the George is worn outside the Mantle and fixed to the shoulders with white satin bows.

The *Mantle* is of dark blue velvet lined with white taffeta. On the left side is an escutcheon of St. George within the Garter, the motto embroidered in gold letters.

The *Hat* is of black velvet lined with white taffeta. It is furnished with a plume of white ostrich feathers fastened to the hat by a badge bearing the design of the Garter enamelled blue with the motto in gold, and within a white enamelled shield with the Cross of St. George.

The *Garter* is dark blue velvet riband edged with gold with the motto of the Order, "Honi soit qui mal y pense", in gold letters and with gold-embroidered roses edged with gold chains. It is worn by ladies, *Ladies of the Garter*, around the left upper arm and by the Knights, *Knights of the Garter*, below the knee of the left leg.

The *George* is a gold and richly enamelled representation of St. George on horseback slaying the Dragon. As stated, it is worn suspended from the Collar.

The *Lesser George* is of gold, and consists of St. George slaying the Dragon, surrounded by an oval band bearing the motto. It is worn suspended on the sash of Saxon blue. The sash passes over the left shoulder and under the right arm, and the Badge rests on the right hip.

The *Collar* is of gold and weighs 30 troy ounces. The design consists of twenty four red-enamelled Tudor roses within dark blue-enamelled Garters bearing the motto in gold letters, and twenty-four lovers' knots. The roses and knots are placed alternately and joined to each other by gold links.

The *Star* is eight-pointed and of chipped silver. At its centre is a white-enamelled medallion bearing the Cross of St. George in red enamel and surrounded by a dark blue-enamelled Garter edged with gold bearing the motto in gold letters.

All the insignia must be returned on the death of the holder. Frederik IX of Denmark is one of the "Extra Knights" now living.

70–72. The Most Ancient and Most Noble Order of the Thistle. Although it seems probable that a Scottish Order of Chivalry existed in the fifteenth and sixteenth centuries, the Order of the Thistle did not become an established Order of Chivalry until it was revived by King James II of England (VII of Scotland) on the 29th May 1687. It was to continue to consist of The Sovereign and twelve Knights, an allusion to The Saviour and his Twelve Apostles. On the death of the King the Order fell into disuse, until it was revived by Queen Anne in 1703, and remodelled on the lines of the Order of the Garter. In 1821 King George IV temporarily increased the number of Knights to sixteen, and in 1827 this number became permanent. Members of the Royal Family are known as "Royal Knights". King Olaf V of Norway is an "Extra Knight" and he is the only Foreigner to be admitted to the Order for over 200 years. The confer-ment of the Order entails admission to Knighthood, and the right to bear the title "Sir". This, however, does not apply to foreigners. Holders of the Order are also entitled to add the letters "K.T." (Knight of the Thistle) after their name. The banners and coats of arms of the Knights are hung in the Chapel of the Order, St. Giles' Cathedral, Edinburgh. The reigning Monarch is The Sovereign of the Order, and 30th November, St. Andrew's Day, is the Day of the Order. The fee for admittance to the Order is £50.

The insignia consist of the Badge Appendant (70) which is worn on the Collar (71), the Star (72) and the Sash with the Investment Badge.

The Collar and Badge Appendant is only worn on Collar Days, or on special occasions as commanded by The Sovereign. At ceremonies in St. Giles Cathedral, the Knights wear the Mantle of the Order, made of green velvet lined with white taffeta and bearing an embroidered design of the Star on the left shoulder. The Collar and Badges are worn outside the mantle and secured on the shoulders by white satin bows.

The *Badge Appendant* is a gold image of St. Andrew in a green habit and purple surcoat, bearing before him a white-enamelled Cross of St. Andrew, the whole surmounted by gold rays.

The *Collar* is of gold and consists of alternate sprigs of Pine enamelled green and Thistles with white-enamelled heads.

The *Star* is of silver and is a combination of St. Andrews' Cross and a four-pointed star. Both Star and Cross are faceted. In the centre is a gold medallion charged with a green enamelled thistle surrounded by a green enamelled band bearing the motto "Nemo me impune lacessit".

The *Riband* is green and is worn over the left shoulder and under the right arm so that the *Investment Badge* rests on the right hip. This Badge is a plain gold one, oval in shape with, in the centre, the figure of St. Andrew holding the Cross of St. Andrew before him, and bearing the motto on the surrounding band.

The Order of the Bath: Star of the Order, Military, Knight Grand Cross

All insignia must be returned on the death of the holder.

73–77. The Most Honourable Order of the Bath. Although the Knighthood of the Bath is of great antiquity, the Order as we know it now was created by George I in 1725. It was reorganized in 1815. The Order may be conferred upon the military as a reward for outstanding war service, and on civilians as a reward for outstanding services in the Home Civil Service. The highest class of the Order is recognised as the highest British military honour to be obtained. Investment with the two highest classes of the Order entails admission to Knighthood and the right to bear the title "Sir". This, however, does not apply to foreigners who can only be admitted as "Honorary Members". A total of 34 Knights Grand Cross (22 Military and 12 Civil) are allotted Stalls in the Chapel of the Order, King Henry VII Chapel in Westminster Abbey. These Knights Grand Cross are entitled to have their Banners, Crests and Stall Plates affixed to their Stalls. The reigning Monarch is The Sovereign of the Order. The Great Master of the Order, at present the Duke of Gloucester, is appointed by The Monarch.

The Order has *Military* and *Civil* Divisions, each of three classes. The number of members in each class is limited.

Classes and insignia of the Military Division are:

1. *Knight Grand Cross.* (G.C.B.) which wears the Badge of the Order (77), but larger, on a crimson sash or on a collar (74) and also the Star of the Order.

2. *Knight Commander* (K.C.B.) which wears the Badge of the Order (77) on a crimson neckband and the Star of the Order (76).

3. *Companion* (C.B.), which wears the Badge of the Order (77), but smaller on a crimson neckband.

The Classes and insignia for the Civil Division are:

1. *Knight Grand Cross* (G.C.B.) which wears the Badge of the Order (73) on a crimson sash or on a collar (74) and the Star of the Order (75).

2. *Knight Commander* (K.C.B.), which wears the Badge of the Order (73) on a crimson neckband and the Star of the Order.

3. *Companion* (C.B.), which wears the Badge of the Order (73) on a crimson neckband.

The Collar of the Order is only worn on the special Collar Days or by Royal Command. The Knights Grand Cross wear the Mantle of the Order during the installation ceremonies in the Chapel of the Order.

The Badge Knight Grand Cross (Military Division) is a gold ball-tipped Maltese Cross enamelled white and edged with gold, with gold lions rampant between the arms. The centre medallion enamelled white bears a rose, a thistle and a shamrock, symbolizing England, Scotland and Ireland radiating from a sceptre between three gold Imperial Crowns, all within a red enamelled band bearing the motto "Tria Juncta in Uno" in gold letters, and surrounded by two laurel branches enamelled green. Beneath the medallion is a blue enamelled scroll with the inscription "Ich Dien" in gold letters. The Badges for Knights Commanders and Companions of the Military Division are exactly the same but smaller, according to the Class.

The Badge Knights Grand Cross (Civil Division) is a gold medallion in the centre of which are a rose, thistle and shamrock radiating from a sceptre between three Imperial Crowns, all within an oval band bearing the motto "Tria Juncta in Uno". The Badges of Knights Commanders and Companions of the Civil Division are exactly the same but smaller, according to the Class.

The Star–Knights Grand Cross (Military Division) is a silver faceted eight-pointed star with a gold Maltese Cross superimposed. In the centre is a white-enamelled medallion bearing three gold Imperial Crowns in relief, encircled by a red-enamelled band with the motto "Tria Juncta in Uno" in gold letters. The band is surrounded by a wreath of laurels enamelled green, the stems of which issue from a blue-enamelled scroll with the inscription "Ich Dien" in gold.

The Star–Knights Commanders (Military Division) is a silver pattée, with five graduated short rays issuing between the arms. The medallion,

crowns, band and motto, and the scroll and motto are exactly the same as in the Star of the Knight Grand Cross, but the laurel wreath is wider.

The Star–Knights Grand Cross (Civil Division) This is similar to the Star of the Knight Grand Cross, Military Division, but without the superimposed Maltese Cross, laurel wreath and scroll.

The Star–Knights Commanders (Civil Division) This is similar to the Star of the Military Division but without the laurel wreath and scroll.

The Collar which is common to both Divisions is gold and consists of nine Imperial Crowns and eight groups comprising a rose, thistle and shamrock* issuing from a sceptre all enamelled in their proper colours. Linking the Crowns and groups are seventeen white-enamelled knots.

The *Riband of the Order* is of one colour, crimson, without moire. It is worn over the right shoulder and under the left arm with the badge resting on the left hip.

The *Mantle*, only worn by a G.C.B., is of rich crimson satin lined with white taffeta, with the Star of the appropriate Division embroidered on the left shoulder.

The Collar of the Order must be returned on the death of the holder. The other insignia are personal property.

78–81. The Most Distinguished Order of Saint Michael and Saint George was founded on 12th August 1818 by King George III as a reward to the inhabitants of the Ionian islands and Malta, who had come under British sovereignty in 1814, for meritorious services to the British Crown, and to Britons for meritorious services in the Mediterranean. The Order is today conferrable upon diplomats and others in the Foreign Service, as well as on persons who have perfomed valuable administrative services in Commonwealth countries. It may also be conferred on foreigners, but it is rare for persons who are not

---

*In the Collar illustrated, on the left-hand side the rose, thistle and shamrock

have been incorrectly reversed with the Imperial Crown.

British nor under British sovereignty to be admitted into the Order. The conferment of the two highest classes of the Order entails admission to Knighthood and the right to bear the title, "Sir", and for ladies "Dame". This, however, does not apply to foreigners, who may be admitted only as "Honorary Members". The banners and the coats of arms of the Knights Grand Cross are hung in the Chapel of the Order in *St. Paul's Cathedral*, London. The reigning Monarch is The Sovereign of the Order.

The Order has three classes, with a limited number of members in each:

1. *Knight Grand Cross or Dame Grand Cross* (G.C.M.G.) which wears the Badge of the Order (78) on a sash or collar (79), and the Star of the Order (80).

2. *Knight Commander or Dame Commander* (K.C.M.G. or D.C.M.G.) which wears the Badge of the Order (78) on a necklet (gentlemen) or on a bow (ladies) and the Star of the Order (81).

3. *Companion* (C.M.G.) which wears the Badge of the Order (78) on a necklet (gentlemen) or on a bow (ladies.)

The ladies wear the insignia in a smaller form.

The Collar of the Order is worn only on the special Collar Days or by Royal Command. The Knights also wear the Mantle of the Order during the ceremonies in the Chapel of the Order.

The Badge of the Order which varies in size according to its class is a gold seven pointed star with v-edged extremities enamelled white and edged with gold, surmounted by an Imperial Crown. On the obverse of the medallion is a representation of the Archangel St. Michael holding a flaming sword in his right hand, and trampling upon Satan. This device is surrounded by a band enamelled blue and edged with gold, bearing the motto "Auspicium Melioris Aevi" in gold letters. On the reverse side of the medallion is a representation of St. George in armour and on horseback and the Dragon.

The *Stars of the Order*, 1st and 2nd Class, are a 7-armed faceted silver star with gold pencils of rays between the arms, and a faceted silver cross in the form of a Maltese Cross respectively, both with a red Cross of Saint George beneath the centre medallion, which has the same motive and inscription as the obverse medallion of the Badge.

The *Collar of the Order*, which is in gold, consists of 8 crowned lions symbolizing England, 8 white-enamelled Maltese Crosses symbolizing Malta, 4 Saint Michael and 4 Saint George monograms, and a pair of winged lions in the centre from which is suspended the Badge of the Order. These lions are crowned with a large Imperial Crown and in one fore-paw hold a book and a bunch of seven arrows.

The *Riband of the Order* is blue with a red centre stripe.

The Collar of the Order must be returned on the death of the holder unless he received it prior to the 14th December 1948. The other insignia are personal property.

The Belgian Foreign Secretary, Henri Spaak; the former German Chancellor, Konrad Adenauer, and the President of Pakistan, Field Marshal Mohammed Ayub Khan, are among the "Honorary Members" alive today.

The *Mantle* is of saxon-blue satin lined with scarlet silk. On the left side is a representation of the Star of the Order.

82. The Order of Merit was founded on 23rd June 1902 by King Edward VII as The Monarch's personal reward for specially eminent service in the armed forces and for unusually deserving achievement in the promotion of the arts, literature and science. The Order ranks after the Grand Cross of the *Order of the Bath* (73–77). The number of ordinary Members, citizens of countries within the British Commonwealth, is restricted to 24, not including foreigners. Foreigners are only admitted as "Honorary Members". The holders of the Order are entitled to add the letters "O.M." after their name.

The Order has a *Military* and a *Civil* Division, each of one class, *Member*, who wears the Badge of the Order (82) on a riband.

The *Badge of the Order* is a gold and red-enamelled cross pattée, convexed with dark blue-enamelled edges and surmounted by a Tudor Crown. In the centre upon blue enamel, and surrounded by a laurel wreath are the words "For Merit" in letters of gold. On the reverse, also surrounded by a laurel wreath, is the Royal Cypher.

The Badge given for distinguished Military Service has two silver swords with gold hilts placed saltire-wise through the angles of the Cross, the hilts downwards. The Badge is suspended by a ring attached to the top of the Crown fitted with a gold laurel chased loop through which the riband, half Garter-blue and half Bath-red passes. The Order is worn round the neck, by men and on a bow by women. It is not worn in miniature, but it is correct for the riband to be worn when ribands of other orders, decorations and medals are worn with various uniform.

Florence Nightingale received the Order in 1902, the only woman to receive it up to 1965 when the Order was awarded to Dr. Dorothy Hodgkin. Sir Winston Churchill was decorated with the Civil Division of the Order. Dr. Albert Schweitzer was an "Honorary Member" of the Civil Division. The former President of the U.S.A., Dwight D. Eisenhower, and the President of India, Dr. Radhakrishnan, are the "Honorary Members" alive today.

83. The Order of the Companions of Honour was founded on 4th June 1917 by King George V. It ranks after the Grand Cross of the *Order of the British Empire* (92–97). The Order may be conferred on men and on women for recognised services of national importance. Prime Ministers of the Commonwealth countries may make nominations. The number of ordinary Members is restricted to 65, not including foreigners, who are only admitted as "Honorary Members". The holders of the Order are entitled to add the letters "C.H." after their name.

The Order has one Class, *Member*, who wears the Badge of the Order (83) on a necklet (gentlemen) and on a bow (ladies).

The Badge is oval consisting of a gold medallion with a representation of an oak tree. Hanging from a branch is a shield of the Royal Arms and on the right a Knight armed and in armour mounted on a horse. Surrounding the medallion is a blue-enamelled border bearing the motto of the Order "In action faithful and in honour clear" in gold.

The *Riband of the Order* is crimson with border threads in gold. The Badge is not worn in miniature, but it is correct for the riband to be worn when the ribands of other orders, decorations and medals are worn with undress uniform.

84–85. The Royal Victorian Chain was instituted by King Edward VII in 1902. The Chain does not form part of the Royal Victorian Order (86–91) and it confers no precedence or addition to the style or title of the holder, but it indicates a rare token of the highest distinction and special esteem on the part of The Sovereign. It may be conferred upon Royalty or other distinguished personages, foreign as well as British.

The Chain is worn by men around the neck, and by ladies pinned to the left side of the dress.

The Chain is of gold, composed of three Tudor roses, two thistles, two shamrocks and two lotus flowers symbolizing England, Scotland, Ireland and India connected by a double chain. In the centre within a wreath is the cypher E.R.I. enamelled red, surmounted by the Imperial Crown, and pendant from the wreath the Badge of the Royal Victorian Order, the Cypher V and the Crown in the Badge being set in brilliants. Ladies wear the chain superimposed on a bow of Royal Victorian Order riband which is blue with a narrow edge of three stripes red, white and red on each side.

The chain must be returned upon the death of the holder.

The Royal Victorian Chain: Bow of the Order with Badge of the Order, Knight Commander and Commander of the Victorian Order

86–91. The Royal Victorian Order was founded on 21st April 1896 by Queen Victoria as a reward for personal services performed for The Sovereign. As a Family Order, it is beyond the influence of the Government. The Order may be conferred on Britons and on foreigners. It is used, inter alia, for The Sovereign's official visits abroad and for the visit of foreign Heads of State to Great Britain. Conferment of the two highest classes of the Order entails admission into Knighthood, and the right to bear the title "Sir", and "Dame" in the case of ladies. This, however, does not apply to foreigners who are admitted only as "Honorary Members". Owing to the lack of spaces no banners are hung, but members of the Royal Family and other Knights and Dames Grand Cross have had stall plates showing the arms placed in the chapel, The *Queen's Chapel of Savoy*, London. The reigning Monarch is The Sovereign of the Order, and 20th June, the date of Queen Victoria's

accession to the throne, is the Day of the Order. The Grand Master of the Order, at present The Queen Mother, is appointed by The Sovereign. Ladies were admitted to the Order in 1936.

The Order has five classes:

1. *Knight Grand Cross* or *Dame Grand Cross* (G.C.V.O.) which wears the Badge of the Order (86) on a sash or on a collar and the Star of the Order (88).

2. *Knight Commander* or *Dame Commander* (K.C.V.O. or D.C.V.O.) which wears the Badge of the Order (85) on a neckband (gentlemen) and on a bow (ladies), and the Star of the Order (89).

3. *Commander* (C.V.O.) which wears the Badge of the Order (85) on a neckband (gentlemen) and on a bow (ladies).

4. *Member, 4th Class* (M V.O.) which wears the Badge of the Order (86) in the same size as the Knight's Cross (90) on a chest riband (gentlemen) and on a bow (ladies).

5. *Member 5th Class* (M.V.O.) which wears the Badge of the Order (90) on a

chest riband (gentlemen) and on a bow (ladies).

The Collar of the Order is worn only on the special Collar Days or by Royal Command.

The *Badge of the Order* is a white-enamelled Maltese Cross of eight points. In the centre is an oval of crimson enamel with the Royal Cypher V.R.I. in gold, and surrounding this is a blue-enamelled riband with the motto of the Order "Victoria" in letters of gold, and above this is the Imperial Crown enamelled in proper colours. Badges of the 1st, 2nd, 3rd and 4th Classes are similar but vary in size according to the class.

The Badge of the 5th Class is similar to the Badge of the 4th Class except that the Cross is of frosted silver instead of white enamel.

The *Star of the 1st Class* (G.C.V.O.) is an eight-pointed chipped star with a representation of the Badge of the Order superimposed in the centre.

The *Star of the 2nd Class* (K.C.V.O. and D.C.V.O.) is a silver-faceted Maltese Cross with smaller rays between the angles of the Cross. Superimposed on the Centre is a representation of the Badge of the Order in frosted silver.

The *Collar of the Order* is of gold and is composed of octagonal pieces and oblong perforated and ornamental frames alternately, linked with gold, the said pieces being edged and ornamented with gold, and each piece containing upon a blue-enamelled ground a gold rose jewelled with a carbuncle. Each frame contains a portion of the inscription "Victoria . . . Britt' . . . Reg . . . Def. Ind . . . Ind. Imp." in letters of white enamel. In the centre of the Collar is, within a gold frame, an octagonal piece, enamelled blue, edged with red and charged with a white saltire, with a gold medallion of the effigy of Queen Victoria, from which hangs the Badge of the Order.

The *Riband of the Order* is blue with red-white-red border stripes.

The Collar of the Order must be returned on the death of the holder;

the other insignia are personal property.

Associated with the Order is the Royal *Victorian Medal* (91) with three grades: gold, silver, and bronze. This is worn on the chest riband of the Order and, in the case of foreigners, the riband has a white centre line. When awarded more than once, a clasp is conferred. The obverse bears the effigy of the reigning Sovereign. On the reverse is the Royal Cypher upon an ornamental shield within a laurel wreath, and below a scroll with the words "Royal Victorian Medal".

92–97. The Most Excellent Order of the British Empire was founded on 4th June 1917 by King George V. The Order is the Order of the British Democracy. It was designed to reward British and Allied subjects who had rendered conspicuous service at home, in India, and in the Dominions and Colonies other than those rendered by the Navy and Army. It could be conferred upon Naval, Military and Air Force Officers for services of a non-combatant nature. In 1918 the Order was divided into *Civil* and *Military* Divisions. The Order is now used to reward service in every activity. Conferment of the two highest classes of the Order entail admission into Knighthood and the right to bear the title "Sir", and "Dame" in the case of ladies. This, however, does not apply to foreigners, who are only admitted as "Honorary Members". The reigning Monarch is The Sovereign of the Order. The Grand Master of the Order, at present The Duke of Edinburgh, is appointed by The Monarch.

The Order has a *Civil* and a *Military* Division, each with five classes:

1. *Knight Grand Cross* or *Dame Grand Cross* (G.B.E.) which wears the Badge of the Order (92) on a sash or on a collar, and the Star of the Order (93).

2. *Knight Commander* or *Dame Commander* (K.B.E. or D.B.E.) which wears the Badge of the Order (94) on a neckband (gentlemen) and on a bow (ladies), and the Star of the Order (95).

The Order of the British Empire: Collar of the Order with Badge of the Order, Knight Grand Cross

3. *Commander* (C.B.E.) which wears the Badge of the Order (94) on a neckband (gentlemen) or on a bow (ladies).

4. *Officer* (O.B.E.) which wears the Badge of the Order (96) on a chest riband (gentlemen) or on a bow (ladies).

5. *Member* (M.B.E.) which wears the Badge of the Order (96) in silver on a chest riband (gentlemen) or on a bow (ladies).

The insignia are common to both Divisions, but the Riband of the Order for the *Military* Division has a narrow grey centre stripe.

The Collar of the Order is worn only on the special Collar Days or by Royal Command. The Knights Grand Cross also wear a special Habit of the Order at Services of the Order held in St. Paul's Cathedral, which contains the Chapel of the Order.

The Badge of the Order

For Knights and Dames Grand Cross the Badge consists of a cross, enamelled pearl, surmounted by the Imperial Crown. In the centre is a medallion bearing the crowned effigies of King George V and Queen Mary, within a circle inscribed with the motto "For God and the Empire" on a red background. The reverse of the medallion bears the Royal Cypher of King George V.

The Badge for a Knight and Dame Commander and for a Commander is similar to that of a Knight and Dame Grand Cross but slightly smaller.

The Badge of an Officer is similar to that of a Commander, but is smaller and made of silver gilt.

The Badge of a Member is the same as that of an Officer but is made of silver.

The *Stars of the Order* for 1st and 2nd Classes are both 8-pointed faceted silver stars, the latter with every second point shortened. In the centre is a gold medallion bearing the crowned effigies of their late Majesties King George V and Queen Mary within a circle inscribed with the motto of the Order.

The *Collar of the Order*, which is in silver gilt, consists of 6 medallions with the Royal Cypher of King George V and 6 medallions with the Royal coat of arms of the founder, alternately linked together with 12 chain links bearing an Imperial Crown between two sea lions with tridents.

The *Riband of the Order* is rose pink with grey border stripes; for the Military Division with a narrow grey centre stripe also. The Military Grand Cross Riband for ladies, however, has no centre stripe.

The Collar of the Order must be returned on the death of the holder; the other insignia are personal property.

Associated with the Order is the British Empire Medal (97) which has a *Civil* and a *Military* Division and which, according to the Statutes of 21st April 1941 valid at present, may be conferred on people who have given deserving service which justifies such a token of Royal appreciation. The Medal is worn irrespective of any other decoration held within the Order. The holders of the Medal are entitled to add "B.E.M." after their name.

The Medal has one class, silver, and is worn on the chest riband of the Order. If awarded more than once it is provided with an oak leaf in silver. The obverse bears a picture of Britannia, the symbol of Great Britain, with the legend "For God and Empire" and the subscription "For Meritorious Service". The reverse bears the monogram of the founder with the inscription "Instituted by King George V".

In December 1957 a new Statute was published differentiating between appointments to the Order or awards of the Medal which were made to reward acts of gallantry as opposed to rewards for meritorious service. Since this date all appointments and awards made for gallantry are distinguished by the wearing of an emblem composed of two silver oak leaves on the appropriate riband.

98. The Victoria Cross. the most highly coveted decoration, was instituted on 29th January 1856 by Queen Victoria at the request of Prince Albert. The decoration may be conferred upon officers, non-commissioned officers and men of all the armed forces who qualify by outstanding valour or devotion to their country in the face of the enemy, and also, in special cases, to civilian personnel of the Merchant Navy and auxiliaries; it may also be conferred posthumously. The decoration ranks above all other British Orders and Decorations. This, however, has not been established by Statute, but rests only on custom. The holders of the Decoration receive a tax-free life annuity of £100, and are entitled to add the letters "V.C." after their name.

The Cross is a cross pattée of bronze from captured Russian guns of the Crimean War. Above the Royal Crown the obverse bears a lion guardant, and below the crown a scroll with the device "For Valour". On the reverse, the date of the feat of valour is engraved. The Cross is worn on a crimson chest riband with a mounting on which the Cross is hung on a "V" on the lower side. If awarded with a bar. The front of the mounting is ornamented with laurel leaves, and on the back is engraved the holder's name, rank and regiment.

The riband worn alone with uniform is provided with a miniature of the Cross in bronze.

The total of Crosses which have been awarded is 1348 which includes 3 Bars. A recent award was to Lance Corporal Rambahadur Limbu, 10th Princess Mary's Own Gurkha Rifles, who won the Cross in Sarawak.

99. The George Cross was instituted on 24th September 1940 by King George VI. The decoration may be conferred as a reward for valour and outstanding gallantry displayed under dangerous conditions, primarily for civilians of the British Commonwealth but also to members of the Armed Forces for actions for which military decorations are not normally awarded. It may also be conferred posthumously. The decoration ranks after the *Victoria Cross* (98) but before all other British Orders and decorations. The holders of the decoration are entitled to add the letters "G.S." after their name and are entitled to an annual tax free annuity of £100.

The Cross is a George Cross in silver with the Royal Cypher GVI in the angles of the cross. The motive of the centre medallion is Saint George and the Dragon surrounded by the words "For Gallantry". The reverse bears the name of the holder and the date of award. The Cross hangs by a ring from a silver bar adorned with oak leaves, and the ribbon is Garter-blue. When awarded to women the Cross is worn suspended from the ribbon tied in a bow. If awarded a second time, the riband is provided with a Bar.

The riband worn alone with uniform is provided with a miniature of the Cross in silver.

The Cross took the place of the Medal of the Order of the British Empire for Gallantry (commonly known as The Empire Gallantry Medal). A holder of this Medal was required to return it to the Central Chancery of the Order of Knighthood, when a George Cross was issued in its place.

The *George Medal* was instituted at the same time as the George Cross. The Medal is awarded in circumstances when the action is not so outstanding as to merit the award of the George Cross.

The Medal is of silver, and hangs by a ring suspended on a riband consisting of six red and four medium blue stripes. The obverse bears the Crowned effigy of Her Majesty with the legend "Elizabeth II Dei Gratia Regina F.D."

The reverse bears St. George on horseback killing the Dragon and the inscription, "The George Medal". The holder is entitled to place the letters G.M. after his or her name. (For illustration, see frontispiece.)

100. The Distinguished Service Order was instituted on 6th September 1886 by Queen Victoria. The Order may be conferred on officers of all the armed forces for distinguished services in war, and also on officers of the Merchant Navy, who, when operating with the Navy, qualify for the decoration. Nomination for the Order may be made only if the person concerned has been mentioned in dispatches. Holders of the Order are entitled to add the letters "D.S.O." after their name.

The Order has only one class, and the Badge of the Order (100) is worn on a chest riband.

The Badge is a gold cross pattée, enamelled white and edged gold. The obverse bears within a laurel wreath enamelled green, the Imperial Crown in gold on a red background. On the reverse within a similar wreath and on the same background is the Royal Cypher of the Reigning Sovereign. The riband is red with blue border stripes.

The Badge hangs from its riband by a gold clasp, with a similar clasp at the top of the riband. Both clasps are ornamented with laurel leaves. If awarded a second time, a Bar is worn on the riband, and when the riband is worn alone with undress uniform a Bar is denoted by a small silver rose. The Distinguished Service Order takes precedence immediately after Commander of the Order of the British Empire.

101. The Distinguished Service Cross was instituted in 1901 by King Edward VII as The Conspicuous Service Cross, which was altered in October 1914 by King George V into the present decoration for Naval and Royal Marine officers. The decoration may be conferred upon officers of the rank of Commander and below and equivalent ranks including officers of the Royal Air Force serving with the Fleet Air Arm, for distinguished services which do not permit the award of the *Distinguished Service Order* (100). It may be awarded to officers of the Women's Royal Naval Service for gallant and distinguished conduct on shore during enemy action and it may also be awarded to officers of the Merchant Navy who, when working with the Royal Navy, qualify for the decoration. Holders of the decoration are entitled to add the letters "D.S.C." after their name. A recipient must have been mentioned in dispatches.

The design consists of a plain silver Cross pattée convexed bearing in the centre the Royal Cypher of the reignign surmounted by the Crown. The reverse side is plain. The Cross is suspended by a ring from the riband which is blue, white and blue stripes of equal width. If awarded a second time, the Riband is provided with a Bar.

The Riband worn alone with undress uniform is provided with a rose in silver to denote a Bar.

102. The Military Cross was instituted on 31st December 1914 as a decoration for the Army which, according to the decree of 5th February 1931 may be awarded to officers of the rank of Major and below and also to Warrant Officers for gallant and distinguished services in action. It may also be awarded to officers and warrant officers of the Royal Air Force for gallant service on the ground as opposed to gallant service whilst flying. The decoration is worn after British Orders, but before war medals. Holders of the decoration are entitled to add the letters "M.C." after their name.

The design is an ornamented silver cross with narrow straight arms which widen at the extremities. Each extremity is surmounted by an Imperial Crown. In the centre is the Royal Cypher of the reigning Sovereign. The reverse is plain and reserved for engraving the name of the recipient and the date of the award.

The Cross is suspended by small links attached to a ring on the Cross and to a silver bar at the bottom of the riband. The riband consists of white, purple and white stripes of equal width. If awarded a second time the riband is provided with a Bar.

The Riband worn alone with undress uniform is provided with a rose in silver to denote a Bar.

103. The Distinguished Flying Cross was instituted on 3rd June 1918 by King George V. The decoration may be awarded to officers and Warrant Officers of the Royal Air Force for having displayed valour, gallantry and devotion to duty on one or more occasions while flying on active operations against the enemy. Holders of the decoration are entitled to add the letters "D.F.C." after their name.

The Cross is an elaborate design in silver. It is a Cross flory the upper arm terminating with a rose and the horizontal and lower arm with bombs. The upper and lower arms are surmounted with a single bladed propeller and the horizontal arm with outspread wings. In the centre is a Tudor rose charged with the letters R.A.F., surmounted by the

Imperial Crown and surrounded by a laurel wreath. On the reverse is the Royal Cypher of the Founder above the date 1918. The Cross is attached to the clasp and riband by two sprigs of laurel. The riband is violet and white in alternate diagonal stripes running at an angle of 45 degrees from left to right. If awarded a second time, the riband is provided with a Bar.

The riband when worn alone with undress uniform is provided with a rose in silver, if awarded a second time.

DENMARK
104–107. The Order of the Elephant *(Elefantordenen)* is thought to have had its origin in the *Society of the Mother of God* referred to by King Christian I in a Charter of 9th October 1464 for the Chapel of the Epiphany in the Cathedral at Roskilde. The Society was a Catholic Brotherhood, instituted by the King about 1462, and consisted of 50 noble men and women who wore as a badge of membership a Collar of the Order on which was hung a medallion bearing a picture of the Holy Virgin. It is possible that the Collar was composed of elephants, but the connection between the Brotherhood and the Elephant has only been dated with certainty from 1508, when Prince Christian, later King Christian II, invested the Father Confessor of the Brotherhood, Dean Erik Walkendorf, with an escutcheon of office which bore on a blue shield a golden elephant with a tower on its back, surrounded by fleur de lis. Further, on the tombstone of King Hans in St. Knud's Church at Odense dating from about 1513 there can be seen the King wearing a collar composed of elephants and spurs. King Christian II still awarded Badges of the Order of the Elephant, but with the dethronement of the King and the introduction of the Reformation, the Catholic Brotherhood disappeared. It was not until 1580, under King Frederik II, that the Elephant reappeared as an independent Order, whose Badge was a golden elephant

bearing a tower on its back and worn pendant on a golden collar. Under King Christian IV, the Elephant was combined with the *Order of the Arm in Armour* (Væ bnede Arms Orden) instituted in 1616, which itself ceased in 1634. After this the Elephant was worn alone on a triple gold collar. In 1663, under King Frederik III, the golden collar was replaced by a blue sash, and from this came the designation "Blue Knight" for a Knight of the Elephant as opposed to "White Knight" for a Knight of the Dannebrog. Further, an embroidered breast star was introduced. The Order did not assume its final form, however, until the reign of Christian V, in the statutes of 1st December 1693. These established the number of Knights at not more than 30, apart from the King and his sons, the minimum age being 30 years, but 20 years for Royalty. By a Royal Ordinance of 9th April 1958 it was established that women as well as men should have access to decoration with the Order. In addition to the members of the Royal Family, the Order is today mainly conferred on foreign Heads of State. The coats of arms of the Knights are hung in the Chapel of the *Castle of Frederiksborg at Hillerød.* The reigning Monarch is the Master of the Order, and 1st January is the Day of the Order. The festival days of the Order are the reigning Monarch's birthday and 28th June, King Valdemar II's birthday.

The Order has one class, *Knight,* which wears the Badge of the Order (104–105) on a sash or collar (106) and the Star of the Order (107).

The *Badge of the Order* is a white-enamelled golden elephant with a blue cover, bearing on its back a watch tower and a blackamoor with a spear. It weighs about 125 grammes and is richly studded with precious stones. The obverse bears a cross in diamonds and the reverse the monogram of the reigning Monarch.

The *Collar of the Order,* which is in gold, consists of towers and elephants alternateley. The cover of the elephant bears a "D" for "Dacia", mediæval Latin for "Denmark".

The *Star of the Order* is an 8-pointed silver star with plane rays, the centre medallion bearing a Latin cross formed of 6 silver pearls on a red background surrounded by a laurel wreath in silver.

The *Riband of the Order* is plain blue, and is worn as a sash across the *left* shoulder.

All the insignia must be returned on the death of the holder.

There are three commoners among the Danish Knights of the Elephant of this century: the philologist, Professor Vilh Thomsen (1912), the founder of The East-Asian Company; titular Councillor of State, H. N. Andersen (1919); and the nuclear physicist, Professor Niels Bohr (1947).

Among living foreign Knights of the Elephant are: the former President of the U.S.A., General Dwight D. Eisenhower (1945), Lord Bernard L. Montgomery (1945) and the President of France, General Charles de Gaulle (1965).

Sir Winston Churchill was also a Knight of the Elephant (1950).

108–117. The Order of the Dannebrog was founded on 12th October 1671 by King Christian V as, it is said, a renewal of the older Order of the Dannebrog founded by King Valdemar II, the Conqueror, after the Battle of Reval in 1219. According to the statutes of 1st December 1693, the Order was to comprise 50 noble Knights in one class only, but by letters patent of 28th June 1808 King Frederik VI extended it to become "an outward token of recognised civic merit" for "all subjects irrespective of position or class". It was also divided into four classes: Grand Commander, Knight Grand Cross, Commander and Knight. Under a Royal Ordinance of 21st February 1842, the Grand Commander class was placed before and above the three other classes of the Order, and only Royal personages were admitted to the Grand Commander class. Under Royal Ordinances of 21st March 1864 and 21st March 1952, the Commander and Knight classes were each divided into two grades: Commander 1st Degree

and Commander, and Knight 1st Degree and Knight. Finally, it was made possible for women to be decorated with the Order by a Royal Ordinance of 10th October 1951. The Order may be conferred for distinguished service, both civil and military. It may also be conferred on foreigners. The coats of arms of the Grand Commanders and Knights Grand Cross are hung in the *Chapel of the Castle of Frederiksborg* at *Hillerød*. The reigning Monarch is the Master of the Order. The 28th January, King Frederik VI's birthday, and 15th April, King Christian V's birthday, are the Days of the Order. The reigning Monarch's birthday and 28th June, King Valdemar II's birthday, are the Festival Days of the Order.

The Order has a Grand Commander Class and three Classes of the Order, the 2nd and 3rd Classes each being divided into two grades:

1*. *Grand Commander*, which wears the Badge of the Order (108) on a necklet (gentlemen) and on a bow (ladies) and the Star of the Order. (112).

1. *Grand Cross*, which wears the Badge of the Order (109) on a sash or collar (110) and the Star of the Order (112). If awarded "with diamonds" a Star of the Order with a Badge of the Order studded with table-cut stones (111) is worn.

2. (i) *Commander 1st Degree*, which wears the Badge of the Order (113) on a necklet and a breast cross (114) (gentlemen) or the breast cross only (ladies).

(ii) *Commander*, which wears the Badge of the Order (113) on a necklet (gentlemen) or on a bow (ladies).

3. (i) *Knight 1st Degree*, which wears the Badge of the Order (115) on a chest riband (gentlemen) and on a bow (ladies), both with rosette.

(ii) *Knight*, which wears the Badge of the Order (116) on a chest riband (gentlemen) and on a bow (ladies).

The Grand Commander Class stands apart from the Order, and only those related to the Royal Family are admitted as Grand Commanders, but not more than seven. As a special distinction, the 1st Class of the Order, the Grand Cross

Class, may be awarded "with diamonds".

The *Badge of the Order* is a red-bordered white-enamelled Latin Cross in gold (in silver for knights), pendant on a royal crown above the monogram of the reigning Monarch. The obverse bears King Christian V's crowned monogram with the legend "Gud og Kongen" (God and the King), the motto of the Order, and the reverse the crowned monograms of the Kings Valdemar II and Frederik VI, with the dates "1219", "1671" and "1808". There are royal crowns in the angles of the cross. The Grand Commander Badge of the Order bears on the obverse 14 table-cut stones instead of white enamel, and diamonds in the remaining ornamentations of the cross. The reverse bears the crowned monograms of the Kings Valdemar II, Christian V and Frederik VI together with the motto of the Order on white enamel.

The *Star Grand Cross* is an 8-pointed, faceted silver star with the Badge of the Order. When awarded "with diamonds", this Badge is studded with table-cut stones. The *Breast Cross* for the Commander 1st Degree is a Badge of the Order with faceted silver background instead of white enamel; the cross bears King Valdemar II's crowned monogram with the legend "Gud or Kongen" (God and the King).

The *Collar of the Order*, which is in gold, consists of alternate links: the crowned monograms of Kings Valdemar II and Christian V and red-bordered white-enamelled Latin crosses.

The *Riband of the Order* is white with red border stripes, the national colours of Denmark. It is worn as a chest riband mounted in a crossed form.

All insignia must be returned on the death of the holder.

The *Silver Cross of the Order of the Dannebrog* (117) is associated with the Order. It was founded on 28th June 1808 as the *Silver Cross of the Order of the Dannebrog*, but changed to the present decoration on 1st April 1952. The decoration, which wears a Badge of the Order in silver on a chest riband with rosette, may only be conferred on

Danish citizens who have already been awarded the Order of the Dannebrog.

THE NETHERLANDS
118–121. The Military Order of William *(De Militaire Willems-Orde)* was founded on 30th April 1815 by King William I. Its present statutes date from 30th June 1941. The Order may be conferred on the military for outstanding courage, leadership and loyalty towards Monarch and Country. In special cases it may also be conferred on civilians and foreigners. The 4th Class of the Order may also be conferred on military units. The Order is rarely conferred, and it is therefore highly esteemed. It is recognized as the highest Dutch military decoration it is possible to obtain; and holders are saluted when they wear their insignia visibly. As it is the only Dutch Order, it may be applied for by those who think they are entitled to it. Knights of the 3rd and 4th Classes of the Order who are below the rank of officer receive a pension, which may also be awarded to civilians and foreigners. The Order is irrevocably attached to the Dutch Crown. The reigning Monarch is the Master of the Order.

The Order has four classes:

1. *Knight 1st Class* or *Grand Cross*, which wears the Badge of the Order (118) on a sash with the Star of the Order (119).

2. *Knight 2nd Class* or *Commander*, which wears the Badge of the Order (118) on a necklet and the same Badge of the Order as a breast star.

3. *Knight 3rd Class*, which wears the Badge of the Order (120) on a chest riband with rosette.

4. *Knight 4th Class*, which wears the Badge of the Order (121) on a chest riband.

The *Badge of the Order* is a white-enamelled Maltese Cross in gold, in silver for 4th Class, pendant on a royal crown. Between its arms the cross bears the green, diagonal Burgundy Cross and in the centre a tinder-box, the symbols of the House of Burgundy and of the

Order of the *Golden Fleece*, to which King William I could claim a right. The obverse bears the inscription "Voor Moed – Beleid – Trouw" (For courage – leadership – loyalty), and the reverse medallion bears a crowned "W" for "William" surrounded by a laurel wreath.

The *Star Grand Cross* is an 8-pointed silver star with a Badge of the Order without crown.

The *Riband of the Order* is yellow with blue border stripes, the colours of the House of Orange Nassau.

All insignia are personal property and are not returned on the death of the holder.

122–123. The Civil Order of Merit of the Netherland Lion *(De Orde van de Nederlandse Leeuw)* was instituted on 29th September 1815 by King William I. The Order may be conferred on civilians for devotion to the Fatherland, special zeal and loyalty in carrying out civic duties, and outstanding proficiency in science and art. In special cases it may also be conferred on the military and on foreigners. The Order is irrevocably attached to the Dutch Crown. The reigning Monarch is the Master of the Order.

The Order has three classes:

1. *Knight 1st Class* or *Grand Cross*, which wears the Badge of the Order (122) on a sash and the Star of the Order (123).

2. *Knight 2nd Class* or *Commander*, which wears the Badge of the Order (122) on a necklet and the same Badge of the Order as a breast star.

3. *Knight 3rd Class*, which wears the Badge of the Order (122) in the same size as the Knight's Cross (120), on a chest riband.

The *Badge of the Order* is a white-enamelled Maltese Cross in gold, pendant on a royal crown. The obverse medallion bears the inscription "Virtus Nobilitat" (Virtue Ennobles), the device of the Order, on a blue background, and the reverse medallion bears the Netherlands Lion. There is a "W" for "William" between the arms of the cross.

The *Star Grand Cross* is an 8-pointed golden star bearing a Maltese Cross with faceted rays and the obverse medallion of the Badge of the Order.

The *Riband of the Order* is blue with yellow border stripes, the colours of the House of Orange Nassau.

Persons who distinguish themselves by performing useful acts, self-sacrifice or other proof of love for their fellow man may be attached to the Order as *Brothers*. They receive a yearly payment of 200 guilders, of which half is paid to the widow on the death of the holder of the decoration.

The Badge of Honour for Brothers is a silver medal, which is worn on a blue chest riband with a yellow centre stripe. On the obverse the medal bears the Netherlands Lion, and on the reverse the device of the Order.

124. The Bronze Lion Decoration *(Bronzen Leeuw)* was instituted in 1944 by Queen Wilhelmina. The decoration may be awarded to officers, non-commissioned officers and men of the Armed Forces who have distinguished themselves in time of war by bravery or leadership in the face of the enemy. It may also be conferred on civilians, members of the Merchant Navy and foreigners. The decoration replaces the gilt crown formerly used, which was worn on the riband of their war medals by persons who had been mentioned in dispatches.

The decoration is a cross patté in bronze. The centre medallion bears the Netherlands Lion; the reverse is plain. The cross is worn on a blue and yellow striped chest riband. If the award is repeated, Arabic numerals are worn on the riband.

125. The Airman's Cross *(Vliegerkruis)* was instituted on 28th August 1941 by Queen Wilhelmina. The decoration may be awarded to the military for initiative, courage and perseverance on flying duties in time of war, in direct combat as well as in general combat. In some circumstances it may also be awarded to civilians and foreigners. It may also be awarded posthumously.

The Cross is a Teutonic Cross in silver. The centre medallion bears a flying eagle with the legend "Initiatief – Moed – Volharding" (Initiative – courage – perseverance) and the year "1941" beneath a royal crown; the reverse is plain. The Cross is worn on a diagonally striped orange and white chest riband. If the award is repeated, golden Roman numerals are worn on the riband.

126. The Bronze Cross *(Bronzen Kruis)* was instituted on 11th June 1940 by Queen Wilhelmina. The decoration may be awarded to officers, non-commissioned officers and men of the Land and Sea Forces who have distinguished themselves in time of war by courage or by leadership in the face of the enemy. It may also be awarded to civilians and foreigners.

The Cross is a Teutonic Cross in bronze with a crowned "W" for "Wilhelmina" in the centre surrounded by a laurel wreath. The obverse bears the date "1940" in an oak and laurel wreath, and the inscription "Trouw ann Koningin en Vaderland" (True to Queen and Country) on the arms of the Cross. The Cross is worn on an orange chest riband with a blue centre stripe. If the award is repeated, Arabic numerals are worn on the riband.

127. The Cross of Merit *(Kruis van Verdienste)* was instituted on 20th February 1941 by Queen Wilhelmina. The decoration may be awarded to persons, both civilian and military, who have distinguished themselves during enemy action by courageous and resolute behaviour, and have thus acted in the interest of the Fatherland.

It may also be awarded to foreigners.

The Cross is a Greek Cross in bronze with a crowned "W" for "Wilhelmina" in the centre surrounded by a laurel wreath. The reverse bears the Netherlands Lion with the legend "Voor Verdienste" (For Merit). The Cross is

worn on a blue chest riband with a yellow centre stripe. If the award is repeated, Arabic numerals are worn on the riband.

128–133. The Order of Orange-Nassau *(De Orde van Oranje-Nassau)* was instituted on 4th April 1892 by the Queen Dowager Emma on behalf of her daughter, Wilhelmina, as a substitute for Luxembourg's *Order of the Oak Crown* (174–179) which was no longer available to the Dutch Monarch following the abolition in 1890 of the personal union between the Netherlands and Luxembourg. The Order may be conferred on Dutchmen and on foreigners who have proved themselves to be specially deserving towards the Head of State or towards society in general. The Order is irrevocably attached to the Dutch Crown. The reigning Monarch is the Master of the Order.

The Order has five classes:

1. *Knight 1st Class* or *Grand Cross*, which wears the Badge of the Order (131), in the same size as the Grand Cross (122), on a sash and the Star of the Order (128–129).

2. *Knight 2nd Class* or *Grand Officer*, which wears the same Badge of the Order as for 1st Class on a necklet and the Star of the Order (130).

3. *Knight 3rd Class* or *Commander*, which wears the same Badge of the Order as for 1st Class on a necklet.

4. *Knight 4th Class* or *Officer*, which wears the Badge of the Order (131) on a chest riband with rosette.

5. *Knight 5th Class* or *Knight* which wears the Badge of the Order (132) on a chest riband.

Military personnel who are awarded the Order receive the insignia with crossed swords (130 and 132).

The *Badge of the Order* is a white-bordered blue-enamelled Maltese Cross in gold, in silver for 5th Class, pendant on a royal crown. The obverse medallion bears the Netherlands Lion with the legend "Je maintiendrai" (I shall persevere), the device of the Order, and the reverse medallion bears a crowned "W" for "Wilhelmina" with the legend

"God zij met ons" (God be with us). The Badge of the Order for *civilians* bears a laurel wreath between the arms of the cross, and the Badge of the Order for the *military* bears a set of crossed swords.

The *Stars of the Order* for 1st and 2nd Class are respectively an 8-pointed and a 4-pointed silver star with the obverse medallion of the Badge of the Order in the centre. Stars of the Order for the *military* bear a set of crossed swords.

The *Riband of the Order* is yellow with blue-white border stripes, the colours of the House of Orange-Nassau.

The *Honorary Medal (133)* is associated with the Order. It has three degrees, *gold*, *silver* and *bronze*, and is worn on a narrow chest riband in the colours of the Order.

134–139. The Family Order of Orange *(De Huisorde van Oranje)* was instituted on 19th March 1950 by Queen Wilhelmina as a reward for services rendered to the House of Orange. The Order may be conferred on Dutchmen and on foreigners. The reigning Monarch is the Master of the Order, and the right to confer the Order is the Monarch's alone.

The Order has five Classes, the 5th Class being divided into two grades:

1. *Grand Cross*, which wears the Badge of the Order (134) on a sash and the Star of the Order (135).

2. *Grand Officer*, which wears the Badge of the Order (134) on a necklet and the Star of the Order (136).

3. *Commander*, which wears the Badge of the Order (134) on a necklet.

4. *Officer*, which wears the Badge of the Order (137) as a breast star.

5. (i) *Knight 1st Class*, which wears the Badge of the Order (134), in the same size as the Knight's Cross (138), on a chest riband.

(ii) *Knight 2nd Class*, which wears the Badge of the Order (134) in silver and in the same size as the Knight's Cross (138) on a chest riband.

The *Badge of the Order* is a red-enamelled Latin Cross in gold, in silver for Knights 2nd Class, with arms

widened. The obverse medallion bears the coat of arms of the House of Orange with the legend "Je maintiendrai" (I shall persevere), the device of the Order, and the reverse medallion bears a crowned "W" for "Wilhelmina". There is a wreath of orange leaves between the arms of the cross.

The *Stars of the Order* for 1st and 2nd Classes are respectively an 8-pointed and a 4-pointed silver star with the obverse medallion of the Badge of the Order in the centre.

The *Riband of the Order* is plain orange, the colour of the House of Orange.

The following medals and badges of honour are associated with the Order:

The Honorary Medal for Art and Science and *The Honorary Medal for Initiative and Inventiveness*, both of which have two grades, *gold* and *silver*. They are worn on a necklet by gentlemen and on a bow on the left shoulder by ladies. The obverse of both medals bears the portrait of the founder, and the reverse bears the coat of arms of the House of Orange with the heading "Je maintiendrai". The first medal bears the inscription "Voor Kunst en Wetenschap" (For Art and Science), and the second medal the inscription "Voor Voortvarendheid en Vernuft" (For Initiative and Inventiveness). The medals in gold are equivalent in rank to Grand Officer, and those in silver to Officer.

The Cross of Merit, which has two grades, *gold* and *silver*, wears a Badge of the Order (138) on a chest riband (gentlemen) or a smaller Badge of the Order on a bow (ladies).

The Honorary Medal (139), which has three grades, *gold*, *silver* and *bronze*, is worn on the chest riband of the Order. The obverse bears the coat of arms of the House of Orange with the legend "Je maintiendrai" and the reverse bears a crowned "W" for "Wilhelmina" beneath the inscription "Voor Verdienste" (For Merit).

The Life-saving Medal, which has one grade, matt *silver*, is worn on a chest riband. The obverse bears a Badge of the Order with the legend "Voor Moed en Zelfopoffering" (For Courage and Self-sacrifice) and the reverse bears a crowned "W" for "Wilhelmina" with the legend "Je maintiendrai".

There is also the rank:

Dame of Honour of the Family Order of Orange, which wears a Badge of the Order (134), in the same size as the Cross of Merit for ladies, on a bow.

BELGIUM

140–149. The Order of Leopold *(Ordre de Léopold)* was instituted on 11th July 1832 by King Leopold I as a reward for services rendered to the Fatherland. The Order may be conferred on Belgians and on foreigners, and for civil services as well as for military and maritime services. Military holders of the Order below the rank of officer receive an annual pension. The Order is administered by the Foreign Ministry.

The Order has *Civil*, *Military* and *Maritime* Divisions, each with five classes.

Classes and insignia for the *Civil* Division are:

1. *Grand Cross*, which wears the Badge of the Order (140), but in a larger size, on a sash, and on special occasions the Badge of the Order (140) on a collar (141), and the Star of the Order (142).

2. *Grand Officer*, which wears the Star of the Order (149) without crossed anchors.

3. *Commander*, which wears the Badge of the Order (140) on a necklet.

4. *Officer*, which wears the Badge of the Order (143) on a chest riband with rosette.

5. *Knight*, which wears the Badge of the Order (144) on a chest riband.

The insignia are common to all Divisions, except that the *Military* and *Maritime* Badges of the Order (145–146) and the Stars of the Order (147–149) are provided with crossed swords and anchors respectively.

The *Badge of the Order* is a white-enamelled Maltese Cross in gold, in silver for 5th Class, pendant on a royal crown. The obverse medallion bears the Belgian Lion on a blue background with the legend "L'Union fait la Force – Eendracht maakt Macht" (Unity makes strong) in French and Flemish on a red background, and the reverse medallion bears a "LR" for "Leopold Rex" in a face-to-face monogram. There is an oak and laurel wreath between the arms of the cross.

The *Stars of the Order* for 1st and 2nd Classes are respectively an 8-pointed faceted silver star and a faceted Maltese Cross in silver with plain pencils of rays in the angles of the cross, both with the obverse medallion of the Badge of the Order in the centre.

The *Collar of the Order*, which is in gold, consists of 9 royal crowns, 7 "LR"s for "Leopold Rex" in a face-to-face monogram, and 18 Belgian Lions alternately, connected with ordinary chain links.

The *Riband of the Order* is purple. Civilians decorated who have distinguished themselves in the First or Second World Wars wear a gold or silver star on the riband for 4th and 5th Classes, and also, according to services, a centre stripe or border stripes of gold.

150–155. The Order of the Crown *(Ordre de la Couronne)* was instituted on 15th October 1897 by King Leopold II as an Order for the Congo State, but it became a Belgian Order in 1908 when Belgium took over the Congo as a Colony. The Order may be conferred on those, Belgians as well as foreigners, who have distinguished themselves by artistic, literary and scientific works, or in the commercial or industrial field. It may also be conferred for meritorious services to African civilization or to the country generally, and for both civil and military services. Military holders of the Order below the rank of officer receive a yearly allowance. The Order is administered by the Foreign Ministry.

The Order has five classes:

1. *Grand Cross*, which wears the

Badge of the Order (150) on a sash and the Star of the Order (151).

2. *Grand Officer*, which wears the Star of the Order (152).

3. *Commander*, which wears the Badge of the Order (150) on a necklet.

4. *Officer*, which wears the Badge of the Order (153) on a chest riband with rosette.

5. *Knight*, which wears the Badge of the Order (153) in silver on a chest riband without rosette.

The *Badge of the Order* is a 5-armed, white-enamelled star in gold, in silver for 5th Class, with plain pencils of rays between the arms. The obverse medallion bears a royal crown on a blue background, and the reverse medallion bears an "L" for "Leopold" in a back-to-back monogram. The Badge of the Order has a green-enamelled laurel wreath as a mounting.

The *Star of the Order 1st Class* is a 10-pointed star with faceted pencils of rays in silver and plain pencils of rays in gold alternately. The *Star of the Order 2nd Class* is a 5-armed faceted silver star with plain pencils of rays in gold between the arms. Both stars bear in the centre a Badge of the Order without a wreath mounting.

The *Riband of the Order* is plain bluish-red.

A set of palms (154) with two grades, *gold* and *silver* is associated with the Order as a 6th Class. There is also a Medal (155) with three grades, *gold*, *silver* and *bronze*. Both of these are worn on a bluish-red chest riband with white border stripes. The Medal, which is pendant on a royal crown, bears on the obverse a royal crown in relief with the legend "Travail et Progrès" (Work and Progress), the motto of the Congo before 1908.

156–159. The Order of Leopold II *(Ordre de Léopold II)* was instituted on 24th August 1900 by King Leopold II as an Order for the Congo State, but became a Belgian Order in 1908 when Belgium took over the Congo as a Colony. The Order may be conferred

on civilians and on the military, on Belgians and on foreigners, as a reward for services to the Monarch and as a token of his personal goodwill. The Order is administered by the Foreign Ministry.

The Order has five classes:

1. *Grand Cross*, which wears the Badge of the Order (156) on a sash and the Star of the Order (157).

2. *Grand Officer*, which wears the Star of the Order (152) but with a Badge of the present Order (156).

3. *Commander*, which wears the Badge of the Order (156) on a necklet.

4. *Officer*, which wears the Badge of the Order (158) in gold on a chest riband with rosette.

5. *Knight*, which wears the Badge of the Order (158) on a chest riband.

The *Badge of the Order* is an un-enamelled Maltese Cross in gold, in silver for the 5th Class, pendant on a royal crown. The obverse medallion bears the Belgian Lion on a black background with the legend "L'Union fait la Force – Eendracht maakt Macht" (Unity makes strong) in French and Flemish on a blue background. The reverse medallion bears a crowned "L" for "Leopold" in a back-to-back monogram. There is a palm wreath between the arms of the cross.

The *Star of the Order 1st Class* is a 10-pointed star with faceted pencils of rays in silver and plain pencils of rays in gold alternately. The *Star of the Order 2nd Class* is a 5-armed faceted silver star with plain pencils of rays between the arms. Both crosses have a Badge of the Order in the centre.

The *Riband of the Order* is blue with a black centre stripe. Military personnel decorated who have been mentioned in dispatches during the First or Second World Wars bear on the riband for 4th and 5th Class a gold or silver palm, with an "A" for "Albert" and an "L" for "Leopold" respectively, and also, according to their achievement, a centre stripe or border stripes in gold.

Associated with the Order as a 6th Class is a *Medal* which has three grades, gold, silver and bronze. It is worn on the chest riband of the Order.

160–161. The Military Decoration of Merit (Decoration Militaire) was founded in 1902 and renewed in 1952. The decoration has two Divisions one for seniority and one for special achievement, courage and self-sacrifice. In special cases, the latter may be awarded to foreign Military personnel.

Both Divisions have a Cross in two classes, with and without a chevron on the riband respectively. The 1st Class is for officers, non-commissioned officers and those of equivalent rank, and the 2nd Class for military personnel in general. The insignia are common to both Divisions; only the colours of the riband vary.

The Cross is a crowned Maltese Cross in silver gilt with rays between the arms of the cross. The obverse medallion bears the Belgian Lion with the legend "L'Union fait la Force – Eendracht maakt Macht" (Unity makes strong) in French and Flemish, and the reverse medallion bears the Belgian Lion. The Cross is worn on a chest riband which, for the Division which may also be conferred on foreigners, is red with yellow and black border stripes, the national colours of Belgium. Those decorated who have been mentioned in dispatches in time of war bear a silver palm on the riband with an "A" for "Albert" or an "L" for "Leopold", and since 1954 a silver palm without monogram.

162–163. The Military Cross (Croix Militaire) was instituted on 11th February 1885 as a decoration for seniority. The decoration has two classes. The 1st Class may be awarded for 25 years' military service. In special cases, the decoration may also be conferred on foreigners.

The Cross is a black-enamelled Maltese Cross in gold, with crossed swords between the arms of the cross, pendant on a royal crown. The obverse medallion bears the Belgian Lion, and the reverse medallion bears the reigning Monarch's monogram. The Cross is

worn on a red chest riband with red border stripes. For the 1st Class it is provided with a rosette.

164. The War Cross 1940 (Croix de Guerre 1940) was instituted on 20th July 1941 by the Belgian Government in exile in London as a war decoration for the Second World War. The decoration might be awarded to personnel of the land, air and sea forces for bravery in the face of the enemy, and in special cases also to military units and to foreigners.

The Cross is a Maltese Cross in bronze, with crossed swords between the arms of the cross, pendant on a royal crown. The obverse medallion bears the Belgian Lion and the reverse medallion bears an "L" for "Leopold". The Cross is pendant on a red chest riband with three narrow green stripes on each side. Persons decorated who have been mentioned in dispatches bear a bronze or silver lion on the riband, and sometimes a bronze palm with an "L" for "Leopold".

The War Cross (Croix de Guerre) was founded on 3rd April 1954 as a decoration for future services in war. The Cross is identical with the War Cross (1940) (164), but the obverse medallion bears the royal coat of arms and the reverse medallion bears the Belgian Lion. The Cross is pendant on a green chest riband with three narrow red stripes on each side.

165. The Order of the Lion (Ordre Royal du Lion) was founded in 1891 by King Leopold II as a reward for meritorious service to the Congo State – later the Belgian Congo – and to its Head of State. The Congo having become independent in 1960, the Order is no longer current, although the wording of the statutes still makes conferment possible, for example for services rendered before independence. The Order, which ranks after the Order of the African Star (166), is administered by the Foreign Ministry.

The Order has five classes, and a medal

The Order of the Star of Africa: Star of the Order, Grand Cross

with three grades, *gold, silver* and *bronze*. Classes and insignia are the same as for the *Order of the Crown* (150–155), except that the Knights Grand Cross wear the Badge of the Order on a collar on ceremonial occasions.

The *Badge of the Order* is a blue-bordered white-enamelled cross pattée in gold, in silver for the 5th Class, with a "C" for "Congo" in a back-to-back monogram in the angles of the cross, pendant on a royal crown. The obverse medallion bears the Belgian Lion on a blue background with the legend "Travail et Progrès" (Work and Progress), the motto of the Congo before 1908, and the reverse medallion bears an "L" in a back-to-back monogram with an "S" interlaced for "Leopold Souverain".

The *Stars of the Order* for 1st and 2nd Class are respectively an 8-pointed star with alternate gold and silver rays, and a Maltese Cross in silver with pencils of rays in the angles of the cross, both with the crowned obverse medallion of the Badge of the Order in the centre.

The *Collar of the Order*, which is in gold, is composed of three alternate links: a royal crown, an "L" in a back-to-back monogram with an "S" interlaced, and a medallion with the Belgian Lion on a blue background.

The *Riband of the Order* is bluish-red with blue-edged yellow border stripes, the colours of the Congo.

166. The Order of the Star of Africa *(Ordre de l'Etoile Africaine)* was instituted in 1888 by King Leopold II as a reward for services rendered to the Congo State – later the Belgian Congo – and to African civilization in general. The Congo having become independent in 1960, the Order is no longer current, but the wording of the statutes still makes conferment possible, for example for services rendered before independence. The Order, which ranks before the *Order of the Lion* (165), is administered by the Foreign Ministry.

The Order has five classes and a medal in three grades, *gold, silver* and *bronze*. Classes and insignia are the same as for the *Order of the Crown* (150–155), but on ceremonial occasions the Knights Grand Cross wear the Badge of the Order on a Collar.

The *Badge of the Order* is a 5-pointed blue-bordered white-enamelled star in gold, in silver for the 5th Class, resting on a green-enamelled wreath of palm leaves and pendant on a royal crown. The obverse medallion bears the Star of the Congo on a blue background with the legend "Travail et Progrès" (Work and Progress), the motto of the Congo before 1908, and the reverse medallion bears an "L" in a back-to-back monogram with an "S" interlaced, for "Leopold Souverain".

The *Star of the Order*, which varies in size according to Class, is a 10-pointed star with alternate gold and silver rays. In the centre the Star bears a Badge of the Order.

The *Collar of the Order*, which is in gold, is composed of three alternate links: a royal crown, an "L" in a back-to-back monogram with an "S" interlaced, and a 5-pointed white-enamelled star surrounded by a palm wreath.

The *Riband of the Order* is blue with a yellow centre stripe, the colours of the Congo.

The Decoration for Civil Merit *(Decoration Civique)* was instituted in 1867. The decoration has two Divisions, one for seniority and one for bravery, self-sacrifice and humanitarian actions. Only the latter Division may be conferred on foreigners.

Both Divisions have a Cross in two classes, *gold* and *silver*, and a Medal in three grades, *gold, silver* and *bronze*. The insignia is the same for both Divisions; only the background colours vary.

The Cross is a white-enamelled Maltese Cross, with a Burgundy Cross between the arms of the Cross, crowned by a tinder box, the symbol of the House of Burgundy and the *Order of the Golden Fleece*. The centre medallion bears the reigning Monarch's back-to-back monogram. The Cross pendant on a vertically mounted chest riband which, for the Division which can also be conferred on foreigners, is red with two gold-edged black border stripes.

The Decoration for Civil Merit: Cross and Medal, Division for bravery, self-sacrifice and humanitarian actions

LUXEMBOURG

167–168. The Order of the Golden Lion of the House of Nassau *(Ordre du Lion d'Or de la Maison de Nassau)* was instituted on 29th January 1858 as a common Family Order for the two lines of the House of Nassau, the Ottonian in the Netherlands and the Walramian in Luxembourg. The Order, which was renewed on 20th May 1906, in reserved for Sovereign Princes and Princes of Sovereign Houses and for persons with the title of "Excellency" and the rank of at least Ambassador, Lieutenant-General, Prime Minister, Archbishop, or the highest ranks at Court.

The Order has one Class, *Knight*, which wears the Badge of the Order (167) on a sash and the Star of the Order (168).

The *Badge of the Order* is a white-enamelled Maltese Cross in gold with an "N" for "Nassau" in the angles of the cross. The obverse medallion bears the Lion of Nassau on a blue background, and the reverse medallion bears the inscription "Je maintiendrai" (I shall persevere), the motto of the House of Nassau.

The *Star of the Order* is an 8-pointed silver star with the obverse medallion of the Badge of the Order surrounded by a white scroll with the motto of the House of Nassau in the centre.

The *Riband of the Order* is orange with blue selvage border, the colours of the Houses of Orange and Nassau.

169–173. The Civil and Military Order of Merit of Adolph of Nassau *(Ordre du Mérite Civil et Militaire d'Adolphe de Nassau)* was instituted on 8th May 1858 by Duke Adolph of Nassau. On the incorporation of Nassau into Prussia in 1866, the Order was abolished, but was reinstituted in 1890 when Duke Adolph became Grand Duke of Luxembourg. The Order may be conferred on citizens of Luxembourg and on foreigners for meritorious services to the Grand Duchy and the Ducal House, as well as in the fields of art and science. The reigning Grand Duke is the Grand Master of the Order.

The Order has a *Civil* and a *Military* Division, each with five classes, the three lowest classes each being divided into two grades, *with* and *without crown:*

1. *Grand Cross*, which wears the Badge of the Order (171) on a sash and the Star of the Order (169).
2. *Grand Officer*, which wears the Badge of the Order (171) on a necklet and the Star of the Order (170).
3. *Commander*, which wears the Badge of the Order (171), with or without the mounting crown, on a necklet.

4. *Officer*, which wears the Badge of the Order (171), with or without the mounting crown and in the same size as the Cross of Merit (172), on a chest riband with a rosette.

5. *Knight*, which wears the Badge of the Order (171), with or without the mounting crown and in the same size as the Cross of Merit (172), on a chest riband without rosette.

The insignia are the same for both Divisions, except that the Military Badges and Stars of the Order are provided with crossed swords (170).

The *Badge of the Order* is a white-enamelled Maltese Cross in gold, with or without the mounting crown according to class and grade. The obverse medallion bears a crowned "A" for "Adolphe" on a white background with the legend "Virtute" (For he who excels), the device of the Order, on a blue background. The reverse medallion bears the date "1292", the year Duke Adolph of Nassau, after whom the Order is named, became King of the Germans, and the date "1858", the date of the original foundation of the Order.

The *Stars of the Order* for 1st and 2nd Classes are respectively an 8-pointed silver star and a Maltese Cross-shaped silver cross with pencils of rays in the angles of the cross, both with the obverse medallion of the Badge of the Order in the centre.

The *Riband of the Order* is blue with an orange selvage border, the colours of the Houses Nassau and Orange.

Associated with the Order are:

The *Cross of Merit* (172), which has two grades, *gold* and *silver*, and is pendant on the chest riband of the Order. Military personnel receive the Cross with crossed swords.

The *Cross of Honour for Ladies*, which wears a Badge of the Order (171), in the same size as the Cross of Merit (172) on a ladies' bow.

The *Medal for Art and Science*, which has two grades, *gold* and *silver*, and which is pendant on the chest riband of the Order. The obverse bears a Badge of the Order resting upon a palm wreath, and the reverse bears the inscription "Artibus et Scientiis" (For Art and Science), surrounded by an oak wreath.

The Medal of Merit, which has three grades, *gold, silver* and *bronze,* is pendant on the chest riband of the Order. The obverse bears the portrait of the founder, and the reverse bears the device of the Order.

In 1945, the *1940–1945 Palm* (173) was founded for patriotic services during the Second World War. The Palm, which is silver gilt, is carried on the riband of the Order. Commanders and upwards wear the Palm on the riband of an additional decoration for officers.

174–179. The Order of the Oaken Crown *(Ordre de la Couronne de Chêne)* was founded on 29th December 1841 by William II, King of the Netherlands and Grand Duke of Luxembourg. The Order may be conferred on citizens of Luxembourg and on foreigners as a reward for civil and military services and for outstanding artistic achievement. The reigning Grand Duke is the Grand Master of the Order.

The Order has five classes:

1. *Grand Cross,* which wears the Badge of the Order (174) on a sash and the Star of the Order (175).

2. *Grand Officer,* which wears the Badge of the Order (174) on a necklet and the Star of the Order (176).

3. *Commander,* which wears the Badge of the Order (174) on a necklet.

4. *Officer,* which wears the Badge of the Order (177), with an oak wreath between the arms of the cross, on a chest riband with rosette.

5. *Knight,* which wears the Badge of the Order (177) on a chest riband.

The *Badge of the Order* is a white-enamelled Teutonic Maltese Cross in gold. The 4th Class has an oak wreath between the arms of the cross. The centre medallion bears a crowned Gothic "W" for "William" on a green background.

The *Stars of the Order* for 1st and 2nd Classes respectively are an 8-pointed faceted silver star and a faceted Maltese Cross in silver, both with the centre

medallion of the Badge of the Order garlanded by a red scroll with the inscription "Je maintiendrai" (I shall persevere), the motto of the House of Nassau, and surrounded by an oak wreath.

The *Riband of the Order* is broom-yellow with three green stripes, symbolizing the green oak forests of Luxembourg and flowering broom bushes.

All insignia must be returned on the death of the holder.

Associated with the Order is the *Medal of Merit* (178–179), which has three grades, *gold, silver* and *bronze* and is worn on the chest riband of the Order. The Medal, which is 8-edged, bears a Badge of the Order without enamel on the obverse and an oak garland on the reverse.

180–184. The Order of Merit *(Ordre de Mérite du Grand-Duché de Luxembourg)* was founded on 23rd January 1961 by Grand Duchess Charlotte. The Order may be conferred on citizens of Luxembourg and on foreigners as a reward for outstanding professional achievement and for services rendered in other special fields. The reigning Grand Duke is the Grand Master of the Order.

The Order has five classes:

1. *Grand Cross,* which wears the Badge of the Order (182) on a sash and the Star of the Order (180).

2. *Grand Officer,* which wears the Badge of the Order (182) on a necklet and the Star of the Order (181).

3. *Commander,* which wears the Badge of the Order (182) on a necklet.

4. *Officer,* which wears the Badge of the Order (183) on a chest riband with rosette.

5. *Knight,* which wears the Badge of the Order (183) in silver on a chest riband without rosette.

The *Badge of the Order* is a blue-edged white-enamelled Teutonic Maltese Cross in gold, in silver for the 5th Class. The obverse medallion bears the Luxembourg Lion surrounded by a stylized laurel wreath, and the reverse medallion bears a crowned "C" for

"Charlotte" in a back-to-back monogram.

The *Grand Cross Star* is a 12-pointed gold star, and the *Grand Officer Star* a 12-pointed silver star, both with a Badge of the Order in the centre.

The *Riband of the Order* is red with blue-white border stripes, the national colours of Luxembourg.

The *Order of Merit* (184) is associated with the Order. It has one grade, *silver-gilt*, and is worn on the chest riband of the Order. The Medal has the form of a Badge of the Order with rays between the arms of the cross.

185. The War Cross 1940–1945 *(Croix de Guerre 1940–1945)* was founded on 17th April 1945 by Grand Duchess Charlotte as a token of national gratitude towards persons, citizens of Luxembourg and foreigners, who had taken part in the battle for the liberation of the Grand Duchy during the Second World War.

The Cross is a Maltese Cross in bronze, with crossed swords between the arms of the cross, pendant on a crown. The obverse medallion bears a crowned "C" for "Charlotte" and the reverse medallion bears the date "1940". The Cross is pendant on a blue and orange striped chest riband, the colours of the Grand Ducal House.

The War Cross *(Croix de Guerre)* was founded on 9th May 1951 by Grand Duchess Charlotte as a decoration for future achievement in war. The Cross is identical with the *War Cross 1940–1945* (185), but the reverse medallion bears an oak garland. The Cross is pendant on a blue and orange striped chest riband, the colours of the Grand Ducal House.

FRANCE
186–189. The Legion of Honour *(Légion d'Honneur)* was founded on 19th May 1802 by the First Consul Napoleon Bonaparte, with the object of creating a decoration for courage, honour and heroic services to replace the Orders of the Royal Family, which had been abolished by a decree of 30th July 1791. The Legion was originally divided into four classes, but in 1805 it was extended by a fifth. In the years up to 1816, the classes received their final and present designations which, together with the Division, formed the basis for most of the newer Orders of Merit. The Legion may be conferred on Frenchmen and on foreigners for military bravery and civil achievement. It may also be conferred posthumously. The holders of the highest class of the Legion receive a monthly allowance of 5 francs. The Legion ranks before all French Orders and decorations. The President of France is the Grand Master of the Legion. The Legion is administered by a Chancellery, the Chancellor being elected for life. Nominations and promotions are approved by the President following recommendation by a Minister or by the Chancellery.

The Legion has five classes:

1. *Grand Cross*, which wears the Badge of the Order (186), but larger, on a sash and the Star of the Order (187).

2. *Grand Officer*, which wears the Badge of the Order (188) on a chest riband with rosette and the Star of the Order (187) on the *right* side of the chest.

3. *Commander*, which wears the Badge of the Order (186) on a necklet.

4. *Officer*, which wears the Badge of the Order (188) on a chest riband with rosette.

5. *Knight*, which wears the Badge of the Order (189) on a chest riband.

The *Badge of the Order* is a 5-rayed white-enamelled star in gold, in silver for the 5th Class, with a wreath of oak and laurel leaves between the rays. The obverse medallion bears the symbolic female head of the Republic with the legend "République Française" (The French Republic) on a blue background, and the reverse medallion bears a set of crossed tricolours with the legend "Honneur et Patrie" (Honour and Country). The Badge of the Order has an oak and laurel wreath as a mounting.

The *Star of the Order* is a faceted silver star in the form of the Badge of the Order with plain rays between the arms. The centre medallion bears the female head of the Republic with the legend "République Française – Honneur et Patrie".

The *Riband of the Order* is plain red, the *Military Order of Ludovic the Holy*, which was abolished by the Republic, being used as a pattern.

190–193. The National Order of Merit *(Ordre National du Mérite)* was founded on 3rd December 1963 by President Charles de Gaulle with the object of ensuring simplification and harmony of the French decorations. It was to replace a number of Ministerial Orders founded before and after the Second World War by substituting for them a new National Order, simple in its principle but varied in its conferment, so that the services previously rewarded by the Ministerial Orders might not remain unappreciated. While the *Légion d'Honneur* (186–189) is conferred for eminent services, this Order is awarded for distinguished achievement in official, civic or military office as well as in the execution of private enterprise. Only Frenchmen may become Members of the Order, but the insignia of the Order may be conferred on foreigners as a mark of respect. The Order ranks after the *Order of Liberation* (194) and the *Military Medal* (195). The President of France is the Grand Master of the Order. The Order has a common Chancellor and Chancellery with the *Legion of Honour* (186–189).

The Order has five classes:

1. *Grand Cross*, which wears the Badge of the Order (190), but larger, on a sash and the Star of the Order (191).

2. *Grand Officer*, which wears the Badge of the Order (192) on a chest riband with rosette and the Star of the Order (191) in silver on the *right* side of the chest.

3. *Commander*, which wears the Badge of the Order (190) on a necklet.

4. *Officer*, which wears the Badge of the Order (192) on a chest riband with rosette.

5. *Knight*, which wears the Badge of the Order (193) on a chest riband.

The *Badge of the Order* is a 6-rayed enamelled star in gold, in silver for the 5th Class, with groups of laurel leaves between the rays. The obverse medallion bears the symbolic female head of the Republic with the legend "République Française" (The French Republic), and the reverse medallion bears a set of crossed tricolours with the legend "Ordre National de Mérite – 3 Décembre 1963" (National Order of Merit – 3rd December 1963).

The *Stars of the Order* for 1st and 2nd Classes are respectively a gold and a silver star with 12 scalloped convex plain rays connected by less-pointed fluted rays. The centre medallion bears the symbolic female head of the Republic with the legend "République Française – Ordre National du Mérite", surrounded by a wreath of individual laurel leaves.

The *Riband of the Order* is plain blue.

194. The Order of Liberation *(Ordre de la Libération)* was founded on 16th November 1940 by General Charles de Gaulle as a reward for military and civilian personnel, including military units, who distinguished themselves during the Second World War in a distinctive manner in the work for the liberation of France and the French Empire. The Members of the Order are called *Compagnons de la Libération* (Companions of the Liberation). The Order ranks before the *National Order of Merit* (190–193). Conferment of the Order was discontinued as from 23rd January 1946.

The Order has one class, which wears a Badge of the Order (194) on a chest riband.

The *Badge of the Order*, which is called the Croix de la Libération (the Cross of Liberation), is a rectangular bronze shield bearing an upright sword on whose blade rests a Cross of Lorraine. The reverse bears the inscription "Patriam Servando Victoriam Tuli" (To serve the Fatherland brings victory), the device of the Order.

The *Riband of the Order* is green with black border and centre stripes, symbolizing the country's sorrow and hope.

195. The Military Medal *(Medaille Militaire)* was founded on 22nd January 1852 by the French President at the time, Ludovic Napoleon Bonaparte. The decoration may be awarded to officers, non-commissioned officers and men of the Armed Forces who have distinguished themselves by courageous services or who have been wounded once or more, on foreigners serving in the French Forces, on personnel of the Merchant Navy, and as a token of respect on certain foreign civilian and military leaders. Senior officers must first, however, have been decorated with the Legion of Honour (186–189) in order to emphasize the decoration as the Nation's highest military distinction. It may also be awarded posthumously. The decoration, which ranks before the *National Order of Merit* (190–193), has a common Chancellor and Chancellery with the *Legion of Honour* (186–189).

The Medal is a silver gilt medal pendant on a trophy. The obverse bears the symbolic female head of the Republic with the legend "République Française" (The French Republic) on a black background surrounded by a laurel wreath in silver, and the reverse bears the inscription "Valeur et Discipline" (Valour and discipline). The Medal is worn on a yellow chest riband with green border stripes.

The Medal has been awarded about one million times since its institution.

196. The War Cross 1939–1945 *(Croix de Guerre 1939–1945)* was instituted on 26th September 1939 as a decoration for the Second World War. The decoration was conferrable on officers, non-commissioned officers and men of the Armed Forces, citizens of France and foreigners, who had been mentioned in dispatches, and in special cases also on military units, towns and civilians.

The Cross is a Maltese Cross in bronze with crossed swords between the arms of the cross. The obverse medallion bears the symbolic female head of the Republic with the legend "République Française" (The French Republic), and the reverse medallion bears the date "1939" or sometimes "1939–1945". The Cross is worn on a red chest riband with four green stripes which, according to the nature of the dispatch, is provided with a palm in bronze or a star in bronze or silver.

Identical with the War Cross is:

The War Cross 1914–1918 which was instituted on 8th April 1915 as a decoration for the First World War. The reverse medallion bears the date "1914–1918", and the riband is green with red selvedge borders and five red stripes. Also:

The War Cross 1941, instituted by the Head of the Vichy Government, Marshal Pétain, in 1941. The reverse medallion bears the date "1939–1940" and the riband is green with black selvedge edges and five black stripes.

The War Cross 1943, instituted by the Head of the Free French Forces in North Africa, General Giraud, in 1943. The obverse medallion bears a set of crossed tricolours and the reverse medallion bears the date "1943". The riband is green with red selvedge borders and five red stripes.

By an Order of 7th January 1944 of the French National Committee of Liberation it was confirmed that the War Cross instituted on 26th September 1939 was to be the only Cross valid for the Second World War.

197. The War Cross T.O.E. *(Croix de Guerre des Théatres d'Opérations Extérieurs)* was instituted on 30th April 1921 as a decoration for meritorious services in the theatre of war outside the home country. The Cross is identical with the *War Cross 1939–45* (196), but the reverse medallion bears the inscription "Théatres d'Opérations Extérieurs" (Foreign theatres of war). The Cross is worn pendant on a red chest riband with a wide light blue centre stripe.

The Order of the Black Star: Star of the Order, Grand Cross and Commander with Star

198. The Order of the Black Star (*Ordre de l'Etoile Noir du Bénin*) was instituted on 1st December 1889 as an Order of Merit for the State of Dahomey on the Slave Coast, but was changed in 1896 into a French Colonial Order for meritorious military and civil services for French West Africa. The Order has a common Chancellor and Chancellery with the *Legion of Honour* (186–189), but conferment has been discontinued as from 1st January 1964.

The Order has five classes:

1. *Grand Cross*, which wears the Badge of the Order (198), but larger, on a sash and the Star of the Order.

2. *Commander with Star*, which wears the Badge of the Order (198), but larger, on a necklet and the same Star of the Order as for 1st Class on the *right* of the chest.

3. *Commander*, which wears the Badge of the Order (198), but larger, on a necklet.

4. *Officer*, which wears the Badge of the Order (198) on a chest riband with rosette.

5. *Knight*, which wears the Badge of the Order (198) in silver on a chest riband without rosette.

The *Badge of the Order* is a blue-rimmed white-enamelled Maltese Cross in gold, in silver for the 5th Class, with pencils of rays in the angles of the cross and pendant on a green-enamelled laurel wreath. The Cross bears Bénin's black star in the centre.

The *Star of the Order* is an 8-pointed silver star with a Badge of the Order, without mounting wreath.

The *Riband of the Order* is plain light blue.

199. The Order of the Anjouan Star (*Ordre de l'Etoile d'Anjouan*) was instituted in 1874 as an Order of Merit for the Sultanate of Anjouan in the Comoro Islands, but was changed in 1896 into a French Colonial Order for meritorious military and civil services. The Order has a common Chancellor and Chancellery with the *Legion of Honour* (186–189), but conferment was discontinued as from 1st January 1964.

The Order has five classes. Classes and insignia are the same as for the *Legion of Honour* (186–189).

The *Badge of the Order* is an 8-pointed gold star. The centre medallion bears the Islamic crescent moon with the Hand of God and an Arabic inscription on a white background around the legend "Ordre Royal de l'Etoile d'Anjouan – Comores" (The Royal Order of the Anjouan Star – The Commoros) on a gold background.

The *Star of the Order* is identical with the Badge of the Order.

The *Riband of the Order* is light blue with two orange border stripes.

200. The Order of Nichan-el-Anouar *(Ordre du Nichan-el-Anouar)* or *The Order of the Lights* was instituted in 1887 as an Order of Merit for the Sultanate of Tajurah in French Somaliland, but was changed in 1896 into a French Colonial Order for meritorious military and civil services. The Order has a common Chancellor and Chancellery with the *Legion of Honour* (186–189), but conferment was discontinued as from 1st January 1964.

The Order has five classes. Classes and insignia are the same as for the *Legion of Honour* (186–189).

The *Badge of the Order* is a 10-pointed silver star with 5-pointed gold stars between the points and pendant on a royal crown. The centre medallion bears a 5-pointed silver star on a black background with an Arbaic legend on a red background.

The *Star of the Order* is identical with the Badge of the Order but without mounting crown.

The *Riband of the Order* is dark blue with a wide white centre stripe.

201–202. The Order of the "Palmes Académiques" *(Ordre des Palmes Académiques)* was instituted on 17th March 1808 as a university decoration. In 1850 the decoration was divided into the two known classes: "Officier de l'Instruction Publique" and "Officier d'Académie", usually called "Golden Palms" and "Silver Palms". It was changed on 4th October 1955 into the present Order. The Order may be conferred on French citizens and on foreigners in recognition of valuable services to the universities, in tuition and for scientific work of all kinds. The minimum age of conferment is 35 years. The Order is administered by a Council of the Order, the Minister of Education being its President.

The Order has three classes:

1. *Commander*, which wears the Badge of the Order (201) on a necklet.

2. *Officer*, which wears the Badge of the Order (202) on a chest riband with rosette.

3. *Knight*, which wears the Badge of the Order (202) in silver on a chest riband without rosette.

The *Badge of the Order* consists of a set of violet-enamelled palm branches in gold, in silver for the 3rd Class. The Badge of the Order for the 1st Class has a violet-enamelled laurel wreath as a mounting.

The *Riband of the Order* is plain violet.

203. The Order of "Mérite Agricole" *(Ordre du Mérite Agricole)* was instituted on 7th July 1883 as a reward for professional, meritorious services in the field of national agriculture and in the overseas territories of that time. The Order was expanded in 1887 and in 1900. The minimum age for conferment is 30 years, and at least 10 years' service in agriculture is required. The Order is administered by a Council of the Order, the Minister of Agriculture being its President.

The Order has three classes:

1. *Commander*, which wears the Badge of the Order (203) but larger, on a necklet.

2. *Officer*, which wears the Badge of the Order (203) on a chest riband with rosette.

3. *Knight*, which wears the Badge of the Order (203) without mounting wreath on a chest riband without rosette.

The *Badge of the Order* is a 6-pointed white-enamelled star in gold with a wreath of wheat and maize ears between the points. The obverse medallion bears the symbolic female head of the Republic with the legend "République Française" (The French Republic) on a blue background, and the reverse medallion bears the inscription "Mérite Agricole 1883" (Agricultural Merit 1883). The Badge of the Order for the 1st and 2nd Classes has a wreath of olive and vine leaves as a mounting.

The *Riband of the Order* is green, symbolizing agriculture, with red border stripes.

204. The Order of "Mérite Maritime" *(Ordre du Mérite Maritime)* was instituted on 9th February 1930 and extended in 1948. The Order may be conferred on personnel of the Merchant Navy and on persons who have rendered special services in the promotion of shipping. The minimum age for conferment is 30 years, and at least 15 years' service in the Merchant Navy is required. The Order is administered by a Council of the Order, the Minister for the Merchant Navy being its President.

The Order has three classes:

1. *Commander*, which wears the Badge of the Order (204) but larger, on a necklet.

2. *Officer*, which wears the Badge of the Order (204) on a chest riband with rosette.

3. *Knight*, which wears the Badge of the Order (204) on a chest riband without rosette.

The *Badge of the Order* is a white-enamelled compass card in gold, in silver for the 3rd Class, on which lies an anchor. The obverse medallion bears the symbolic female head of the Republic full face with the legend "République Française" (The French Republic) on a blue background, and the reverse medallion bears the inscription "Mérite Maritime" (Maritime Merit) with the legend "Marine Marchande" (The Merchant Navy).

The *Riband of the Order* is blue with two green border stripes, symbolizing the colours of the sea.

205–206. The Order of "Mérite Social" *(Ordre du Mérite Social)* was instituted on 25th October 1936 as a reward for devoted meritorious service within

institutions and the like which are concerned with social legislation. The Order is administered by the Ministry of Labour but conferment was discontinued as from 1st January 1964.

The Order has three classes:

1. *Commander*, which wears the Badge of the Order (205) on a necklet.

2. *Officer*, which wears the Badge of the Order (206) on a chest riband with rosette.

3. *Knight*, which wears the Badge of the Order (206) in silver on a chest riband without rosette.

The *Badge of the Order* is a 7-pointed blue-enamelled star in gold, in silver for the 3rd Class, with a laurel wreath between the points. The obverse medallion bears the symbolic female head of the Republic full face with the legend "Mérite Social" (Social Merit) on a white background, and the reverse medallion bears the inscription "Ministére du Travail" (The Ministry of Labour). The Badge of the Order for the 1st Class has a laurel wreath as a mounting.

The *Riband of the Order* is red with light blue border stripes.

207. The Order of "Santé Publique" *(Ordre de la Santé Publique)* was instituted on 18th February 1938 as a reward for devoted service in the cause of health, relief of the poor, and for child welfare. The Order is administered by the Ministry of Health, but conferment was discontinued as from 1st January 1964.

The Order has three classes:

1. *Commander*, which wears the Badge of the Order (207), but larger, on a necklet.

2. *Officer*, which wears the Badge of the Order (207) on a chest riband with rosette.

3. *Knight*, which wears the Badge of the Order (207) in silver on a chest riband without rosette.

The *Badge of the Order* is a 5-pointed blue-enamelled star in gold, in silver for the 3rd Class, with scalloped, concave rays between the points. The obverse medallion bears a female head, symbolizing health, which looks towards the light, with the legend "Ordre de la Santé Publique" on a blue background, and the reverse medallion bears a rising sun with the inscription "Jeue – Santé" (Joy – Health).

The *Riband of the Order* is plain dark blue.

208. The Order of "Mérite Commercial" *(Ordre du Mérite Commercial)* was instituted on 27th May 1939 as a reward for meritorious services in the field of the national economy and foreign trade. The Order is administered by the Ministry for Trade and Industry, but conferment was discontinued as from 1st January 1964.

The Order has three classes:

1. *Commander,* which wears the Badge of the Order (208), but larger, on a necklet.

2. *Officer,* which wears the Badge of the Order (208) on a chest riband with rosette.

3. *Knight,* which wears the Badge of the Order (208) on a chest riband without rosette.

The *Badge of the Order* is a compass card in gold resting upon a cog wheel in the colours of the Republic. On the compass card is positioned a caduceus whose wings crown the Badge of the Order at the top. The obverse medallion bears the symbolic female head of the Republic watching over foreign trade symbolized by a ship, and the reverse medallion bears a globe with the inscription "Mérite Commercial" (Services to Trade).

The *Riband of the Order* is grey with gold interwoven border stripes.

209. The Order of "Mérite Touristique" *(Ordre du Mérite Touristique)* was instituted on 27th May 1949 as a reward for meritorious achievement in the field of tourism in France and in the French Union. The Order is administered by the Ministry of Traffic and Tourism, but conferment was discontinued as from 1st January 1964.

The Order has three classes:

1. *Commander,* which wears the Badge of the Order (209), but larger, on a necklet.

2. *Officer,* which wears the Badge of the Order (209) on a chest riband with rosette.

3. *Knight,* which wears the Badge of the Order (209) in silver on a chest riband without rosette.

The *Badge of the Order* is a plaque in gold, in silver for the 3rd Class. The obverse bears the symbolic female figure of the Republic having a map of France as a background with the subscription "République Française" (The French Republic) and the reverse bears a rectangular frame for engraving of the holder's name, with the subscription "Mérite Touristique" (Services to Tourism).

The *Riband of the Order* is pale blue with red and olive-green border stripes.

210. The Order of "Mérite Artisanal" *(Ordre du Mérite Artisanal)* was instituted on 11th June 1948 as a reward for specialist meritorious services in the field of craftmanship and its organisation. The Order is administered by the Ministry for Crafts, but conferment was discontinued as from 1st January 1964.

The Order has three classes:

1. *Commander,* which wears the Badge of the Order (210), but larger, on a necklet.

2. *Officer,* which wears the Badge of the Order (210) on a chest riband with rosette.

3. *Knight,* which wears the Badge of the Order (210) in silver on a chest riband without rosette.

The *Badge of the Order* is a 5-armed star in gold, in silver for the 3rd Class, with pencils of rays between the arms. The obverse medallion bears the symbolic female head of the Republic full face with the legend "République Française 1948" (The French Republic 1948) on a blue background, and the reverse medallion bears an open hand with the legend "Mérite Artisanal, Labeur, Qualité"

(Services to Craftmanship; Labour, Quality). The mounting of the Badge of the Order is a laurel wreath.

The *Riband of the Order* is blue with 4 grey centre stripes.

211. The Order of "Mérite Combattant" *(Ordre du Mérite Combattant)* was instituted on 14th September 1953 as a reward for meritorious services and devotion to ex-servicemen and war victims from the two last wars. The Order is administered by the Minister for Ex-servicemen, but conferment was discontinued as from 1st January 1964.

The Order has three classes:

1. *Commander*, which wears the Badge of the Order (211), but larger, on a necklet.

2. *Officer*, which wears the Badge of the Order (211) on a chest riband with rosette.

3. *Knight*, which wears the Badge of the Order (211) in silver on a chest riband without rosette.

The *Badge of the Order* is a 5-pointed green-enamelled star in gold, in silver for 3rd class, with scalloped convex plain rays behind the points. The obverse medallion bears the symbolic female head of the Republic with the legend "République Française – Mérite Combattant" (The French Republic – Services to Ex-servicemen) on a green background, and the reverse medallion bears two clasped hands before an upright sword with the legend "Honneur et Dévouement" (Honour and devotion).

The *Riband of the Order* is dark green with orange diagonal stripes.

212–213. The Order of "Mérite Postal" *(Ordre du Mérite Postal)* was instituted on 14th November 1953 as a reward for meritorious services, national as well as international, in the field of post and telecommunications. The Order is administered by the Ministry for Post, Telephones and Telecommunications, but conferment was discontinued as from 1st January 1964.

The Order has three classes:

1. *Commander*, which wears the Badge of the Order (212) on a necklet.

2. *Officer*, which wears the Badge of the Order (213) in gold on a chest riband with rosette.

3. *Knight*, which wears the Badge of the Order (213) on a chest riband.

The *Badge of the Order* is a 5-pointed white-enamelled star in gold, in silver for the 3rd Class, with a laurel wreath between the points. The obverse medallion bears a picture of Mercury in profile, and the reverse medallion bears allegorical images representing post and telegraphy with the legend "République Française – Mérite Postal" (The French Republic – Postal Services). The Badge of the Order has the wings of Mercury as a mounting.

The *Riband of the Order* is postal yellow with two black border stripes symbolizing telegraph wires.

214. The Order of "Economie Nationale" *(Ordre de l'Economie Nationale)* was instituted on 6th January 1954 as a recognition of significant services in the field of the French economy. The Order is administered by the Ministry of Finance, but conferment was discontinued as from 1st January 1964.

The Order has three classes:

1. *Commander*, which wears the Badge of the Order (214), but larger, on a necklet.

2. *Officer*, which wears the Badge of the Order (214) on a chest riband with rosette.

3. *Knight*, which wears the Badge of the Order (214) in silver on a chest riband without rosette.

The *Badge of the Order* is a 5-armed white-enamelled star in gold, in silver for the 3rd Class, with yellow points between the arms. The obverse medallion bears the symbolic female head of the Republic within a garland of balls, and the reverse medallion bears a globe on the background of an 8-pointed star with the legend "Ordre de l'Economie Nationale". The mounting of the Badge of the Order is a cog wheel.

The *Riband of the Order* is plain orange.

215–216. The Order of "Mérite Sportif" *(Ordre du Mérite Sportif)* was instituted on 6th July 1956 as a reward for meritorious services in the development of physical education and sport in France and the French Union. The Order is administered by the Ministry for National Education, but conferment was discontinued as from 1st January 1964.

The Order has three classes:

1. *Commander*, which wears the Badge of the Order (215) on a necklet.

2. *Officer*, which wears the Badge of the Order (216) on a chest riband with rosette.

3. *Knight*, which wears the Badge of the Order (216) in bronze on a chest riband without rosette.

The *Badge of the Order* is a blue-enamelled medallion in gold, in silver and bronze without enamel for the 2nd and the 3rd classes respectively, illustrating the Goddess of Victory bearing a laurel wreath above her head. The obverse medallion bears the inscription "Mérite Sportif" (Services to Sport) and the reverse bears the inscription "République Française" (The French Republic).

The *Riband of the Order* is blue with yellow border stripes.

217. The Order of "Mérite du Travail" *(Ordre du Mérite du Travail)* was instituted on 21st January 1957 as a reward for meritorious services in the field of commerce and industry. The Order is administered by the Ministry of Labour, but conferment was discontinued as from 1st January 1964.

The Order has three classes:

1. *Commander*, which wears the Badge of the Order (217), but larger, on a necklet.

2. *Officer*, which wears the Badge of the Order (217) on a chest riband with rosette.

3. *Knight*, which wears the Badge of the Order (217) in silver on a chest riband without rosette.

The *Badge of the Order* is a circular medallion in gold, in silver for the 3rd Class. The obverse bears the symbols of a set-square, calipers and hammers with the legend "Mérite du Travail" (Services to Labour), and in a medallion below the symbolic female head of the Republic wearing a helmet of Hermes bearing the Gallic cock. The reverse bears the inscription "Liberté – Egalité – Fraternité" (Liberty – Equality – Fraternity) with the legend "République Française" (The French Republic).

The *Riband of the Order* is dark green with red-white border stripes.

218–219. The Order of "Mérite Militaire" *(Ordre du Mérite Militaire)* was instituted on 22nd March 1957 as a reward for meritorious, voluntary, instructive and defensive services in the Reserves in peace time. The Order is administered by the Ministry of Defence, but conferment was discontinued as from 1st January 1964.

The Order has three classes:

1. *Commander*, which wears the Badge of the Order (218) on a necklet.

2. *Officer*, which wears the Badge of the Order (219) on a chest riband with rosette.

3. *Knight*, which wears the Badge of the Order (219) in silver on a chest riband without rosette.

The *Badge of the Order* is a blue-enamelled Maltese Cross in gold, in gold and silver without enamel for the 2nd and the 3rd Classes respectively. The obverse medallion bears the symbolic female head of the Republic wearing a steel helmet with the inscription "République Française" (The French Republic), and the reverse medallion bears the inscription "Mérite Militaire" (Military Services). The Badge of the Order for the 1st Class has a wreath of oak leaves as a mounting and groups of laurel leaves in the angles of the cross.

The *Riband of the Order* is blue with white selvedge borders and a wide red centre stripe.

220–221. The Order of "Mérite Civil" *(Ordre du Mérite Civil)* was instituted on 2nd May 1957 as a reward for outstanding services to the State within the field of administration in the Arrondissements, Departments and Municipalities or within public institutions. The Order is administered by the Ministry of the Interior, but conferment was discontinued as from 1st January 1964.

The Order has three classes:

1. *Commander*, which wears the Badge of the Order (220) on a necklet.

2. *Officer*, which wears the Badge of the Order (221) in gold on a chest riband with rosette.

3. *Knight*, which wears the Badge of the Order (221) on a chest riband.

The *Badge of the Order* is an 8-pointed blue-enamelled star in gold, in silver for the 3rd Class, with blue-enamelled radial points between the points. The obverse medallion bears the symbolic female head of the Republic wearing a Phrygian cap – the Cap of Liberty worn by extremists during the French Revolution – with the legend "République Française" (The French Republic), and the reverse medallion bears the inscription "Mérite Civil" (Civilian Services). The Badge of the Order for the 1st Class has an "RF" for "République Française" as a mounting.

The *Riband of the Order* is blue with a white-edged black centre stripe.

222–223. The Order of "Mérite Saharien" *(Ordre du Mérite Saharien)* was instituted on 4th April 1958 as a reward for meritorious humanitarian and social services as well as preparatory scientific work and other pioneering work in the Sahara regions. The Order is administered by the Ministry for the Sahara, but conferment was discontinued as from 1st January 1964.

The Order has three classes:

1. *Commander*, which wears the Badge of the Order (222) on a necklet.

2. *Officer*, which wears the Badge of the Order (223) on a chest riband with rosette.

3. *Knight*, which wears the Badge of the Order (223) in silver on a chest riband without rosette.

The *Badge of the Order* is an ornamented Arabian jewel in gold, in silver for the 3rd Class, from the Sahara. The wreath at the top bears the inscription "République Française" (The French Republic) and the centre of the reverse bears the inscription "Mérite Saharien" (Services to the Sahara).

The *Riband of the Order* is desert-sand yellow with two blue border stripes.

224. The Order of "Arts et Lettres" *(Ordre des Arts et des Lettres)* was instituted on 2nd May 1957 as a reward for meritorious services in the field of the arts and literature. The Order is administered by a Council of the Order, the Minister for Culture being its President.

The Order has three classes:

1. *Commander*, which wears the Badge of the Order (224) on a necklet.

2. *Officer*, which wears the Badge of the Order (224), but smaller, on a chest riband with rosette.

3. *Knight*, which wears the Badge of the Order (224), but smaller and in silver, on a chest riband without rosette.

The *Badge of the Order* is a double-pointed, 8-armed green-enamelled star in gold, in silver for the 3rd Class. The obverse medallion bears an "A" and an "L", for "Arts et Lettres", entwined on a white background with the legend "République Française" (The French Republic) on a gold background, and the reverse medallion bears the symbolic female head of the Republic with the legend "Ordre des Arts et des Lettres". The Badge of the Order for the 1st Class has a twisted ring as a mounting.

The *Riband of the Order* is dark green with four white stripes.

MONACO
225. The Order of Charles the Holy *(Ordre de Saint-Charles)* was instituted on 15th March 1858 by Prince Charles III. The Order may be conferred on citizens of Monaco and on foreigners as a reward for services to Prince and State.

The Order of Charles the Holy: Star of the Order, Grand Cross and Grand Officer

The reigning Prince is the Grand Master of the Order.

The Order has five classes:

1. *Grand Cross*, which wears the Badge of the Order (225) on a sash and Star of the Order.

2. *Grand Officer*, which wears the Badge of the Order (227) on a chest riband with rosette and the same Star of the Order as for the 1st Class on the *right* of the chest.

3. *Commander*, which wears the Badge of the Order (225) on a necklet.

4. *Officer*, which wears the Badge of the Order (225) in the same size as the Knight's Cross (227) on a chest riband with rosette.

5. *Knight*, which wears the Badge of the Order (225) in the same size as the Knight's Cross (227) on a chest riband without rosette.

The *Badge of the Order* is a red-rimmed white-enamelled Maltese Cross in gold with a laurel wreath between the arms of the cross and pendant on a Prince's crown. The obverse medallion bears a crowned "C" for "Charles" in a back to back monogram on a red background with the legend "Princeps et Patria" (Prince and Country) on a

white background, and the reverse medallion bears the red-white rhombs of the State coat of arms with the legend "Deo Juvante" (With God's Help).

The *Star of the Order* is an 8-pointed faceted silver star with a Badge of the Order without mounting crown.

The *Riband of the Order* is red with white selvedge borders and a wide white centre stripe.

226–227. The Order of the Crown *(Ordre de la Couronne)* was instituted on 20th July 1960 by Prince Rainier III. The Order may be conferred on citizens of Monaco and on foreigners as a reward for services to the Prince personally and as a recognition of his respect. Holders of the Order, who wear their insignia visibly, are given a military salute. The reigning Prince is the Grand Master of the Order, and conferment of the Order is the sole right of the Prince.

The Order has five classes:

1. *Grand Cross*, which wears the Badge of the Order (227) in the same size as the Grand Cross (225) on a sash and the Star of the Order (226).

2. *Grand Officer*, which wears the

Badge of the Order (227) in the same size as the Grand Cross (225) on a necklet and the Star of the Order (226) on the *right* of the chest.

3. *Commander*, which wears the Badge of the Order (227) in the same size as the Grand Cross (225) on a necklet.

4. *Officer*, which wears the Badge of the Order (227) on a chest riband with rosette.

5. *Knight*, which wears the Badge of the Order (227) on a chest riband without rosette.

The *Badge of the Order* is a so-called "cross pattée" with fluted silver arms and a golden centre stripe, with the face-to-face monogram of the founder in gold between the arms. The obverse medallion bears a Prince's crown on a white background, and the reverse medallion bears the rhombs of the State coat of arms in gold. The Badge of the Order has a wreath of oak and laurel leaves as a mounting.

The *Star of the Order* is identical with the Badge of the Order but without mounting wreath. The centre medallion is garlanded with a ring of embossed rhombs.

The *Riband of the Order* is olive-green with a red centre stripe.

228–229. The Order of Grimaldi *(Ordre des Grimaldi)* was instituted on 18th November 1954 by Prince Rainier III. The Order is named after the Princely Family of Grimaldi, the parent line of Monaco, and may be conferred on citizens of Monaco and on foreigners as a reward for services to the Prince personally. Holders of the Order, who wear their insignia visibly, are given a military salute. The reigning Prince is the Grand Master of the Order, and conferment of the Order is the sole right of the Prince.

The Order has five classes:

1. *Grand Cross*, which wears the Badge of the Order (229) in the same size as the Grand Cross (225) on a sash and the Star of the Order (228).

2. *Grand Officer*, which wears the Badge of the Order (229) in the same

size as the Grand Cross (225) on a necklet and the Star of the Order (228) on the *right* of the chest.

3. *Commander*, which wears the Badge of the Order (229) in the same size as the Grand Cross (225) on a necklet.

4. *Officer*, which wears the Badge of the Order (229) on a chest riband with rosette.

5. *Knight*, which wears the Badge of the Order (229) in silver on a chest riband without rosette.

The *Badge of the Order* is a white-enamelled Mantua Cross in gold, in silver for the 5th Class, pendant on a Prince's crown. The obverse medallion bears a galloping knight with the coat of arms of the Grimaldi family on his breast, and the legend "Rainer Grimaldi, Prince of Monaco" (Rainer Grimaldi, Prince, of Monaco), and the reverse medallion bears the date "1950" with the legend "Principauté de Monaco" (Principality of Monaco).

The *Star of the Order* is a silver star formed by 16 rhombs, with the same obverse medallion as the Badge of the Order.

The *Riband of the Order* is white with narrow red border stripes.

230. The Order of "Mérite Culturel" *(Ordre du Mérite Culturel)* was instituted on 31st December 1952 by Prince Rainier III. The Order may be conferred on citizens of Monaco and on foreigners who, by their works or teaching activities, have contributed to the development of art, literature and science in Monaco, or who, within the same fields, have contributed to the cultural reputation of the Principality. Conferment is made by order of the Prince, and the minimum age is 40 years.

The Order has three classes:

1. *Commander*, which wears the Badge of the Order (230), but larger and in gold, on a necklet.

2. *Officer*, which wears the Badge of the Order (230) on a chest riband with rosette.

3. *Knight*, which wears the Badge of

the Order (230) in bronze on a chest riband without rosette.

The *Badge of the Order* is a medallion, in gold for the 1st Class, in silver for the 2nd Class, in bronze for the 3rd Class, garlanded by a laurel wreath and pendant on a Prince's crown. The obverse bears the face-to-face monogram of the founder with the legend "Principauté de Monaco 1952" (The Principality of Monaco 1952) surrounded by a circle of rhombs, and the reverse bears tributes for art, literature and science with the inscription "Arts – Lettres – Sciences" (Art – Literature – Science) surrounded by a circle of rhombs.

The *Riband of the Order* is red with a centre stripe consisting of white rhombs.

WESTERN GERMANY
231–239. The Order of Merit of the Federal Republic of Germany *(Der Verdienstorden der Bundesrepublik Deutschland)* was instituted on 7th September 1951 by the Federal President, Theodor Heuss. The Order may be conferred as a visible expression of recognition and gratitude to deserving men and women, German and foreign, who, during the rebuilding of the Federal Republic or later, have rendered services in the political, cultural or economic-social fields. The Order is administered by a Chancellery of the Order, which is administered by the Federal President. Conferment is effected on the recommendation of the President, following nomination by the highest authorities in the Federal Republic.

The Order is divided into three main Divisions which internationally correspond to (1) Grand Cross in three stages, (2) Commander in three stages and (3) Knight in two stages:

1. (i) *Grand Cross Special Class* which wears the Badge of the Order (231), but larger, on a sash and the Star of the Order (232).

(ii) *Grand Cross Special Design*, which wears the same Badge of the Order as for Grand Cross Special Class on a

sash and the Star of the Order (233), both with a laurel wreath in gold around the centre medallion of the Badge of the Order.

(iii) *Grand Cross*, which wears the Badge of the Order (231) on a sash and the Star of the Order (233).

2. (i) *Grand Cross of Merit with Star and Sash*, which wears the Badge of the Order (235) on a sash and the Star of the Order (234).

(ii) *Grand Cross of Merit with Star*, which wears the Badge of the Order (235) on a necklet (gentlemen) or on a bow (ladies) and the Star of the Order (236).

(iii) *Grand Cross of Merit*, which wears the Badge of the Order (235) on a necklet (gentlemen) or on a bow (ladies).

3. (i) *Cross of Merit 1st Class*, which wears the Badge of the Order (237) as a breast cross without riband.

(ii) *Cross of Merit with Riband*, which wears the Badge of the Order (238) on a chest riband (gentlemen) or on a bow (ladies).

The 1st stage of the Grand Cross Division is reserved for foreign Heads of State; the 2nd stage has so far been conferred only once, on the former Federal Chancellor, Konrad Adenauer.

The *Badge of the Order* is a red-enamelled Maltese Cross in gold with slender arms. The centre medallion bears the black German eagle. The Badge of the Order for the Grand Cross Special Design bears a laurel wreath in gold around the centre medallion as a special ornamentation.

According to division and stage, the *Star of the Order* is an 8-, 6-, or 4-pointed gold star with a Badge of the Order, and for Grand Cross Special Design with a laurel wreath in gold around the centre medallion.

The *Riband of the Order* is red with gold-edged black border stripes, the colours of the Federal Republic. The sash of the Grand Cross Division bears interwoven eagles. Ladies wear a bow above the fan on the sash. The ladies' bow for the 2nd and 3rd Divisions is respectively with or without ribands. Persons who celebrate their 50 years' jubilee in German private enterprises wear a bar with the figure "50" on the riband for the 2nd stage of the Cross of Merit Division.

The *Medal of Merit* (239) is attached to the Order. It has one grade, *gold*, and is worn on a red chest riband with narrow gold-edged black border stripes. The obverse bears a Badge of the Order resting on a laurel wreath, and the reverse bears the inscription "Für Verdienste um die Bundesrepublik Deutschland" (For Services to the Federal Republic of Germany) surrounded by a laurel wreath.

All insignia are personal property and are not to be returned on the death of the holder.

240. The Order "Pour le Mérite" for Science and the Arts *(Der Orden "Pour le Mérite" für Wissenschaften und Künste)* was instituted on 31st May 1842 by King Frederick William IV of Prussia as a "Peace Class" of the Order "Pour le Mérite" instituted by King Frederick II of Prussia in 1740, which King Frederick William III had in 1810 limited by statute to be a purely martial Order of Merit. Following a stagnant period after 1935, renewal was effected on 31st May 1952. The Federal Republic acknowledged the Order as a free association of scholars and artists, with the Federal President as its protector, on 18th June 1956. Men and women who have achieved an outstanding reputation through widespread acknowledgement of their services to science and the arts may be admitted into the Order. The number of members, who must be German citizens, is limited to 30, of whom 10 must be in the philosophic-scientific field, 10 in the natural-scientific field and 10 artists. In addition, foreigners, also to a number of not more than 30, may also be awarded the insignia of the Order. The Order is administered by a Chancellor of the Order, who is elected by the members. If a place becomes vacant, the members themselves elect the new member.

The Order has one class, which wears the Badge of the Order (240) on a necklet.

The *Badge of the Order*, which is in gold, consists of a medallion with the Prussian eagle surrounded by a blue-enamelled scroll with the inscription "Pour le Mérite" (For Merit), the device of the Order. Between the medallion and the Scroll, four "F"s in back-to-back monogram and four Roman figures II for "Frederick II" have been inserted. On the outside, the scroll bears the four crowns appertaining to the monograms.

The *Riband of the Order* is black with silver-white border stripes, the colours of Prussia.

The insignia of the Order must be returned on the death of the holder.

Professor Niels Bohr may be mentioned among the foreigners.

241–243. The Iron Cross *(Das Eiserne Kreuz)* was originally instituted on 10th March 1813 by King Frederick William III of Prussia for services during the Wars of Liberation, but it was renewed in 1870 for the Franco-Prussian War and in 1914 for the First World War. Finally, the decoration was renewed on 1st September 1939 by the Reich Chancellor, Adolf Hitler, for the Second World War, during which it might be conferred on Germans and on citizens of countries allied with Germany for exceptional bravery in the face of the enemy and for outstanding services in the leadership of troops.

The Iron Cross was divided in 1813, 1870 and 1914 into two classes and one Grand Cross Class. In 1939 the Iron Cross was divided into four degrees, the 3rd degree being divided in the course of the war into five stages.

1. *Iron Cross 2nd Class*, which wears the Badge of the Order (243) on a chest riband.

2. *Iron Cross 1st Class*, which wears the Badge of the Order (242) as a breast cross without riband.

3. (i) *The Knight's Cross of the Iron Cross*, which wears the Badge of the Order (241) without oak leaves, with swords, on a necklet.

(ii) *The Knight's Cross of the Iron Cross with Oak Leaves*, which wears the Badge of the Order (241) with oak leaves, without swords, on a necklet.

(iii) *The Knight's Cross of the Iron Cross with Oak Leaves and Swords*, which wears the Badge of the Order (241) on a necklet.

(iv) *The Knight's Cross of the Iron Cross with Oak Leaves, Swords and Diamonds*, which wears the Badge of the Order (241) with oak leaves and swords studded with diamonds on a necklet.

(v) *The Knight's Cross of the Iron Cross with Golden Oak Leaves, Swords and Diamonds*, which wears the Badge of the Order (241) with golden oak leaves and swords studded with diamonds on a necklet.

4. *The Grand Cross of the Iron Cross*, which wears the Badge of the Order (241), but larger, without oak leaves, with swords on a necklet.

The last two honours were each conferred once only: the Grand Cross to Field Marshal Hermann Göring; and the Knight's Cross with golden oak leaves, swords and diamonds to the leader of the Immelmann Fighter Squadron, Colonel Rudel; 3 (iv), the Knight's Cross with oak leaves, swords and diamonds, was primarily conferred on officers of the air and submarine forces for successful services.

The *Badge of the Order* is a silver-rimmed black Mantua Cross in the colours of Prussia. The obverse bears a 3-leaved oak twig in the centre, and on the bottom arm the year "1939". The reverse bears on the bottom arm the year "1813". The Badge of the Order conferred during the war bore a swastika, the symbol of the Third Reich, instead of the oak twig, but the law of 26th July 1957 concerning titles, orders and medals of honour permitted the Iron Cross to be worn in future only if the swastika is removed. "Oak leaves" or "Oak leaves with Swords" are carried on the mounting of the Knight's Cross.

The *Riband of the Order* is red with black-white border stripes, the colours of the Third Reich.

Holders of the Iron Cross of 1914 who were awarded the decoration again in the Second World War wear a silver bar with the year "1939" on the riband (2nd Class) or above the Badge of the Order (1st Class).

All insignia are personal property and are not to be returned on the death of the holder.

244–246. The War Cross of Merit *(Das Kriegsverdienstkreuz)* was instituted on 18th October 1939 by the Reich Chancellor, Adolf Hitler, as a recognition for services during the Second World War which could not be recognised by the award of the *Iron Cross* (241–243). The decoration might be conferred "with swords" or "without swords" for, respectively, exceptional services under enemy fire or the execution of special war tasks which did not require direct engagement with the enemy.

The decoration has three degrees, the 3rd Degree, the Knight's Cross, being first instituted on 19th August 1940:

1. *The War Cross of Merit 2nd Class,* which wears the Badge of the Order (245) on a chest riband.

2. *The War Cross of Merit 1st Class,* which wears the Badge of the Order (244) as a breast cross without riband.

3. *The Knight's Cross of the War Cross of Merit,* which wears the Badge of the Order (244), but larger, on a necklet.

For conferment of the Knight's Cross, it was normally a requirement that the person concerned had previously been decorated with the *German Cross* in silver. (247–248)

The *Badge of the Order* is a Maltese Cross in bronze (1st Degree) or in silver (2nd and 3rd Degree). The obverse medallion bears the date "1939" within a stylised laurel wreath. The reverse medallion is plain. Badges of the Order for the decoration conferred "with swords'' bear a set of crossed swords in the angles of the cross. The Badge of the Order conferred during the war bore a swastika on the obverse medallion, the symbol of the Third Reich, and on the reverse medallion the date ''1939''. The law of 26th July 1957 concerning titles, orders and medals of honour, however, permitted the War Cross of Merit to be worn in future only if this symbol is removed.

The *Riband of the Order* is black with red-white border stripes, the colours of the Third Reich.

The *War Medal of Merit* (246), which was instituted on 19th August 1940, is attached to the Order. The Medal, which has one degree, bronze, is worn on a chest riband which is black with red-white border stripes and a narrow red centre stripe. The obverse bears a Badge of the Order embossed, and the reverse bears the inscription ''Für Kriegsverdienst 1939'' (For War Services, 1939).

247–248. The German Cross (*Das Deutsche Kreuz*) was instituted on 28th September 1941 by the Reich Chancellor, Adolf Hitler, as a reward for war services during the Second World War.

The decoration has two classes:

1. *The German Cross in Gold* (247) which was conferred for frequent exceptional bravery in the face of the enemy.

2. *The German Cross in Silver* (248) which was conferred for repeated outstanding services in the leadership of troops.

For the conferment of 1st and 2nd Classes respectively, the person concerned was required to have been previously decorated with the *Iron Cross* 1st class (242) or the *War Cross of Merit* 1st Class (244). Holders of both classes wear only the higher.

The *Badge of the Order*, which is worn on the *right* side of the chest, is an 8-pointed silver star with a stylized laurel wreath, in gold or silver according to class, and with the date ''1941'' below. The Badge of the Order for the 1st Class bears an Iron Cross within the laurel

wreath, and the Badge of the Order for the 2nd Class bears a War Cross of Merit with swords, both without date.

The Badge of the Order conferred during the war bore a black swastika within the laurel wreath for both classes, the symbol of the Third Reich. The law of 26th July 1957 concerning titles, orders and medals of honour permits the German Cross to be worn in future only if this symbol is removed.

EASTERN GERMANY

249. The Order of Karl Marx (*Der Karl Marx Orden*) was instituted on 30th April 1953, the 135th year and 70th year respectively of Karl Marx' birth and death. The Order may be conferred on individuals and collectively for outstanding services in the fields of the arts and of culture, science and the national economy in the struggle for an eternal, independent and peace-loving Germany. It may also be conferred on foreigners. The Order may be conferred on the recommendation of the President of the State Council.

The Order has one class, which wears the Badge of the Order (249) on a chest riband.

The *Badge of the Order* is the 5-pointed red star of Communism in gold with oak leaves between the points. The centre medallion bears in relief a portrait of Karl Marx.

The *Riband of the Order* is red, the colour of Communism. It is worn on a chest riband mounted in a crossed fashion.

Ribands worn on their own with uniform are provided with an oak leaf in gold.

250. The Order of Merit of the Fatherland. (*Vaterländischer Verdienstorder*) was instituted on 21st April 1954. The Order may be conferred on individuals and collectively for special services to the State and to society. It may also be conferred on foreigners. The Order is conferred on the recommendation of the President of the State Council, usually on 7th October, the Day of the Republic. The Order ranks after the Order of the *Star of Friendship between Peoples* (251.)

The Order has three classes, 1st, 2nd and 3rd, which wear the Badge of the Order (250) in gold, silver or bronze, according to class.

The *Badge of the Order* is a ray-shaped star with 10 points. The centre medallion bears the State coat of arms on a red background.

The *Riband of the Order*, which is horizontally striped in the black-red-gold colours of the Republic, is borne on a mounting whose lower bracket consists of stylized oak leaves.

251. The Order of the "Star of Friendship between Peoples" *(Der Orden "Stern der Völkerfreundschaft")* was instituted on 20th August 1959 as a reward for outstanding services to the Republic and for meritorious achievement in the promotion of understanding and friendship between peoples. It may also be conferred on foreigners. The Order is conferred on the recommendation of the President of the State Council. The Order ranks before the *Order of Merit of the Fatherland* (250).

The Order has three classes:

1. *Grand Star*, which wears the Badge of the Order (251), but larger and in gold, on a sash or as a breast cross.

2. *Gold Star*, which wears the Badge of the Order (251) in silver-gilt as a breast cross.

3. *Silver Star*, which wears the Badge of the Order (251) as a breast cross.

The *Badge of the Order* is a 5-pointed star, in gold for 1st Class, in silver-gilt for 2nd Class, and in silver for 3rd Class, with a single-leaf oak wreath between the arms, but arranged so that the wreath lies across the upper arm which bears a dove in relief. The centre medallion bears the State coat of arms on a red background.

The *Riband of the Order*, which is worn as a sash for the 1st Class, is red with border stripes in the black-red-gold colours of the Republic.

252. The Order of the Banner of Work *(Der Orden "Banner der Arbeit")* was instituted on 4th August 1954 as a reward for outstanding services in the promotion of production. It may be conferred on individuals and collectively, but with a maximum number respectively of 70 and 50 a year. The Order is conferred on the recommendation of the President of the State Council, usually on 1st May or on 7th October, the Day of the Republic.

The Order has one class, which wears the Badge of the Order (252) on a chest riband.

The *Badge of the Order* is a gold medallion with the State coat of arms crowned by the Red Flag, with the inscription "Banner der Arbeit" (The Banner of Work).

The *Riband of the Order* consists of two ribands, one in the red colour of Communism, the other in the black-red-gold colours of the Republic. It is worn as a chest riband mounted in a crossed fashion.

The Riband worn alone with uniform is red with black-gold-red centre stripes.

AUSTRIA
253–259. The Decoration of Honour for Merit *(Das Ehrenzeichen für Verdienste um die Republik Österreich)* was instituted by the National Council in a law of 2nd April 1952, amended in 1954 and 1956. The Decoration may be conferred on Austrians and on foreigners, men and women, as a reward for outstanding public achievement and exceptional services to the Republic. The Order is conferred on the recommendation of the Federal President or the proposal of the Federal Government.

The Decoration is divided into five groups corresponding to the five international classes, each group, with the exception of the 4th group, being graded beyond the normal:

1*. *Grand Star*, which wears the Badge of the Order (253) on a sash and the Star of the Order (254) in solid gold.

1. (i) *Grand Decoration of Honour*

in Gold with Sash, which wears the Badge of the Order (253) on a sash and the Star of the Order (254).

(ii) *Grand Decoration of Honour in Silver with Sash*, which wears the Badge of the Order (253) in silver on a sash and the Star of the Order (254), in solid silver.

2. (i) *Grand Decoration of Honour in Gold with Star*, which wears the Badge of the Order (255) on a white red-striped necklet and the Star of the Order (254), but smaller.

(ii) *Grand Decoration of Honour in Silver with Star*, which wears the Badge of the Order (255) in silver on a red white-striped necklet and the Star of the Order (254), but smaller and in solid silver.

3. (i) *Grand Decoration of Honour in Gold*, which wears the Badge of the Order (255) on a white red-striped necklet.

(ii) *Grand Decoration of Honour in Silver*, which wears the Badge of the Order (255) in silver on a red white-striped necklet.

4. *Grand Decoration of Honour*, which wears the Badge of the Order (256) without riband as a breast cross.

5. (i) *Decoration of Honour in Gold*, which wears the Badge of the Order (257) in gold on a white red-striped chest riband.

(ii) *Decoration of Honour in Silver* which wears the Badge of the Order (257) on a red white-striped chest riband.

The Grand Star group is a "special class" reserved for the Federal President and foreign Heads of State.

The *Badge of the Order* is a red-enamelled Maltese Cross, in gold for 1st Degree in all groups, in silver for 2nd Degree, with an inlaid white Greek Cross and crowned with the Austrian Federal coat of arms. For the 4th Group, the Federal coat of arms is in the centre.

The *Star of the Order*, which varies in size according to Group, is an 8-pointed silver star, for the Grand Star Group a gold star, with plain rays. The star bears in the centre the Austrian Federal coat of arms, for the 1st Degree of 1st and 2nd Groups in gold, and for the 2nd Degree in silver.

The *Riband of the Order* is in the red and white colours of the Federal Republic, but in two different patterns. For the sash in the 1st Group and for the silver decorations in the other Groups, the Riband is red with white selvedge borders and a white centre stripe. For the gold decorations it is white with red border stripes. They are worn on a chest riband in a triangular fashion.

Attached to the Decoration is:

The *Decoration of Merit* (258), which has two degrees, *gold* and *silver*, which are worn on the white red-striped and red white-striped chest riband respectively of the 5th Group. The Badge of the Order is an unenamelled Maltese Cross crowned by the Austrian Federal coat of arms.

The *Medal of Merit* (259) has 3 degrees, *gold*, *silver* and *bronze*, which are all worn on the red white-striped breast riband of the 5th Group. On the obverse, the medal bears the Austrian Federal coat of arms, and on the reverse "Für Verdienste um die Republik Österreich" (For Services to the Republic of Austria).

The Star of the Order must be returned on the death of the holder. The other insignia are personal property.

260. The Decoration of Honour for Science and the Arts *(Das Österreichische Ehrenzeichen für Wissenschaft und Kunst)* was instituted by the National Council under a law of 25th May 1955. The decoration may be conferred on persons in Austria and abroad who, by exceptional creative work in the field of science or within the arts, have earned general recognition and repute. The number of persons decorated may not exceed 36 Austrian citizens (18 scientists and 18 artists) and 36 foreigners. The Austrian holders of the Decoration form a senate which, on a place becoming vacant, submits a proposal to the

Federal Government through the Minister for Education for the new occupant. Conferment is made on nomination by the Federal President following proposal by the Federal Government.

The Decoration has one class, which wears the Badge of the Order (260) on a necklet.

The *Badge of the Order* is a red-enamelled Maltese Cross in gold, upon which rests a more slender white-enamelled Maltese Cross. The centre medallion bears the inscription "Litteris et Artibus" (For Science and the Arts). The Badge of the Order is pendant on a mounting ornamented with two laurel twigs.

The *Riband of the Order* is plain red.

The insignia of the Decoration are Government property and must be returned on the death of the holder.

261–262. The Cross of Honour for Science and Art *(Das Österreichische Ehrenkreuz für Wissenschaft und Kunst)* was instituted by the National Council under a law of 25th May 1955. The Decoration may be conferred on persons in Austria and abroad who, in the fields of science and the arts, have acquired merit by recognised works. Conferment is effected on the nomination of the Federal President following proposal by the Federal Government.

The Decoration has two classes:

1. *Cross of Honour 1st Class*, which wears a Badge of the Order (261) without riband as a breast cross.

2. *Cross of Honour*, which wears the Badge of the Order (262) on a chest riband.

The *Badge of the Order* is identical with the Badge of the Order for the *Decoration of Honour for Science and the Arts* (260), but without mounting.

The *Riband of the Order* is plain red. It is worn as a chest riband mounted in a triangular fashion.

The insignia of the Decoration are personal property and are not returned on the death of the holder.

263–264. The Teutonic Order *(Deutscher Orden* or *Der Deutsche Orden St.*

Mariens zu Jerusalem), whose origin and history were described on page 10, was drastically altered in 1929, when Pope Pius XI changed the original Order of Chivalry into a Clerical Order of priests, lay brothers and lay sisters who all take vows. The Order is considered to be a mendicant order, and its field of activity is mainly restricted to Germany, Italy and Austria. Its main objects are missionary and, as concerns the sisters, hospital service.

The Head of the Order, whose headquarters is in Vienna, bears the old title of "Hochmeister" (Grand Master); he is a prelate with the rank of Abbot, and he enjoys the privilege of "pileolus violaceus", that is to say he has the right to wear the violet-coloured hood. As a badge of office, the Grand Master wears a special Badge of the Order on a black necklet and a corresponding breast cross. The members of the Order, the Brothers, wear as a Badge of the Order a silver-rimmed black Latin Cross on the breast or on a black cord around the neck, according to category.

Benefactors of the Order may be admitted as *Honorary Knights* or *Marians*. These so-called "familiares" are entitled to wear on ceremonial occasions as a visible token of affiliation to the Order the Badges of the Order special to them, together with a mantle of the Order with the Badge of the Order sewn upon it.

The Teutonic Order: Badge of the Order, Brother of the Order

The Teutonic Order: Badge of the Order, Marians

A small number of Roman Catholic personalities in prominent social positions who have previously given great services to the Order may be admitted as *Honorary Knights*. They wear as a Badge of the Order a white-rimmed black Latin Cross in gold crowned with a helmet with the crest on a black necklet (263). Women may be admitted as *Honorary Dames*.

A limited number of prominent, strictly Roman Catholic, personalities, doctors and clerics, men and women, who have supported the Order spiritually or financially may be admitted as *Marians*. They wear as a Badge of the Order a white-rimmed black Latin Cross in gold on a black and silver-white necklet. The former *Knights of the Teutonic Order* were able to continue after 1929 as "Alt Marianer" (Old Knights of the Teutonic Order). They wear their old Badge of the Order (264) which, without the centre medallion, is identical with the Badge of the Order for Marians, on a black and silver-white necklet, formerly worn on a chest riband.

The former German Federal Chancellor, Konrad Adenauer, is one of the Honorary Knights. He was admitted into the Order in 1958.

265–267. The Order of St. John of Jerusalem and of Malta for the Grand Priorate of Austria and Bohemia *(Der Johanniter-Malterser-Ordenen für das Grosspriorat Österreich und Böhmen)*, which is a branch of the *Order of Malta* whose origin and history was described on page 9 has its headquarters in Vienna. It is occasionally possible for Knights of Orders of confessions other than the Roman Catholic to be admitted into the Grand Priorate.

The Grand Prior and the other Knights of the Order wear, as Badges of Office and of the order, in addition to the so-called "Profess Cross" (265) as a breast cross, a Maltese Cross with the old Austrian Double Eagle between the arms and crowned by an Imperial Eagle (266). This latter cross varies in size and in the accessories above the crown, and is worn on a sash, necklet or chest riband, according to the office of the holder.

In 1916, the Grand Prior at that time instituted a *Cross of Merit* (267), which was extended in 1928 by the Grand Master in Rome to cover the whole *Maltese Order* (see Nos. 411–412).

LIECHTENSTEIN
268–269. The Order of Merit of the Principality of Liechtenstein *(Der fürstliche liechtensteinische Verdienstorden)* was instituted on 22nd July 1937 by Prince Franz I. The Order may be conferred on citizens of Liechtenstein and on foreigners who have acquired special merit, official as well as social, in relation to the Principality. The reigning Prince is the Grand Master of the Order.

The Order has five classes:
1. *Grand Star*, which wears the Badge of the Order (268) on a sash and the Star of the Order (269) in gold.
2. *Grand Cross*, which wears the Badge of the Order (268) on a sash and the Star of the Order (269).
3. *Commander with Star*, which

wears the Badge of the Order (268) on a necklet and the Star of the Order (269), with shorter pencils of rays in the cross angles of the Badge of the Order.

4. *Commander*, which wears the Badge of the Order (268) on a necklet.

5. *Knight*, which wears the Badge of the Order (268), in the same size as the Knight's Cross (229), on a chest riband.

The insignia of the four highest classes may, according to more detailed rules, be replaced by the Knight's Cross by adding to the riband of this, as an indication, the following miniature badges: for 1st Class, an 8-pointed gold star; for 2nd Class, an 8-pointed silver star; for 3rd Class, a 4-pointed silver star; and for 4th Class, a miniature Badge of the Order.

The *Badge of the Order* is a red-rimmed blue-enamelled so-called "cross pommé" in gold. The obverse medallion bears a Gothic "L" for "Liechtenstein" and the reverse medallion bears the monogram of the founder.

The *Star of the Order* is an 8-pointed faceted star, in gold for 1st Class, in silver for 2nd and 3rd Classes, and in 3rd Class with shorter pencils of rays in the angles of the cross of the Badge of the Order resting upon the Star.

The *Riband of the Order* consists of two equally wide stripes in red and blue, the colours of the Principality. As a chest riband, it is worn mounted in triangular fashion.

The *Medal of Merit*, which has two degrees, *gold* and *silver*, is attached to the Order. It is worn on the chest riband of the Order. The Badge of the Order is a Knight's Cross with unenamelled arms.

CZECHOSLOVAKIA

270–274. The Order of the White Lion *(Ceskoslovenský rád bílého Lva)* was instituted on 7th December 1922. Its present statutes date from 11th January 1961. The Order, which is reserved for foreigners, may be conferred on persons who have acquired outstanding merit in relation to the Czechoslovakian State or who have contributed to the promotion of co-operation and scientific relations with it. Political and public personalities and representatives of international organisations, inter alia within the fields of culture and the economy, are given preference. The Order is conferred on the nomination of the President, whose Chancellery administers the Order.

The Order has a *Civil* and a *Military* Division, each of three classes:

1. *1st Class*, which wears the Badge of the Order (270) on a sash or collar (271) and the Star of the Order (272).

2. *2nd Class*, which wears the Badge of the Order (273–274) on a necklet and the Star of the Order (272).

3. *3rd Class*, which wears the Badge of the Order (273–274) on a necklet.

The Collar of the Order, which may be conferred separately or in conjunction with 1st Class, is mainly reserved for Heads of State.

The insignia is the same for both Divisions, but the Badge of the Order for the *Civil* Division bears, in its mounting wreath, a set of crossed palm branches (274), and the Badge of the Order for the *Military* Division bears a set of crossed swords (273).

The *Badge of the Order* is a 5-armed red-enamelled gold star with double-forked arms and pendant on a wreath of lime leaves symbolizing the Czechoslovakian national tree, the lime. There are also lime leaves between the arms. The obverse bears the white Czech lion with the State coat of arms employed since 1960, and the reverse bears the monogram "CSSR" for "Ceskoslovenský socialistický republika" (The Czech Socialist Republic) with the legend "Pravda vitesi" (Truth is victorious).

The *Star of the Order* is a radiating 8-pointed silver star. The obverse medallion bears the white Czech lion on a red background with the legend "Pravda vitesi", and the reverse medallion bears the monogram "CSSR".

The *Collar of the Order*, which is gold, is composed of 10 medallions and 10 monograms, the former with the same motif as the obverse medallion of the

Star of the Order, the latter with the monogram "CSSR" entwined on a background of lime leaves. The lowest monogram, on which the Badge of the Order is pendant, is white-enamelled with green-enamelled lime leaves.

The *Riband of the Order* is red with white border stripes.

275–277. The Military Order of the White Lion *(Ceskoslovenský vojenský rád bílého Lva "Za vitezstvi")* was instituted on 9th February 1945. The Order is the highest Czech military decoration, and consequently ranks before the *Order of the White Lion* (270–274) if both are worn together. The Order may be conferred on Czechs and on foreigners as a reward for outstanding military services, including personal bravery in battle.

The Order has three degrees, the 1st and 3rd Degrees each being divided into two stages:

1. (i) *Star 1st Class*, which wears a Star of the Order (275).

(ii) *Star 2nd Class*, which wears a Star of the Order (275), the crossed swords of the centre medallion being in silver.

2. *Cross*, which wears a Cross of the Badge (276) on a chest riband.

3. (i) *Gold Medal*, which wears a medal (277) on a chest riband.

(ii) *Silver Medal*, which wears a medal (277) in silver on a chest riband.

The *Star of the Order* for the 1st Degree is a ray-shaped 8-pointed silver star. The centre medallion bears the Czech white lion with the State coat of arms employed before 1960 on a red background with the legend "Za Vitezstvi" (For Victory) on a blue background, and also, under the lion, a set of crossed swords, in gold for 1st stage and in silver for 2nd stage.

The *Cross of the Order* for the 2nd Degree is a red-enamelled Maltese Cross in gold with double-forked arms. The obverse medallion is identical with the centre medallion of the Star of the Order, and the reverse medallion bears the Czech State monogram employed before 1960, "CSSR" for "Ceskoslovenska republika" (The Republic of Czechoslovakia) with the legend "Pravda vitesi" (Truth is victorious).

The *Medal* for the 3rd Degree, which is in gold for the 1st stage and in silver for the 2nd stage, bears on the obverse the centre medallion of the Star of the Order, and on the reverse the reverse medallion of the Cross of the Order, both stamped on.

The *Riband of the Order* is red with white border stripes.

Ribands worn alone with uniform are provided with miniature reproductions of the insignia for the degrees and stages concerned.

278–280. The Military Order "For Liberty" *(Ceskoslovenský vojenský rád "Za svobodu")* was instituted by decree on 2nd April 1946 as a military decoration for Czechs and for foreigners who, during the Second World War, rendered military service abroad or in the Republic of Czechoslovakia, and in doing so fought for the liberation of the country. The Order ranks after the *Officer's Order of Jan Zizka of Trochnova* (281–283).

The Order has three degrees:

1. *Gold Star*, which wears a Star of the Order (278).

2. *Silver Medal*, which wears a Medal (279) on a chest riband.

3. *Bronze Medal*, which wears a Medal (280) on a chest riband.

The *Star of the Order* for the 1st Degree is a 5-pointed gold star resting on a silver wreath of lime leaves. The centre medallion bears in profile two soldiers' heads with steel helmets with the legend "Za svobudo Ceskoslovenska" (For the Freedom of Czechoslovakia).

The *Medal* for the 2nd and 3rd Degrees, in silver and bronze respectively, bears on the obverse the same motif and legend as the centre medallion of the Star of the Order, and on the reverse a set of crossed swords with a lime branch between the blades. Beneath the hilts of the swords is the date "1939-1945", and on a scroll in the top curvature of the medal is the inscription "Pravda vitesi" (Truth is victorious).

The *Riband of the Order* is blue with red-white border stripes, the national colours of Czechoslovakia.

Ribands worn alone with uniform for the 1st and 2nd Degrees are provided with miniature reproductions of the insignia for the degrees concerned.

281–283. The Officers' Order of Jan Zizka of Trochnova *(Ceskoslovenský velitelský rád Jana Zizky z Trocnova)* was instituted on 14th June 1946 as a military decoration for Czech and foreign officers. The Order is named after Jan Zizka, the leader of the Hussites in the battles against the German armies in 1420–1422. It ranks before the *Military Order "For Liberty"* (278–280) and has been conferred, inter alia, for leadership in the battles for liberation during the Second World War.

The Order has three degrees:

1. *Gold Star*, which wears a Star of the Order (281).
2. *Silver Star*, which wears a Star of the Order (282).
3. *Medal*, which wears a Medal (283) on a chest riband.

The *Star of the Order* for the 1st and 2nd degrees is an 8-pointed gold or silver star, according to degree. The Star and the *Medal* for the 3rd Degree, which is silver, bear on the obverse a portrait in profile of Jan Zizka, with the legend "Neprátel se nelekejte na mnozstvi" (Do not fear the enemy, whatever his number). The Medal also bears on the reverse the inscription "Jana Zizky z Trocnova" (Jan Zizka of Trochnova) and a set of crossed clubs with the legend "Ceskoslovenský velitelský rád" (The Officers' Order of Czechoslovakia).

The *Riband of the Order* is black with a narrow red centre stripe, the colours of the Hussites.

Ribands worn alone with uniform are provided, for 1st and 2nd Degrees, with a set of crossed miniature clubs, in gold and silver respectively.

The War Cross, 1939

The War Cross 1939 *(Ceskoslovenský válecny kriz z roku 1939)* was instituted on 20th December 1940 as a war decoration for the Second World War. It was conferrable for feats of valour at the risk of life on Czechs at home and on personnel of the Czech armies, including foreigners, who participated in the War on the side of the Allies outside the frontiers of the country.

The Cross is a Greek Cross in bronze with rhomb-shaped ends and with crossed swords in the angles of the Cross. The centre shield of the obverse bears the Czech lion. The centre shield of the reverse bears the coat of arms of Bohemia and the date "1939". The arms of the Cross of the reverse bear the coats of arms of Slovakia, Moravia, Silesia and Ruthenia. The Cross is pendant on a vertically mounted red-white striped chest riband with a blue centre stripe in each of the white stripes, the national colours of Czechoslovakia.

HUNGARY

284. The Order of Merit of the People's Republic of Hungary *(Magyar Népköztársaság Erdemrendje)*, similarly to the

Hungarian Orders following, received its present form under Law No. 5 of 1953 and Legal Decree No. 35 of 1963. They may all be conferred as a reward for meritorious services in the promotion of Socialism in the service of the Peoples' Republic and for meritorious services in the fight for peace and for co-operation between the nations. The Order of Merit may be conferred on civilians and on the military. The Order is conferred on nomination by the President of the Ministerial Council for the People's Republic, after proposal by the Council.

The Order has one class, which wears the Badge of the Order (284) on a chest riband.

The *Badge of the Order* is the 5-pointed red star of Communism in gold, with the State coat of arms in the centre and pencils of rays between the points. The reverse bears the registration number of the Badge of the Order.

The *Riband of the Order* is white with border stripes in the red-white-green colours of Communism and the People's Republic respectively. It is worn on a chest riband mounted in a triangular fashion.

285. The Order of the Flag of the Hungarian People's Republic *(Magyar Népköztársaság Zászlórendje)* is reserved for civilians. See also the *Order of Merit of the People's Republic of Hungary* (284).

The Order has three degrees, 1st – 3rd Degrees, which wear a Star of the Order (285), varying in size according to degree, on the left side of the breast.

The *Star of the Order* is an 8-pointed gold star with short points between. In the centre, the Star bears the Hungarian flag surrounded by an open laurel wreath with 10 rubies; in special cases with 10 diamonds.

286. The Order of Merit of the Red Flag of Work *(Munka Vörös zászló Erdemrendje)* is reserved for civilians. See also the *Order of Merit of the People's Republic of Hungary* (284).

The Order has one degree, which

wears the Badge of the Order (286) on a chest riband.

The *Badge of the Order*, which is gold, consists of a red banner resting on a laurel wreath, with the State coat of arms at the base of the wreath.

The *Riband of the Order* is red with a white-edged, red-white-green centre stripe. It is worn on a chest riband mounted in a triangular fashion.

287. The Order of the Red Flag *(Vörös Zászló Erdemrend)* is reserved for the military. See also the *Order of Merit of the People's Republic of Hungary* (284).

The Order has one degree, which wears the Badge of the Order (287) on a chest riband.

The *Badge of the Order* is identical with the Badge of the Order for the *Order of Merit of the Red Flag of Work* (286), but the banner is bordered with a serrated edge in the red-white-green colours of the People's Republic.

The *Riband of the Order* is red with a white-edged, red-white-green centre stripe. It is worn as a chest riband mounted in triangular fashion.

288. The Order of Merit of Work *(Munka Erdemrend)* is reserved for civilians. See also the *Order of Merit of the People's Republic of Hungary* (284).

The Order has one degree, which wears the Badge of the Order (288) on a chest riband.

The *Badge of the Order* is an oval medallion in gold with a 5-pointed red star on a white background in the centre, garlanded with golden wheat-ears. At the base, the medallion bears a hammer and a torch, crossed together with a ribbon in the red-white-green colours of the People's Republic. The reverse is plain.

The *Riband of the Order* is plain dark red. It is worn as a chest riband mounted in triangular fashion.

Hungary's Order of Merit for Work *(Magyar Munka Erdemrend)* is reserved for civilians. See also the *Order of Merit of the People's Republic of*

Hungary (284).

The Order has three degrees, *gold, silver* and *bronze*, which wear the Badge of the Order on a chest riband.

The *Badge of the Order* is identical with the Badge of the Order for the *Order of Merit for Work* (288), but the Star in the centre is on a blue background and the wheat-ears are in gold, silver or bronze according to degree.

The *Riband of the Order* is plain dark red. It is worn as a chest riband mounted in triangular fashion.

Ribands worn alone with uniform are provided with miniature reproductions of the insignia of the respective grades.

289. The Order of the Red Star *(Vörös Csillag Erdemrend)* is reserved for the military. See also the *Order of Merit of the People's Republic of Hungary* (284).

The Order has one degree, which wears the Badge of the Order (289) on a chest riband.

The *Badge of the Order* is the 5-pointed red star of Communism in gold resting on a laurel wreath. In the centre, the star bears the State coat of arms, and at the base of the garland a riband in the red-white-green colours of the People's Republic. The reverse is plain.

The *Riband of the Order* is plain dark red. It is worn as a chest riband, mounted in triangular fashion.

290. The Order of Merit for Special Services *("Kivalo Szolgalatert" Erdemerem)* is reserved for the military; see also the *Order of Merit of the People's Republic of Hungary* (284).

The Order has one degree, which wears the Badge of the Order (290) on a chest riband.

The *Badge of the Order* is the 5-pointed red star of Communism in gold with silver pencils of rays between the points and garlanded by a laurel wreath. In the centre, the star bears the State coat of arms, and the wreath bears at the base a riband in the red-white-green colours of the People's Republic, with a

set of crossed rifles above.

The *Riband of the Order* is red with a white-edged double red-white-green centre stripe. It is worn as a chest riband mounted in triangular fashion.

291. The Official Order of Merit *(Szolgalati Erdemerem)* was reserved for the military. Conferment was discontinued as from 1st January 1964.

The Order has one degree, which wears the Badge of the Order (291) on a chest riband.

The *Badge of the Order* is a blue-enamelled medallion in gold. It has in the centre the State coat of arms above a set of crossed sub-machine guns garlanded by a laurel wreath in silver. At the base, the wreath bears a riband in the red-white-green colours of the People's Republic.

The *Riband of the Order* is red with three white-edged red-white-green stripes. It is worn as a chest riband, mounted in triangular fashion.

RUMANIA

292–293. The Order of the Star of the People's Republic of Rumania *(Ordinul "Steaua Republicii Populare Romine")* was instituted on 12th January 1948. The Order may be conferred on civilians and on the military, Rumanians and foreigners, as a reward for political, cultural, social or scientific services for the promotion of the interests of the people, fulfilment of the freedom of democracy and the construction of the Rumanian People's Republic. Conferment is effected on nomination by the State Council of the People's Republic.

The Order has five classes:

1. *1st Class*, which wears the Badge of the Order (292) as a breast star.

2. *2nd Class*, which wears the Badge of the Order (292) in silver as a breast star.

3. *3rd Class*, which wears the Badge of the Order (293) on a chest riband.

4. *4th Class*, which wears the Badge of the Order (293) in silver on a chest riband.

5. *5th Class*, which wears the Badge of the Order (293) in bronze on a chest riband.

The *Badge of the Order*, which varies in size according to the manner in which it is worn, is a 5-pointed, blue-rimmed red star, in gold for 1st and 3rd Classes, in silver for 2nd and 4th Classes, and in bronze for 5th Class, with plain pencils of rays between the points. On the Badge of the Order for 1st and 2nd Classes, the obverse medallion bears the inscription "30 Decembrie 1947" (30th December 1947), the date of King Michael I's abdication, within a garland of laurel leaves. On the Badge of the Order for 3rd to 5th Class, the obverse medallion bears the monogram "RPR" for "Republica Populare Romine" (The Rumanian People's Republic). The reverse medallion on the Badge of the Order for 3rd and 5th Classes bears the inscription "30 Decembrie 1947".

The *Riband of the Order* is plain red; it is worn as a chest riband, mounted in crossed fashion.

Ribands worn alone with uniform are provided with miniature reproductions of the insignia, in some cases combined with the stripes of the respective classes.

294–295. The Order of "23rd August" (*Ordinul "23 August"*) was instituted on 3rd June 1959 as a reward for services in connection with the revolution of 23rd August 1944, but at present it may be conferred on civilians and on the military, Rumanians and foreigners, for services involving political or scientific activities, military instruction, organization and leadership, as well as for acts of bravery and devotion in battle. Conferment is effected on nomination by the State Council of the People's Republic.

The Order has five classes:

1. *1st Class*, which wears the Badge of the Order (294) as a breast star.
2. *2nd Class*, which wears the Badge of the Order (294), without "stones" in the radial rays, as a breast star.
3. *3rd Class*, which wears the Badge

of the Order (295) on a chest riband.
4. *4th Class*, which wears the Badge of the Order (295) in silver on a chest riband.
5. *5th Class*, which wears the Badge of the Order (295) in bronze on a chest riband.

The *Badge of the Order*, which varies in size according to the manner in which it is worn, is a 10-pointed star, in gold for 1st to 3rd Classes, silver for 4th Class, and bronze for 5th Class, with radial rays. For 1st Class it is studded with 60 "stones". The centre medallion bears the State coat of arms within a laurel wreath, surrounded by a garland of 25 "stones" for 1st and 2nd Classes.

The *Riband of the Order* is red with narrow blue-yellow border stripes, the colours of the People's Republic. It is worn as a chest riband, mounted in crossed fashion.

The riband worn alone with uniform is provided with miniature reproductions of the insignia, or with extra stripes for the respective classes.

296–297. The Order of "The Defence of the Fatherland" (*Ordinul "Apararea Patriei"*) was instituted on 23rd July 1949. The Order may be conferred on the military and on civilians, Rumanians and foreigners, as a reward for outstanding services in the field of political or scientific activities, as well as for proposals for and planning of military operations for the promotion of the defence of the Fatherland and the freedom of the workers' democracy. Conferment is effected on the nomination of the State Council of the People's Republic.

The Order has three classes:

1. *1st Class*, which wears a Badge of the Order (296) in gold with crossed swords in silver, as a breast star.
2. *2nd Class*, which wears a Badge of the Order (296) as a breast star.
3. *3rd Class*, which wears the Badge of the Order (297) on a chest riband.

The *Badge of the Order*, which varies in size according to the manner in which it is worn, is a 5-pointed red star in gold with crossed silver swords for 1st and 3rd Classes, and in silver with crossed swords in gold for 2nd Class, with pencils of rays between the points and the State coat of arms in silver in the centre.

The *Riband of the Order* is red with narrow border stripes in the red-yellow-blue colours of the People's Republic. It is worn as a chest riband, mounted in crossed fashion.

Ribands worn alone with uniform are provided with extra stripes, according to class.

298–299. The Order of Work *(Ordinul Muncii)* was instituted on 29th April 1948. The Order may be conferred on persons, Rumanians and foreigners, who in their work have rendered special service to the Rumanian People's Republic or to the cultural and material freedom and well being of the people. The Order is conferred on nomination by the State Council of the People's Republic.

The Order has three classes:

1. *1st Class*, which wears a Badge of the Order (298) as a breast star.

2. *2nd Class*, which wears a Badge of the Order (299) as a breast star.

3. *3rd Class*, which wears a badge of the Order (299) (all bronze) as a breast star.

The *Badge of the Order* is an oval medallion, in gold for 1st Class with ornamentation in silver, and in silver for 2nd Class with ornamentation in gold, and all bronze for 3rd Class, which bears the hammer and sickle symbols above a 5-pointed red star garlanded with wheat-ears and laurel branches on a background of a sun surrounded by pencils of rays. The medallion bears a red scroll at the base with the monogram "RPR" for "Republica Populare Romine" (The Rumanian People's Republic).

300. The Medal of Work *(Medalia Muncii)* was instituted on 26th April 1949. The Medal may be conferred on persons who have distinguished themselves in cultural, artistic or scientific activities. The Order is conferred on nomination by the State Council of the People's Republic.

The Medal has one class, silver, and is worn on a red chest riband with yellow selvage mounted in crossed fashion. The obverse bears the same motif in relief as the *Order of Work* (298–299) and the reverse bears the inscription "Pentru merite deosebite in munca" (For special services in work).

BULGARIA

301. The Hero of Socialistic Work *(Geroj na sotsialistitjeskija trud)* is a title instituted on 15th June 1948 which can be conferred for outstanding and lasting services, such as initiative or efficiency, of the greatest importance for the whole country in conjunction with unique devotion to the Bulgarian People's Republic. As an outward token of the title conferred, the holder receives a special badge of distinction together with the highest Order of the Bulgarian People's Republic, the Order of "*Georgi Dimitrov*" (302).

The *Badge of Distinction* (301) is a 5-pointed golden star with the hammer and sickle symbols in the centre. The star is worn on a plain red chest riband mounted between two yokes.

302. The Order of "Georgi Dimitrov" *(Orden "Georgi Dimitrov")* was instituted on 17th June 1950. The Order is named after the Bulgarian Communist leader Georgi Dimitrov, Prime Minister of Bulgaria from 1946 to 1949. The Order may be conferred on Bulgarians and on foreigners for outstanding services in the defence of the freedom and independence of the Bulgarian People's Republic, as well as for unique contributions to the construction of Socialism. It is the highest Order of the Bulgarian People's Republic.

The Order has one degree, which wears the Badge of the Order (302) on a chest riband.

The *Badge of the Order* is a gold medallion which bears a portrait of Georgi Dimitrov in the centre garlanded by wheat-ears. At the top, the medallion bears the 5-pointed star, and at the base a red scroll with the name "Georgi Dimitrov" in Cyrillic script. Beneath these are the hammer and sickle symbols.

The *Riband of the Order* is red with selvedges of a lighter shade. It is worn as a chest riband mounted in crossed fashion.

303. The Order of "The People's Republic of Bulgaria". *(Orden "Narodne Repoublika Balgaria")* was instituted on 19th June 1947. The Order may be conferred on Bulgarians and on foreigners for services in connection with the construction of the defence, freedom and independence of the Bulgarian People's Republic. In war-time it may also be conferred on officers and leaders of the People's Army for outstanding leadership of troops and for the planning of military operations.

The Order has three degrees.

1. *1st Degree*, which wears the Badge of the Order (303) on a chest riband.

2. *2nd Degree*, which wears the Badge of the Order (303) in silver with the centre medallion in gold on a chest riband.

3. *3rd Degree*, which wears the same Badge of the Order as for 2nd Degree, but smaller, on a chest riband.

The *Badge of the Order*, which varies in size according to degree, is a star with uncentred rays, in gold with centre medallion in silver for 1st Degree, in silver with centre medallion in gold for 2nd and 3rd Degrees. The State coat of arms is in the centre.

The *Riband of the Order* is white with red-green border stripes, the colours of the People's Republic. It is worn as a chest riband, mounted in crossed fashion.

304. The Order of "9th September 1944" *(Orden "9. Septembri 1944 g.")* was instituted on 14th September 1945

for services in connection with the revolt of the Army on 9th September 1944 and the formation of the Bulgarian People's Republic. In war-time, the Order may be conferred on Officers and leaders of the People's Army who have distinguished themselves in the fight for the Fatherland by displaying courage, bravery and efficient leadership in military operations. In peace-time it may be conferred on the military and on civilians, Bulgarians and foreigners, for faultless execution of tasks set by the Government for the consolidation of the People's Republic.

The Order has a *military* and a *civil* division, each of three degrees.

1. *1st Degree*, which wears the Badge of the Order (304), but larger and with the inscription on the centre medallion on the reverse, on a chest riband.

2. *2nd Degree*, which wears the Badge of the Order (304) on a chest riband.

3. *3rd Degree*, which wears the same Badge of the Order as for 2nd Degree, but red-enamelled, on a chest riband.

The insignia is the same for both divisions, but the *Military* Badge of the Order is provided with crossed swords.

The *Badge of the Order*, which varies in size according to degree, is a 5-pointed gold star, white-enamelled for 1st and 2nd Degrees and red-enamelled for 3rd Degree. The centre medallion bears a portrait of the Bulgarian champion of liberty, the monk Vasil Levski, the leader of the unsuccessful revolt against the Germans in 1872, surrounded by a stylized garland of leaves on a green background. For 2nd and 3rd Degrees, the medallion bears the inscription "9th September 1944". This is on the reverse for the Badge of the Order for 1st Degree.

The *Riband of the Order* is red, with green-white border stripes for 1st degree, with white border stripes and a white centre stripe for 2nd degree, and with green border stripes for 3rd Degree. It is worn as a chest riband, mounted in crossed fashion.

305. The Order "For the Liberation of the People 1941–1944" *(Orden "Narodna svoboda 1941–1944 g.")* was instituted on 14th September 1945 and was confirmed by the statutes of 30th December 1955. The Order may be conferred on Bulgarians who, as partisans or in other ways, contributed or displayed devotion during the fight for liberation before 9th September 1944, and also on foreigners who, during the same period, have merited the gratitude of the Bulgarian people in the fight against Fascism.

The Order has two degrees:

1. *1st Degree*, which wears the Badge of the Order (305) on a chest riband.

2. *2nd Degree*, which wears the same Badge of the Order as for 1st Degree, but in silver and red-enamelled, on a chest riband.

The *Badge of the Order*, which is worn on the right side of the breast, is a 5-pointed star, in gold and white-enamelled for 1st Degree and in silver and red-enamelled for 2nd Degree, with pencils of rays between the points. The centre medallion bears a portrait of the Bulgarian champion of liberty, the poet Cristo Botev, the leader of the unsuccessful revolt against the Germans in 1867, with the legend "Za narodna svoboda 1941–1944" (For the Liberation of the People 1941–1944) in Cyrillic script on a green background.

The *Riband of the Order* is red with silver-white border stripes and for 2nd Degree also with a light blue selvedge. It is worn as a chest riband mounted in crossed fashion.

306. The Order of "The Red Flag of Work" *(Orden "Tjervéno znamé na truda")* was instituted on 13th December 1950. The Order may be conferred on individuals and collective groups, working physically and intellectually in production, for outstanding success in the cultural, political, social or economic life of the People's Republic. It may also be conferred for civic achievement and other services.

The Order has one degree, which wears the Badge of the Order (306) on a chest riband.

The *Badge of the Order* is a gold medallion, garlanded by wheat-ears, bearing the hammer and sickle symbols in the centre on a blue background surrounded by a white cog wheel, with the inscription "Za sotsialistitjeski trud" (For socialistic work) in Cyrillic script and crowned by a red flag with the monogram "NRB" for "Narodna Repoublika Balgaria" (The People's Republic of Bulgaria), also in Cyrillic script. The medallion bears a 5-pointed red star at the top.

The *Riband of the Order* is red with a white centre stripe. It is worn as a chest riband, mounted in crossed fashion.

The Order of "Kyrillos and Methodios" *(Orden "Kiril i Metodij")* is named after the brothers Kyrillos and Methodios, the apostles of the Slav people, the first

The Order of "Kyrillos and Methodios": Badge of the Order

of whom created the Slavonic (Cyrillic) script and is the father of Slavonic literature, and the second of whom was the Archbishop who made the Slavonic language the ecclesiastical language of the Slavonic countries and who, together with his brother, translated the Bible into Slavonic. The Order may be conferred on statesmen, scientists, authors and artists, Bulgarians and foreigners, for long, untiring and devoted cultural services for the benefit of the Bulgarian people.

The Order has three degrees, *1st–3rd Degrees,* which wear a medallion, varying in design according to degree, on a chest riband.

The *Badge of the Order* is a medallion, in gold for 1st and 2nd Degree with red and blue enamel background respectively, and in silver on a blue background for 3rd Degree. The medallion bears portraits of Kyrillos and Methodios in relief, the former characterised by a scroll with the first four letters of the Cyrillic alphabet "ABVG" and the latter by the book (the Bible) he holds in his arms. At the top the medallion bears a 5-pointed star.

The *Riband of the Order* is plain light blue. It is worn as a chest riband in crossed fashion.

POLAND
The Order of "The Re-builder of the Polish People's Republic" *(Order Budowniczych Polski Ludowej)* was instituted in 1945. The Order may be conferred on Poles and on foreigners who, during the re-building of the Polish nation, performed special services, particularly in public administration, culture and art, national economy, public health, science and national defence. It may also be conferred on institutions, organisations and the like. The Order is the highest Polish decoration and has been conferred on only about 50 persons.

The Order has one class, which wears the Badge of the Order on a chest riband.

The Order of "The Re-builder of the Polish People's Republic": Badge of the Order

The *Badge of the Order* is a gold medallion with eight red and white-enamelled scallops divided by small pencils of rays. The obverse medallion has the motif of a soldier planting the red flag, as a symbol of victory, on a blue background. The reverse medallion bears the monogram "PRL" for "Polska Rzeczpospolita Ludowa" (The Polish People's Republic).

The *Riband of the Order* is red with narrow blue border stripes and a wide white centre stripe.

307–308. The Order of "Polonia Restituta" *(Order Odrodzenia Polski)* was instituted on 4th February 1921 and renewed on 22nd December 1944 by the National Polish Liberation Committee. The Order may be conferred for services in public activities, culture and art, national economy, physical education, public health and the national defence. It may also be conferred on foreigners.

The Order "Virtuti Militari": Badge of the Order, Grand Cross, here shown on a necklet

The Order has five classes:

1. *Grand Cross*, which wears the Badge of the Order (308), in Grand Cross size (231), on a sash and the Star of the Order (307).

2. *Commander with Star*, which wears the Badge of the Order (308) in Commander size (235), on a necklet and the Star of the Order (307).

3. *Commander*, which wears the Badge of the Order (308), in Commander size (235), on a necklet.

4. *Officer*, which wears the Badge of the Order (308) on a chest riband with rosette.

5. *Knight*, which wears the Badge of the Order (308), but smaller, on a chest riband without rosette.

The *Badge of the Order*, which varies in five sizes according to class, is a white-enamelled Maltese Cross in gold. The obverse medallion bears the white Polish eagle on a red background with the legend "Polonia Restituta" (The

Rebuilt Poland) on a blue background. The reverse medallion bears the date "1944", and on Badges of the Order dating from 1921, the date "1918".

The *Star of the Order* is an 8-pointed silver star with plain rays. The centre medallion bears the monogram "PRL" for "Polska Rzeczpospolita Ludowa" (The Polish People's Republic) on a white background with the legend "Polonia Restituta" on a blue background.

The *Riband of the Order* is red with white border stripes, the national colours of Poland.

309–310. The Order of "Virtuti Militari" *(Order Virtuti Military)* was instituted in 1792 by King Stanislaus II. It was renewed in 1919, and again in 1944 by the National Polish Liberation Committee. The Order is for services in war, and may be conferred on Poles and on foreigners as a reward for outstandingly heroic achievement and services in battle.

The Order has five classes:

1. *Grand Cross*, which wears the Badge of the Order on a sash and the Star of the Order (309).

2. *Commander*, which wears the same Badge of the Order as for 1st Class, but smaller, on a necklet.

3. *Knight*, which wears the same Badge of the Order as for 2nd Class, but smaller and without the mounting, on a chest riband.

4. *Gold Cross*, which wears the Badge of the Order (310) on a chest riband.

5. *Silver Cross*, which wears the Badge of the Order (310) in silver, with obverse and reverse medallion in gold, on a chest riband.

The *Badge of the Order*, which varies in size accordng to class, is a black-enamelled Maltese Cross in gold. For 4th and 5th Classes, in gold and silver respectively, it is un-enamelled with a black contour and inscription, and concave arms. Within a laurel garland, the obverse medallion bears the white Polish eagle, and the reverse medallion bears the inscription "Honor i Ojczyzna" (Honour and Country), the motto of the Order, and the year "1792". The Badge of the Order for 1st and 2nd Classes has a mounting of a laurel garlanded medallion with the monogram "RP" for "Rzeczpospolita Polska" (The Polish Republic), the designation of the State after the 1st World War. All Badges of the Order bear on the obverse side the title of the Order in the arms of the cross.

The *Star of the Order* is an 8-pointed silver star with plain rays, and with a reproduction of the Badge of the Order in the centre, but with the inscription "Honor i Ojczyzna" as a legend within the laurel garland of the obverse medallion.

The *Riband of the Order* is azure with wide black border stripes.

The *Medal for Merit on the Field of Honour* is attached to the Order. It is of two types, instituted in 1943 and 1944 respectively. The first type was conferred for participation in the battles around Lenino on 12th – 13th October 1943, and the second may be conferred for war services generally.

The Medal has three degrees, *gold, silver* and *bronze*, and is worn on a black chest riband with wide azure border stripes.

The 1943 medal bears on the obverse

The Medal for Merit on the Field of Honour: 1943 Medal and 1944 Medal

medallion a Badge of the Order flanked by the flags of Poland and the Soviet Union. On the reverse it bears the inscription "Zazluzonym na Polu Chwaly" (For Merit on the Field of Honour) and the date "12th – 13th October 1943 Lenino".

The 1944 medal is without flanking flags on the obverse. It bears on the reverse, in addition to the inscription "Zasluzonym na Polu Chwaly", only the date "1944".

The Order of the "Grünwald Cross" *(Order Krzyza Grunwaldu)* was instituted in 1944 as a reward for Poles and foreigners who had acquired outstanding merit during the 2nd World War or had rendered special services in the training of the Armed Forces of the Polish people. The Order takes its name from the historic battle at Grünwald in 1410 between a Polish-Lithuanian army and the Teutonic Order.

The Order has three classes, *Classes 1–3*, which wear the Badge of the Order, varying in size and design according to class, on a chest riband.

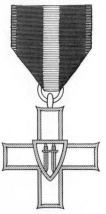

The Order of the Grünwald Cross: Badge of the Order, 2nd Class

The *Badge of the Order* is a Greek Cross with concave ends, for 1st Class completely in gold, for 2nd Class in silver with ornamentation and edges of the Cross and centre shield in gold, for 3rd Class completely in silver. The obverse shield bears two swords, one blunt and one pointed. The reverse shield bears the dates "1410" above and "1944" below the monogram "KG" for "Krzyza Grunwaldu" (The Grünwald Cross). The two swords symbolize the episode before the battle at Grünwald when the German knights sent the Polish-Lithuanian army a blunt sword to make it realise that it was ill-armed and should lay down its arms. They received in return a pointed sword together with the blunt sword as a token that the Poles and Lithuanians were ready for battle.

The *Riband of the Order* is red with green selvedges and a white centre stripe.

311. The Cross of Merit *(Krzyz Zaslugi)* was instituted in 1923 and renewed by the National Polish Liberation Committee in 1944. The decoration may be conferred on deserving persons, Poles and foreigners, for services of a professional or public character.

The decoration has three degrees:

1. *The Cross of Merit in Gold*, which wears the Badge of the Order (311) in gold on a chest riband.

2. *The Cross of Merit in Silver*, which wears the Badge of the Order (311) on a chest riband.

3. *The Cross of Merit in Bronze*, which wears the Badge of the Order (311) in bronze and unenamelled on a chest riband.

The *Badge of the Order* is a red-enamelled Maltese Cross, in gold for 1st Degree, in silver for 2nd Degree, in bronze and unenamelled for 3rd Degree, with plain rays between the concave arms. The centre medallion bears the monogram "PRL", for "Rzeczpospolita Polska" (The Polish Republic), the designation of the State after the 1st World War. The reverse is plain.

The *Riband of the Order* is reddish brown with narrow azure border stripes.

Until 1944, the decoration could also be conferred "with swords".

312. The War Cross of 1944 *(Krzyz Walecznych 1944)* was instituted in 1944 by the National Polish Liberation Committee as a renewal of the *War Cross of 1920* as a reward for acts of valour and courage in battle during the Second World War.

The Cross is a Mantua Cross in bronze. The obverse bears the inscription "Na Polu Chwaly 1944" (On the Field of Honour, 1944) and the Polish eagle in a shield in the centre. The reverse bears a laurel-garlanded upright sword and the inscription "Walecznym" (For the Brave). The Cross is worn on a reddish brown chest riband with wide white border stripes.

313. The Partisan Cross *(Krzyz Partyzancki)* was instituted in 1945 as a reward for meritorious services in the partisan war during the German occupation in the Second World War.

The Cross is a Greek Cross in gilded bronze. The obverse bears the inscription "Za Polske Wolnosc i Lud" (For Polish Freedom and for the People) and in the centre the Polish eagle. The reverse bears the dates "1939" above and "1945" below the inscription "Partyzantom" (For the Partisans). The Cross is worn on a green chest riband with black border stripes.

THE SOVIET UNION
314. The Medal of "The Golden Star" *(Medalj "Zolotaja Zvezda")* was instituted on 1st August 1939 by the Presidium of the Chief Soviet of the Soviet Union as a decoration for civilians and for the military on whom the title "Hero of the Soviet Union" is bestowed. The holder simultaneously receives the highest Order of the Soviet Union, *The Order of Lenin* (316), and a diploma issued by the Presidium. Further, as a token of distinction, a bronze plate bearing his name is hung in the Kremlin,

and his bust is set up in his native area. The honorary title "Hero of the Soviet Union" was instituted on 29th July 1936 as an award of the highest degree to be conferred on Soviet citizens for personal or collective meritorious services to the State in connection with the execution of acts of valour. It may also be conferred on foreign citizens for meritorious acts or for meritorious services in the strengthening of co-operation and friendship between the Soviet Union and the peoples of other nations. If the title is conferred a second or third time an additional decoration is awarded, together with a Badge of the Order and a diploma.

The Medal has one class, which wears a Decoration (314) on the left side of the breast above other decorations.

The Decoration is a 5-pointed gold star. The obverse is faceted and without ornamentation, and the reverse is plain and bears the inscription "Geroj SSSR" (Hero of the Soviet Union). The star is worn on a plain red chest riband mounted between two yokes. The riband cannot be worn alone.

315. The Gold Medal of the "Hammer and Sickle" *(Zolotaja Medalj "Serp i Molot")* was instituted on 22nd May 1940 by the Presidium of the Chief Soviet of the Soviet Union as a decoration for civilians, on whom the honorary title "Hero of Socialist Work" is bestowed. The holder simultaneously receives the highest order of the Soviet Union, *The Order of Lenin* (316), together with a diploma issued by the Presidium and, as a token of distinction, his bust may be erected in his native area. The honorary title of "Hero of Socialist Work" was instituted on 27th December 1938 as a decoration of the highest degree, which may be conferred on Soviet citizens who, by specially outstanding and creative achievement in the field of cultural and economic reconstruction, have rendered to the State exceptional services, and have contributed to progress and to the greatness and glory of the Soviet Union. It may also be conferred on Soviet citizens for exceptionally meritorious achievement in State or other public activities. It may further be conferred on foreign citizens for meritorious acts or meritorious services towards the strengthening of co-operation and friendship between the Soviet Union and the peoples of other nations. If the title is conferred a second or third time, an additional decoration is awarded, together with a Badge of the Order and a diploma.

The Medal has one class, which wears a Badge of the Decoration (315) on the left side of the breast above other decorations.

The Badge of the Decoration is a 5-pointed gold star. The obverse is faceted and bears the hammer and sickle symbols in relief in the centre. The reverse is plain and bears the inscription "Geroj Sotsialistitjeskoto Truda" (Hero of Socialist Work). The Star is worn on a plain red chest riband, mounted between two yokes. The riband cannot be worn alone.

316. The Order of Lenin (*Orden Lenina*) was instituted on 6th April 1930 by the Central Executive Committee of the Soviet Union, whose Presidium affirmed the regulations of the Order on 5th May 1930. The Order is the highest civilian Order of the Soviet Union, and may be conferred on individual Soviet citizens, workers' collectives, institutions, organisations and undertakings for socialist reconstruction, for outstanding achievements in the field of research, art, technology and economics, and for the solution of special tasks vital to the State. It may also be conferred on persons who have been awarded the honorary titles of "Hero of the Soviet Union" and "Hero of Socialist Work". It may further be conferred on foreign citizens for meritorious acts and meritorious services in strengthening co-operation and friendship between the Soviet Union and the peoples of other nations.

The Order has one class, which wears the Badge of the Order on a chest riband.

The *Badge of the Order* is a gold medallion, bearing a portrait of Lenin in the centre, crowned by the red flag bearing Lenin's name in Cyrillic script, and garlanded with wheat-ears. On the right side, the medallion bears the 5-pointed red star, and at the base the hammer and sickle symbols.

The *Riband of the Order* is red with two yellow border stripes. It is worn as a chest riband, mounted in a crossed fashion.

317. The Order of Victory (*Orden "Probeda"*) was instituted on 8th November 1943 by the Presidium of the Chief Soviet of the Soviet Union as the highest military Order of the Soviet Union. The Order may be conferred on officers in the highest ranks of command in the Soviet Army and on Commanders-in-Chief of Allied Nations for the successful execution of operations in battle on one or more fronts contributing to a decisive change in the situation to the advantage of the Soviet Army. Conferment may be repeated. This has occurred three times.

The Order has one class, which wears the Badge of the Order (317) as a breast star.

The *Badge of the Order* is a 5-pointed star in platinum with faceted rubies in the points. Its borders and intermediate pencils of rays are studded with 120–150 diamonds to a total weight of about 16 carats. The motif in relief on the centre medallion is part of the wall of the Kremlin with the Lenin mausoleum in front of the Spaskija Tower, which bears the 5-pointed red star beneath the monogram "SSSR" for "Sojuz Sovjetskih Sotsialistitjeskih Respublik" (The Union of Soviet-Socialist Republics) in Cyrillic script. The motif is framed by an oak wreath bearing a red scroll at the base with the inscription "Pobeda" (Victory).

For wear with uniform, a red *Riband of the Order* was introduced on 18th August 1944. The riband is flanked by green, dark blue, red, light blue, and yellow-black-yellow stripes, the riband colours of the Soviet military Orders.

The insignia of the Order must be

returned on the death of the holder.

The Order has been conferred fourteen times on Soviet Marshals, of whom three have received it twice. It has also been conferred on the former President of the U.S.A., General Dwight D. Eisenhower, Field Marshal Lord Montgomery, Marshal Tito and ex-King Michael of Rumania.

318. The Order of the Red Flag (*Orden "Krasnoe Znamja"*) was instituted on 16th September 1918 and renewed on 1st August 1924 by the Central Executive Committee of the Soviet Union, whose Presidium affirmed the statutes of the Order on 11th January 1932. The Order may be conferred on officers and men of the Soviet Army and on civilians for fearlessness, devotion and bravery displayed in battle, and on military units for having contributed decisively to the successful outcome of a battle or operation of war for the Soviet Union under unfavourable conditions. It may also be conferred on foreigners.

The Order has one class, which wears the Badge of the Order (318) on a chest riband.

The *Badge of the Order* is a gold medallion garlanded by a laurel wreath which, on a white background, bears a red flag and a torch crossed in the centre, as well as a hammer, a plough and a 5-pointed red star. It also bears, within a smaller laurel wreath, the hammer and sickle symbols. The flag bears the inscription "Proletari i Vsekh Stran Soendinjajtej" (Workers of the world, unite), and the scroll at the bottom bears the monogram "SSSR" for "Sojuz Sovjetskih Sotsialistitjeskih Respublik" (The Union of the Soviet Socialist Republics) in Cyrillic script. The reverse bears the registration number in the Order.

The *Riband of the Order* is red with white selvedges and a wide white centre stripe. It is worn as a chest riband, mounted in a crossed fashion.

319. The Order of the Red Flag of Work (*Orden "Trudovoe Krasnoe Znamja"*) was instituted on 7th September 1928 by the Central Executive Committee of the Soviet Union and the Council of the People's Commissars. The Order may be conferred on individuals, workers' collectives, institutions, organisations and undertakings for specially meritorious services for the benefit of the Soviet Union in the fields of research, production, public administration and services of State. It may also be conferred on foreigners. The Order ranks after the *Order of War for the Fatherland* (326).

The Order has one class, which wears the Badge of the Order (319) on a chest riband.

The *Badge of the Order* is a gold medallion surrounded by a cog wheel, in whose centre are the hammer and sickle symbols on a background of a power station garlanded by an oak wreath and crowned by a red flag with the monogram "SSSR" for "Sojuz Sovjetskih Sotsialistitjeskih Respublik" (The Union of the Soviet Socialist Republics) in Cyrillic script. The cog wheel bears the inscription "Proletarii Vsekh Stran Soendinjajtesj" (Workers of the World, unite), also in Cyrillic script.

The *Riband of the Order* is blue with border stripes one shade darker. It is worn as a chest riband mounted in a crossed fashion.

320. The Order of Suvorov (*Orden Suvorova*) was instituted on 29th July 1942. The Order is named after the Russian General Aleksandr Sovorov who, *inter alia*, suppressed the revolt in Poland in 1794 and who, as Commander-in-Chief of the Russo-Austrian Army during the Second Coalition, drove the French from northern Italy in 1799. The Order may be conferred on officers of the Soviet Army for outstanding leadership of troops and for faultlessly organised and successfully executed operations in war, during which the person concerned displayed resoluteness and perseverance resulting in a victorious outcome of the operation. It may also be conferred on foreign officers.

The Order has three degrees, *1st to 3rd Degrees*, which wear the Badge of the Order (320), varying in design according to degree, as a breast star on the *right* side of the chest.

The *Badge of the Order* is a 5-pointed star, in platinum for 1st Degree, in gold for 2nd Degree and in silver for 3rd Degree, with centred pencils of rays. The centre medallion, which is gold for 1st Degree and in silver for 2nd and 3rd Degrees, bears a portrait of General Suvorov in relief, with his name as legend. The Badge of the Order for 1st degree bears a 5-pointed red star at the top.

When worn with uniform, a green *Riband of the Order* is worn, with an orange centre stripe for 1st Degree, an orange border stripe for 2nd Degree and three narrow orange stripes for 3rd Degree.

321. The Order of Usjakov *(Orden Usjakova)* was instituted on 3rd March 1944. The Order is named after the Russian Admiral Theodore Usjakov who *inter alia*, when Commander of the Russian Black Sea Fleet in 1799, drove the French from the Ionic Islands occupied by General Bonaparte and thus consolidated Russian influence in the Adriatic. The Order may be conferred on naval officers for outstanding planning and execution of naval operations in which victory was won over an enemy superior in number. It may also be conferred on foreign naval officers.

The Order has two degrees, *1st and 2nd Degrees*, which wear the Badge of the Order (321), varying in design according to degree, as a breast star on the *right* side of the chest.

The *Badge of the Order* is a 5-pointed star, in platinum for 1st Degree and in gold for 2nd Degree, with centred rays which bear an anchor in silver. The centre medallion, which is in gold for 1st Degree and in silver for 2nd Degree, bears a portrait of Admiral Usjakov in relief with his name as legend. The Badge of the Order for 1st Degree bears a set of oak and laurel branches beneath the centre medallion.

When worn with uniform, a *Riband of the Order* is worn. This is blue with white border stripes for 1st Degree, and white with blue border stripes for 2nd Degree.

Attached to the Order is the *Usjakov Medal*, which has one degree, *silver*. It is worn on a light blue chest riband with blue-white border stripes mounted in a crossed fashion. The Medal, which may be conferred on petty officers and ratings, has the same motif as the centre medallion of the Badge of the Order.

322. The Order of Kutuzov *(Orden Kutuzova)* was instituted on 29th July 1942 and extended on 8th February 1943. The Order is named after the Russian General Mihail Kutuzov who *inter alia*, when Russian Commander-in-Chief in the campaign against Napoleon in 1812, by cautious and clever strategy, for example the abandonment of Moscow, contributed to the ruin of the Grand Army. The Order may be conferred on officers of the Soviet Army for faultless planning and successful execution of operations involving an Army or a Front during which the enemy was heavily defeated. It may also be conferred on foreign officers.

The Order has three degrees, *1st to 3rd Degrees*, which wear the Badge of the Order (322), varying in design according to degree, as a breast star on the *right* side of the chest.

The *Badge of the Order* is a 5-pointed star, in gold and silver for 1st and 2nd Classes respectively with platinum pencils of rays between the points, and all in silver for 3rd Degree with centred rays. The centre medallion, which is in gold for 1st Degree and in silver for 2nd and 3rd Degrees, bears a portrait in relief of General Kutuzov on a background of the Kremlin wall with the Spaskija Tower crowned by the red star, and the General's name as legend. The Badge of the Order for 1st Degree bears a laurel garland around the outside of the centre medallion.

When worn with uniform, a blue *Riband of the Order* is worn. It has an orange centre stripe for 1st Class, orange border stripes for 2nd Class and three narrow orange stripes for 3rd Class.

323. The Order of Nakhimov *(Orden Nakhimova)* was instituted on 3rd March 1944. The Order is named after the Russian Admiral Paul Stephanovitsch Nakhimov who, *inter alia*, during the Crimean War attacked and destroyed the Turkish Navy in the Black Sea. The Order may be conferred on naval officers for outstanding planning and execution of naval operations in which enemy attacks were repulsed and the main forces of the enemy received significant damage. It may also be conferred on foreign naval officers.

The Order has two degrees, *1st and 2nd Degrees*, which wear the Badge of the Order (323), varying in design according to degree, as a breast star on the *right* side of the chest.

The *Badge of the Order* is a 5-pointed, red-enamelled star whose points are surrounded by split anchors in silver. The centre medallion, which similarly to the pencils of rays between the points is in gold for 1st Degree and in silver for 2nd Degree, bears a portrait in relief of Admiral Nakhimov with his name as legend.

When worn with uniform, an orange *Riband of the Order* is worn. This has black selvedges and a wide black centre stripe for 1st Degree and two black stripes for 2nd Degree.

Attached to the Order is the *Nakhimov Medal*, which has one degree. It is worn on a light blue chest riband with three white stripes and in a crossed fashion. The Medal, which may be conferred on petty officers and ratings, has the same motif as the centre medallion of the Badge of the Order.

324. The Order of Bogdan Khmelnitskij *(Orden Bogdana Khmelnitskogo)* was instituted on 10th October 1943 as a war decoration which may be conferred on non-commissioned officers and men of the Soviet Army and Navy, and also on the guerilla forces, for resoluteness, efficiency, patriotism, devotion and bravery displayed in the fight for the Fatherland. It may also be conferred on foreigners. The Order is named after the military Commander Bogdan Khmelnitskij who, in the first half of the seventeenth century, attempted to liberate the Ukraine from Polish oppression and to make the country into an independent Cossack State, but who eventually put himself and his army under Russian protection, whereby the Ukraine came under Russian rule.

The Order has three degrees, *1st to 3rd Degrees*, which wear the Badge of the Order (324), varying in size and design according to degree, as a breast star on the *right* side of the breast.

The *Badge of the Order* is a 5-pointed star in silver, with gold pencils of rays between the points for 1st Degree and all in silver for 2nd and 3rd Degree, with centred rays. The centre medallion, which is in gold for 1st and 2nd Degrees and in silver for 3rd Degree, bears a portrait in relief of Bogdan Khmelnitskij within an ornamented circle in silver and with his name as legend. For 3rd Degree the legend is in the top half of the circle. The Badge of the Order for 3rd Degree is smaller than the Badge of the Order for 1st and 2nd Degrees.

When worn with uniform, a blue *Riband of the Order* is worn, having a white centre stripe for 1st Degree, white border stripes for 2nd Degree, and three narrow white border stripes for 3rd Degree.

325. The Order of Alexander Nevskij *(Orden Aleksandra Nevskogo)* was instituted on 29th July 1942. The Order is named after Grand Duke Alexander Jaroslavitsch Nevskij who, during the first half of the thirteenth century, fought the Swedes and the Teutonic Knights of the Sword at the Neva river and thus consolidated and expanded Russian influence on the Baltic coast – a feat for which Czar Peter I instituted the Order in his honour and under his name already in 1722. The Order may be conferred on officers of the Soviet Army who, in battle for the Fatherland, have displayed personal courage, bravery and valour and who, by astute leadership, have contributed to a successful outcome of the actions of their troops with a minimum loss of life. It may also be conferred on foreign officers.

The Order has one degree, which wears the Badge of the Order (325) as a breast star on the *right* side of the breast.

The *Badge of the Order* is a 5-pointed red-enamelled star in gold with pencils of rays in silver between the points. The centre medallion, which is garlanded with laurel branches, bears above a shield with the hammer and sickle symbols a portrait in relief of Alexander Nevaskij with his name as legend. As a further ornamentation, the Badge of the Order bears a set of crossed battle axes, a bow with quiver and a set of crossed swords at the base.

When worn with uniform, a bluish-white *Riband of the Order* with a red centre stripe is worn.

326. The Order of the Patriotic War *(Orden Otetjestvennoj Vojni)* was instituted on 20th May 1942 as a war decoration for the Second World War. The Order might be conferred on personnel of the Soviet Army, Navy and Air Force and on security and partisan forces who, in the battle against the German occupation forces, displayed fearlessness, perseverance and bravery, or otherwise contributed to the furtherance of the battle operations of the Soviet Forces. It might also be conferred on foreigners. The Order ranks before the *Order of the Red Flag of Work* (319).

The Order has two degrees; *1st Degree*, which was conferred on combattants, and *2nd Degree* which was conferred on non-combattants. Both degrees wear the Badge of the Order (326), varying in design according to degree, as a breast star on the *right* side of the breast.

The *Badge of the Order* is a 5-pointed red-enamelled star in gold, with pencils of rays between the points in gold for 1st Degree and in silver for 2nd Degree. The centre medallion bears the hammer and sickle symbols on a red background within a white scroll with the inscription

"Otetjestvennoj Vojni" (The Patriotic War) in Cyrillic script. As a further ornamentation, the Badge of the Order bears in crossed fashion a gun with fixed bayonet and a sabre.

When worn with uniform, a reddish-brown *Riband of the Order* is worn, with a red centre stripe for 1st Degree and red border stripes for 2nd Degree.

327. The Order of Honour *(Orden Slavi)* was instituted on 8th November 1943. The Order may be conferred on non-commissioned officers and men of the Soviet Army and lieutenants of the Air Force who, in battle for the Soviet Union, have displayed audacity, fearlessness and bravery in the face of the enemy by, for example, being the first to break through an enemy position, or by similar positive acts. It may also be conferred on foreigners.

The Order has three degrees, *1st to 3rd Degrees*, which are conferred according to rank. They wear the Badge of the Order (327), varying in design according to degree, on a chest riband.

The *Badge of the Order* is a 5-pointed star, in gold for 1st Degree and in silver for 2nd and 3rd Degrees. The centre medallion, which is in gold for 1st and 2nd Degrees and silver for 3rd Degree, has as its motif in relief the Spaskija Tower in the Kremlin crowned by the 5-pointed red star and garlanded by a laurel wreath bearing a red scroll at the the base with the inscription "Slava" (Honour) in Cyrillic script. The reverse bears within a circle the monogram "SSSR" for "Sojuz Sovjetskih Sotsialistitjeskih Respublik" (The Union of Soviet Socialist Republics), also in Cyrillic script.

The *Riband of the Order* is orange with three black stripes, probably taking the *Order of Saint George* from Czarist times as a model. It is worn as a chest riband mounted in crossed fashion.

328. The Order of the Red Star *(Orden "Krasnaja Zvezda")* was instituted on 6th April 1930 by the Central Executive Committee of the Soviet Union, whose Presidium affirmed the statutes of the

Order on 5th May 1930. The Order may be conferred on units and personnel of the Soviet Army, Navy and Air Force and also on works collectives, institutions, organisations and undertakings for outstanding services in the defence of the Soviet Union in times of war and of peace. It may also be conferred on civilians for courage and bravery displayed in the preservation of public order and socialist property and for saving the lives and property of Soviet citizens. It may also be conferred on foreigners.

The Order has one degree, which wears the Badge of the Order (328) as a breast star.

The *Badge of the Order* is a 5-pointed red-enamelled star in silver. The centre medallion, above the hammer and sickle symbols, bears in relief a Soviet soldier with fixed bayonet with the legend "Proletarii Vsekh Stran Soedinjaitesi" (Workers of the World, unite) and the monogram "SSSR" for "Sojuz Sovjetskih Sotsialistitjeskih Respublik" (The Union of Soviet Socialist Republics) both in Cyrillic script.

When worn with uniform, a red *Riband of the Order* with a silver-grey centre stripe is worn.

PORTUGAL
The Riband of the Three Orders *(Banda das Três Ordens)* is a special decoration worn by the Portuguese President in his capacity as Grand Master of the Orders of the Republic. It may also be conferred on foreign Heads of State.

Holders of the decoration wear a sash with three stripes of equal width in green, red and lilac, on which is pendant a medallion in gold bearing reproductions of the Badges of the *Order of Christ* (332–333), the *Order of Aviz* (334–335) and the *Order of Sant' Iago* (336–339). They also wear an 8-pointed breast star in gold with a corresponding medallion.

329–331. The Order of the Tower and the Sword *(Ordem Militar da Torre e Espada, do Valor, Lealdade e Mérito)*

The Riband of the Three Orders: Medal

was instituted in 1459 by King Alphonso V, and renewed in 1808, 1832 and 1917. Its present statutes date from 24th November 1963. The Order may be conferred on the military and on civilians, Portuguese and foreigners, for outstanding services to the National and Overseas Governments or in command of troops in the field, and also for heroic acts and outstanding proof of devotion and sacrifice for country and mankind. The Portuguese President is the Grand Master of the Order.

The Order has a Grand Collar and five classes:

1*. *Grand Collar*, which wears the Badge of the Order (329) on a Grand Collar and insignia as for the Grand Cross.

1. *Grand Cross*, which wears the Badge of the Order (329) on a sash and the Star of the Order in gold.

2. *Grand Officer*, which wears the Star of the Order in gold.

3. *Commander*, which wears the Star of the Order in silver.

The Riband of the Three Orders:
Breast Star

4. *Officer*, which wears the Badge of the Order (331), but in this case larger, on a chest riband with rosette.

5. *Knight*, which wears the Badge of the Order (331), but in this case larger, on a chest riband.

The Grand Collar Class is a special class which is conferred exclusively on foreign Heads of State. On ceremonial occasions, the other classes wear, as well as the appropriate insignia, the Badge of the Order (329) on a collar (330), but both in silver for the Knights' Class.

The *Badge of the Order* is a 5-pointed, white-enamelled star in gold crowned by a tower and resting upon an oak wreath. The obverse medallion bears a sword garlanded by laurel branches on a white background with the legend "Valor, Lealdade e Mérito" (Bravery, Loyalty and Service) on a blue background. The reverse medallion bears the Portuguese State coat of arms with the legend "Republica Portuguesa" (The Portuguese Republic).

The *Star of the Order* is a pentagonal star in gold, in silver for the Commander Class, with faceted rays. The star bears in the centre a Badge of the Order without oak wreath.

The *Collar of the Order* and the *Grand Collar*, which are both in gold, are composed respectively of longitudinal and transverse laurel-garlanded swords and towers. In addition the Grand Collar has as a mounting a larger tower between two dragons armed with swords.

The *Riband of the Order* is plain blue. As a chest riband, it is worn with a silver-gilt metal bar.

332–333. The Order of Christ *(Ordem Militar de Christo)* is a branch of the *Order of the Knights Templar*, whose origin and history were described on pages 8–9. The Order of the Knights Templar, which because of its enormous riches had become a dangerous power factor by about 1300, was abolished in 1312 by Pope Clement V on the instigation of King Philip the Fair of France. In Portugal, however, King Dionysus allowed the Order to be re-established in 1317 under its original name, "The Knights of Christ" – or the Order of Christ – and allowed them to have the property there of the Order of the Knights Templar. This was affirmed in 1319 by Pope John XXII on condition that the Pope also received the right to award the Order. In this way the

The Order of the Tower and the Sword: Grand Collar with Badge of the Order and Star of the Order

foundation was laid for the split in the Order of Christ into a Portuguese and a Papal branch, which still exists today. The Order was secularized in 1789 into a military and civil Order of Merit of three classes, which were extended in 1918 by another two. The present statutes of the Order date from 24th November 1963. The Order may be conferred on Portuguese and on foreigners for outstanding services to the Republic in the government, the diplomatic service, the public authorities or in administration. The Portuguese President is the Grand Master of the Order. The Order ranks after the *Order of Aviz* (334–335).

The Order has five classes:

1. *Grand Cross*, which wears the Badge of the Order (333), but larger, on a sash and the Star of the Order (332).

2. *Grand Officer*, which wears the Badge of the Order (333), but larger, on a necklet and the Star of the Order (332).

3. *Commander*, which wears the Badge of the Order (333), but larger, on a necklet and the Star of the Order (332) in silver.

4. *Officer*, which wears the Badge of the Order (333) on a chest riband with rosette.

5. *Knight*, which wears the Badge of the Order (333) on a chest riband.

The Badge of the Order for 4th and 5th Classes is worn on a necklet in the same size as the Commander Cross on ceremonial occasions.

The *Badge of the Order*, which varies in size according to class, is a red-enamelled Latin Cross in gold with outward-bent arms and with a white Latin Cross in the centre. The obverse and the reverse are the same.

The *Star of the Order* is a multi-pointed star in gold, in silver for the Commander class, with asymmetrical rays. The centre medallion, which is gold for all classes, bears the Badge of the Order on a white background within a laurel wreath.

The *Riband of the Order* is plain red. As a chest riband, it is worn with a silver-gilt bar.

334–335. The Order of Aviz *(Ordem Militar de Aviz)* owes its origin to a society of aristocratic Portuguese established about 1140 to fight against the Moors. It was called "The New Militia". The Order was affirmed in 1162 by King Alphonso I and converted into a clerical Order of Knighthood under the Benedictine rule. The Order was secularized in 1789 to become a naval and military Order of Merit of three classes, which were extended in 1918 by a further two. The present statutes of the Order date from 24th November 1963. The Order may be conferred on naval officers, Portuguese and foreign, as a reward for outstanding achievement during service. The Portuguese President is the Grand Master of the Order. The Order ranks before the *Order of Christ* (332–333).

The Order has five classes:

1. *Grand Cross*, which wears the Badge of the Order (335) on a sash and the Star of the Order (334).

2. *Grand Officer*, which wears the Badge of the Order (335) on a necklet and the Star of the Order (334).

3. *Commander*, which wears the Badge of the Order (335) on a necklet and the Star of the Order (334) in silver.

4. *Officer*, which wears the Badge of the Order (335), but smaller, on a chest riband with rosette.

5. *Knight*, which wears the Badge of the Order (335), but smaller, on a chest riband without rosette.

The Badge of the Order for 4th and 5th Classes is worn on a necklet in the Commander size on ceremonial occasions.

The *Badge of the Order*, which varies in size according to class, is a green-enamelled fleury cross of Latin form in gold. The obverse and reverse are alike.

The *Star of the Order* is an 8-pointed star in gold, in silver for the Commander Class, with faceted rays. The centre medallion, which is gold for all classes, bears the Badge of the Order on a white background within a laurel wreath.

The *Riband of the Order* is plain green.

As a chest riband it is worn with a silver-gilt metal bar.

336–339. The Order of Sant' Iago *(Ordem Militar de Sant' Iago da Espada)* was a Portuguese branch separated in 1290 from the Spanish *Order of Saint Jacob of the Sword*. It was affirmed in 1320 by Pope John XXII as an independent Order. The Spanish Order had its origin in an Order of Knighthood founded in 1170 for the protection of pilgrims journeying to Santiago de Compostella in North-Western Spain. According to tradition, it was here that the earthly remains of the Apostle Jacob the Elder – Saint Iago – had been found in 829 in a field indicated by a star – campus stella – "the field of stars". The increasing riches and power of the two branches of the Order eventually led to the dignities of Grand Master in Castile (Spain) and in Portugal coming under the Crown. The Portuguese Order was secularized in 1789 and changed in 1862 into an Order of Merit for science, literature and art. It may today be conferred on Portuguese and on foreigners for acknowledged services in these fields. The present statutes of the Order date from 24th November 1963. The Portuguese President is the Grand Master of the Order.

The Order has a Grand Collar and five classes:

The Order of Sant' Iago: Grand Collar with Badge of the Order

1*. *Grand Collar*, which wears the Badge of the Order (337), without palm branches but garlanded with a laurel wreath, on a Grand Collar, and the insignia as for Grand Cross.

1. *Grand Cross*, which wears the Badge of the Order (337) on a sash and the Star of the Order (338) in gold.

2. *Grand Officer*, which wears the Star of the Order (338) in gold.

3. *Commander*, which wears the Star of the Order (338).

4. *Officer*, which wears the Badge of the Order (339) on a chest riband, with rosette.

5. *Knight*, which wears the Badge of the Order (339) on a chest riband.

The Grand Collar Class is a special class which is exclusively conferred on foreign Heads of State. As well as the appropriate insignia, the other classes wear on ceremonial occasions the Badge of the Order (337) on a collar (336), but both are in silver for the Knight's Class.

The *Badge of the Order* is a red-enamelled fleury cross in gold, whose lower arm forms a sword. The cross rests on two palm branches which bear a scroll at the base with the inscription "Ciencia Letras e Artes" (Science, literature and art). It has a laurel wreath as a mounting.

The *Star of the Order* is a multi-pointed star in gold, in silver for the Commander Class, with asymmetrical rays. The centre medallion, which is gold for all classes, bears the Badge of the Order on a white background within a laurel wreath, with the inscription on the scroll as a legend on a red background.

The *Collar of the Order* and the *Grand Collar*, which are both gold, are composed of Badges of the Order, laurel wreaths and shells respectively, the symbols of the pilgrims. In addition, the Grand Collar has as a mounting the ancient Christian fish symbol for "Jesus Christ, the Son of God, Saviour" (the first letters of the corresponding Greek words form the work "IXTYZ", meaning "fish").

The *Riband of the Order* is plain lilac. As a chest riband, it is worn with a silver-gilt metal bar.

340–343. The Order of Infante Dom Henrique *(Ordem do Infante Dom Henrique)* was instituted on 2nd June 1960 as a tribute to the Portuguese Prince Henry, who bore the nickname "The Navigator", and to his discoveries, on the occasion of the 500th anniversary of the Prince's death. The Order may be conferred on individuals and on institutions, Portuguese and foreign, for outstanding services in connection with enterprises or investigations which have made maritime history and for spreading the knowledge of Portugal's discoveries to the world. The present statutes of the Order date from 24th November 1963. The Portuguese President is the Grand Master of the Order. The Order ranks after the *Imperial Order* (344).

The Order has a Grand Collar and five classes:

1*. *Grand Collar*, which wears the Badge of the Order (341) on a Grand Collar (340) and insignia as for the Grand Cross.

1. *Grand Cross*, which wears the Badge of the Order (341), without supporting wreath, on a sash and the Star of the Order (342).

2. *Grand Officer*, which wears the Badge of the Order (341), without supporting wreath, on a necklet and the Star of the Order (342).

3. *Commander*, which wears the Badge of the Order (341), without supporting wreath, on a necklet and the Star of the Order (342) in silver.

4. *Officer*, which wears the Badge of the Order (341), without supporting wreath and in Knight's Cross size (344), on a chest riband with rosette.

5. *Knight*, which wears the Badge of the Order (341), without supporting wreath and in Knight's Cross size (344), on a chest riband without rosette.

The Grand Collar Class is a special class which is conferred exclusively on foreign Heads of State.

The Imperial Order: Star of the Order

The *Badge of the Order* is a red-enamelled Mantau Cross in gold, with an oak wreath as a mounting for the Grand Collar. The obverse and reverse are alike.

The *Star of the Order* is a 9-pointed star in gold, in silver for Commander Class, with plain rays, on which rests a smaller 9-pointed star. The centre medallion, which is gold for all classes, bears a Badge of the Order on a white background with the legend "Talant de bie' faire" (It is a gift to be able to do well) garlanded by a laurel wreath on a black background.

The *Grand Collar*, which is gold, is composed of double oak wreaths and Badges of the Order.

The *Riband of the Order* consists of three equally wide stripes in blue, white and black. As a chest riband it is worn with a silver-gilt metal bar.

The *Infante Dom Henrique Medal* is attached to the Order. It has two degrees, *gold* and *silver*, and is worn on the chest riband of the Order. The obverse bears a portrait in relief of Henry the Navigator. The reverse bears a Badge of the Order with the same legend as the centre medallion of the Star of the Order.

344. The Imperial Order *(Ordem do Imperio)* was instituted on 13th April 1932 as a reward for Portuguese and foreigners for services to the government, in administration or in the diplomatic and military defence of the overseas territories, and also for meritorious services to colonization or of a valuable cultural, political or economic nature. It may also be conferred as a reward for outstanding services in the merchant navy, airways and other means of communication between the various parts of the Portuguese Empire. Holders of the three highest classes of the Order, who wear their insignia visibly, are given a military salute in the overseas territories. The present statutes of the Order date from 24th November 1963. The Portuguese President is the Grand Master of the Order. The Order ranks before the *Order of Infante Dom Henrique* (341–343).

The Order has five classes:

1. *Grand Cross*, which wears the Badge of the Order (344), but larger and in gold, on a sash and the Star of the Order in gold.

2. *Grand Officer*, which wears the Badge of the Order (344), but larger

and in gold, on a necklet and the Star of the Order in gold.

3. *Commander*, which wears the Badge of the Order (344), but larger and in gold, on a necklet and the Star of the Order in silver.

4. *Officer*, which wears the Badge of the Order (344) in gold on a chest riband with rosette.

5. *Knight*, which wears the Badge of the Order (344) on a chest riband.

The *Badge of the Order*, which varies in size according to class, is a red-enamelled Greek Cross in gold, in silver for the Knight's Class, with arms bent outwards, bearing a white Greek Cross in the centre. The cross bears in the centre in the form of a medallion the Portuguese State coat of arms in gold. The reverse is plain.

The *Star of the Order* is an 8-pointed faceted star in gold, in silver for Commander Class, with a Badge of the Order in gold in the centre.

The *Riband of the Order* is red with black selvedges and a narrow black centre stripe. As a chest riband it is worn with a silver-gilt metal Bar.

345–346. The Order of Merit *(Ordem da Benemerência)* was instituted on 30th January 1929 as a reward to Portuguese and foreigners for civil services in general within the fields of administration and private industry. It may also be conferred as a reward for special services to public welfare and health. The present statutes of the Order date from 24th November 1963. The Portuguese President is the Grand Master of the Order.

The Order has five classes:

1. *Grand Cross*, which wears the Badge of the Order (346), but larger, on a sash and the Star of the Order (345) in gold.

2. *Grand Officer*, which wears the Badge of the Order (346), but larger, on a necklet and the Star of the Order (345) in gold.

3. *Commander*, which wears the Badge of the Order (346), but larger, on a necklet and the Star of the Order (345).

4. *Officer*, which wears the Badge of the Order (346) on a chest riband with rosette.

5. *Medal*, which wears the Badge of the Order (346), with arms of the cross and mounting wreath in silver, on a chest riband without rosette.

The *Badge of the Order*, which varies in size according to class, is a blue-enamelled Maltese Cross in gold, in silver for 5th Class, pendant on a laurel wreath. The obverse medallion bears a 5-pointed star with the legend "Benemerência" (Well Deserved) on a white background. The reverse medallion bears the Portuguese State coat of arms with the legend "República Portuguesa" (The Portuguese Republic).

The *Star of the Order* is a blue-enamelled Maltese Cross in gold, as is the Badge of the Order, and in silver for the Commander Class. Its centre medallion, which is gold for all classes, is garlanded by a laurel wreath.

The *Riband of the Order* is black with a wide, yellow centre stripe. As a chest riband it is worn with a silver-gilt metal Bar; for 5th Class it is a silver Bar.

347–348. The Order "Instruçao Publica" *(Ordem da Instruçao Publica)* was instituted on 30th January 1919 as a reward for civil servants and teachers, Portuguese and foreigners, for meritorious services to administration and teaching. It may also be conferred on private persons as a reward for services to teaching and education. The present statutes of the Order date from 24th November 1963. The Portuguese President is the Grand Master of the Order.

The Order has five classes:

1. *Grand Cross*, which wears the Badge of the Order (348), but larger, on a sash and the Star of the Order (347), both in gold.

2. *Grand Officer*, which wears the Badge of the Order (348), but larger, on a necklet and the Star of the Order (347), both in gold.

3. *Commander*, which wears the Badge of the Order (348), but larger and in gold, on a necklet and the Star of

the Order (347).

4. *Officer*, which wears the Badge of the Order (348) in gold on a chest riband with rosette.

5. *Medal*, which wears the Badge of the Order (348) on a chest riband.

The *Badge of the Order*, which varies in size according to class, consists of two palm branches in gold, for 5th Class in silver, which form an oval garland.

The *Star of the Order* is an 8-pointed star in gold, for the Commander Class in silver, with plain rays, on which rests a smaller 8-pointed, blue-enamelled star. The centre medallion, which is gold for all classes and garlanded by the palm branches of the Badge of the Order, bears the Portuguese State coat of arms with the legend "Instruçao Publica" (Public teaching) on a white background.

The *Riband of the Order* is plain yellow. As a chest riband it is worn with a silver-gilt metal Bar; for 5th Class it is a silver Bar.

349–350. The Order of "Mérito Agricola e Industrial" *(Ordem do Mérito Agricola e Industrial)* was instituted on 4th June 1893 and renewed on 13th November 1926. Its present statutes date from 24th November 1963. The Portuguese President is the Grand Master of the Order.

The Order has two divisions, one for *agricultural services* as a reward for special services in the promotion and improvement of the Republic's agriculture, cattle breeding and forestry, and one for *industrial services* as a reward for special services in the promotion and improvement of the Republic's industry and trade in general and for encouraging the qualification and co-operation of workers and technicians.

Each division has five classes:

Classes and insignia for the division for *agricultural services* are:

1. *Grand Cross*, which wears the Badge of the Order (349) on a sash and the Star of the Order in gold.

2. *Grand Officer*, which wears the Badge of the Order (349) on a necklet and the Star of the Order in gold.

3. *Commander*, which wears the Badge of the Order (349) on a necklet and the Star of the Order in silver.

4. *Officer*, which wears the Badge of the Order (349) in Officer's Cross size (346) on a necklet with rosette.

5. *Medal*, which wears the Badge of the Order (349) in Officer's Cross size, with rays and mounting wreath in silver, on a chest riband without rosette.

The *Badge of the Order* is a 9-pointed star in gold, in silver for 5th Class, with fluted rays, on which rests a smaller 9-pointed, green-enamelled faceted star with nine small 5-pointed green-enamelled stars between the points. The centre medallion which, as with the other ornamentation of the Badge of the Order, is in gold for all classes, bears the Portuguese State coat of arms with the legend "Mérito Agricola" (Agricultural services) on a white background. The Badge of the Order has a green-enamelled laurel wreath as a mounting.

The *Star of the Order* is a Badge of the Order in gold, for the Commander Class in silver, but without mounting wreath. The centre medallion and the other ornamentation of the Star is in gold for all classes.

The *Riband of the Order* is green with a wide white centre stripe. As a chest riband it is worn with a silver-gilt metal Bar; for 5th Class it is a silver Bar.

Classes and insignia for the division for *industrial services* are:

1. *Grand Cross*, which wears the Badge of the Order (350) on a sash and the Star of the Order in gold.

2. *Grand Officer*, which wears the Badge of the Order (350) on a necklet and the Star of the Order in gold.

3. *Commander*, which wears the Badge of the Order (350) on a necklet and the Star of the Order in silver.

4. *Officer*, which wears the Badge of the Order (350), in Officer's Cross size (346), on a chest riband with rosette.

5. *Medal*, which wears the Badge of the Order (350) in Officer's Cross size and with rays and supporting wreath in silver, on a chest riband without rosette.

The *Badge of the Order* and the *Star of the Order* are identical with the corresponding insignia for the division for *agricultural services*, except that the 9- and 5-pointed stars superimposed as ornamentation are red-enamelled, and the centre medallion bears the legend "Mérito Industrial" (Industrial services) on a white background.

The *Riband of the Order* is red with a wide white centre stripe. As a chest riband it is worn with a silver-gilt metal Bar; for 5th Class it is a silver Bar.

SPAIN
351–354. The Order of Charles III *(Muy Distinguida Orden de Carlos III)* was instituted on 19th September 1771 by King Charles III. The Order was dissolved in 1809 by Joseph Bonaparte, but was reinstituted in 1814 by King Ferdinand VII. After being again dissolved and reinstituted several times, it was finally re-established and provided with new statutes on 10th May 1942. The Order may be conferred on Spaniards and on foreigners for outstanding services to the Fatherland. The Spanish Head of State is the Grand Master of the Order.

The Order has five classes:

1. *Grand Cross with Collar*, which wears the Badge of the Order (351) on a collar, the Badge of the Order (354) on a sash of a special colour pattern and the Star of the Order (352) with the fleur-de-lis between the arms of the cross in gold.

2. *Grand Cross*, which wears the Badge of the Order (354) on a sash and the Star of the Order (352).

3. *Commander by Number*, which wears the Star of the Order (353).

4. *Commander*, which wears the Badge of the Order (351) on a necklet.

5. *Knight*, which wears the Badge of the Order (354) on a chest riband (gentlemen) or on a bow (ladies).

The Grand Cross with Collar is conferred exclusively on foreign Heads of State. The designation "Commander by Number" originates from 1815 when, after reinstitution, an excess number of Knights was found beyond the number established in the statutes. The members within the established number were hereafter called "Commanders by Number".

The *Badge of the Order* is a white-edged, blue-enamelled Maltese Cross in gold with the golden fleur-de-lis of the House of Bourbon between the arms of the cross (the Bourbons inherited the Spanish throne in 1700 when the House of Hapsburg became extinct in Spain) and pendant on a laurel wreath. The obverse medallion bears a portrait of St. Mary, the patron saint of the Order, on a silver cloud symbolizing the Immaculate Conception, and the reverse medallion bears the face-to-face monogram of the founder with the legend "Virtuti et Merito" (For the Brave and the Meritorious), the motto of the Order.

The *Stars of the Order* for *1st and 2nd Classes* are both a faceted Maltese Cross in silver, for 1st Class with the fleur-de-lis between the arms of the cross in gold. The gold centre medallion has the same motif as the obverse medallion of the Badge of the Order, but with the motto of the Order as a legend on a white scroll and with the face-to-face monogram of the founder in a shield beneath the medallion. The *Star of the Order* for *3rd Class* is a blue-enamelled faceted Maltese Cross in silver, whose centre medallion bears the face-to-face monogram of the founder within a green-enamelled laurel wreath in gold.

The *Collar of the Order*, which is of gold, consists of seven links with the monogram of the founder, 14 links of a lion connected to a tower, six links with a trophy, and on neck link.

The *Riband of the Order* is light blue with a wide white centre stripe. As a chest riband it is worn with a supporting bar. The sash of the Grand Cross with Collar is blue with narrow white border stripes.

355–358. The Order of Isabella the Catholic *(Orden de Isabel la Catolica)* was instituted on 24th March 1815 by King Ferdinand VII in memory of his

The Order of Charles III: Collar of the Order with Badge of the Order, Grand Cross with Collar

return to the Spanish throne after the withdrawal of the French troops in 1813, and as a tribute to the great and wise Queen Isabella who, during the second half of the fifteenth century, by her marriage to King Ferdinand II, united and, by supporting Columbus, expanded Spain beyond the seas. The original name of the Order was *The Royal American Order of Isabella the Catholic.* Its present statutes date from 15th June 1938. The Order is preferably conferred for services of a civil nature for the benefit of the country. It may also be conferred on foreigners, *inter alia* diplomats, for services to Spain. The

The Order of Isabella the Catholic: Collar of the Order with Badge of the Order, Grand Cross with Collar

Spanish Head of State is the Grand Master of the Order.

The Order has five classes:

1. *Grand Cross with Collar*, which wears the Badge of the Order (355) in Commander size (351) on a collar and the insignia of the Grand Cross.

2. *Grand Cross*, which wears the Badge of the Order (355) on a sash and the Star of the Order (356).

3. *Commander by Number*, which wears the Star of the Order (356), but smaller and with a different medallion motif.

4. *Commander*, which wears the Badge of the Order (355), in Commander size (351), on a necklet.

5. *Knight*, which wears the Badge of the Order (355) on a chest riband (gentlemen) or on a bow (ladies).

Grand Cross with Collar is conferred exclusively on high-ranking Spaniards and foreign Heads of State and Chiefs of Governments, but to a total of not more than 25.

The *Badge of the Order* is a red-enamelled Maltese Cross in gold with double-cleft arms and pencils of rays in the angles of the cross. The obverse medallion bears within a white ring with the inscription "A la Lealtad Acrisolada" (For Loyalty shown) the two columns of Hercules, symbolizing the Straits of Gibraltar, beyond which there was thought in ancient times to be no more land, entwined with a scroll bearing the inscription "Plus – Ultra" (More on the other Side) as a triumph after Columbus' discovery of America. Further, it bears two globes, symbolizing the old world and the new world, beneath a crown. The reverse medallion bears a crowned "FY" for "Ferdinand and Isabella" on a blue background with the legend "Por Isabel la Catolica" (For Isabella the Catholic) on a white background. The cross is pendant on a green-enamelled laurel wreath.

The *Star of the Order*, which varies in size according to class, is identical with the Badge of the Order, but the centre medallion, which has the same motif as the obverse medallion of the Badge of the Order for 1st and 2nd Classes, is surrounded by a green-enamelled laurel wreath entwined with a white scroll bearing the inscriptions "A la Lealtad Acrisolada" at the top and "Por Isabel la Catolica" at the base. The medallion bears a crowned shield at the top with the monogram "FY" for "Ferdinand and Isabella". The centre medallion for 3rd Class bears only the two columns of Hercules entwined with a scroll bearing the inscription "Plus – Ultra" and crowned by a royal and an imperial crown respectively.

The *Collar of the Order*, which is gold, consists of 15 links, eight links with the "yoke and arrows" symbol, (five arrows penetrating a yoke, an old Spanish symbol of the Moorish yoke which the Spaniards broke, and which is now the emblem of the Spanish Phalangist Party), flanked by an "F" for "Ferdinand" and a "Y" for "Isabella", and seven medallions with the same motif as the obverse medallion of the Badge of the Order and garlanded by a laurel wreath. The Collar has as a mounting the Spanish State coat of arms from the sixteenth century.

The *Riband of the Order* is white with wide yellow border stripes. As a chest riband it is worn with a supporting bar. The sash of the Grand Cross with Collar is yellow with narrow white border stripes.

The *Silver Cross* (357) is attached to the Order. It was instituted in 1903 and consists of a Badge of the Order on a chest riband. There is also the *Medal of Isabella the Catholic* (358), instituted in 1907, which has two degrees, *silver* and *bronze*, and is worn on the chest riband of the Order.

359–361. The Civil Order of Mercy *(Orden Civil de Beneficencia)* was instituted on 17th May 1856 in recognition of heroism and acts of mercy in all layers of society during the cholera epidemic and other disasters which struck the Iberian Peninsula in 1854 and 1855. The Order, which is a revival and an extension of the *Epidemic Cross* of 1838, may today be conferred for services during catastrophies, and in individual cases where human life or property is saved, where the consequences of an accident are alleviated or where there is a clear example of benefaction to people. It may be conferred irrespective of sex or nationality. The Order is administered by the Ministry of State.

The Order has four divisions, each characterised by special colours in the otherwise common insignia. The "violet with black borders" division in conferred for services to public health if the services have been rendered at the risk of one's own life. If this element of risk is lacking, the "purple with white borders" division is conferred. The "white with black borders" division is conferred for charitable services at personal risk. The "all white" division is conferred for outstanding acts of mercy.

Each division has four classes:

Classes and insignia for the "white with black borders" division are:

1. *Grand Cross*, which wears the Badge of the Order (359) on a sash and the Star of the Order (361).

2. *Cross 1st Class*, which wears the Star of the Order (361).

3. *Cross 2nd Class*, which wears the Star of the Order (361), but smaller, on on a necklet.

4. *Cross 3rd Class*, which wears the Badge of the Order (359) on a chest riband.

The *Badge of the Order* is an 8-pointed gold star resting upon a red-enamelled Maltese Cross. The star is enamelled in colours corresponding to the divisions of the Order: violet with black borders (360), purple with white borders, white with black borders (359) and all white. The centre medallion, within a white scroll bearing the inscription "Fortitudo – Charaitas – Abnegation" (Fearlessness – Charity – Abnegation), bears an 8-petalled pale blue rose, and below is a symbolic picture group representing charity. The reverse medallion bears only the rose.

The *Star of the Order*, which varies in size according to class, is identical with the Badge of the Order corresponding to the respective division, except that the Star bears a filigree ornamentation between the points.

The *Riband of the Order*, according to division, is violet with black border stripes (360), purple with white border stripes, white with black border stripes (359) or plain white. As a chest riband it is worn with a supporting bar.

362. The Order of "Mérito Agricola" *(Orden Civil del Mérito Agricola)* was instituted on 1st December 1905 and renewed on 14th October 1942. Its present statutes date from 14th December 1942. The Order may be conferred on Spaniards and on foreigners for eminent services to Spanish agriculture, its institutions and industry. The number of members in the two highest classes of the Order is restricted. The Order is administered by the Ministry of Agriculture.

The Order has three classes, the 2nd Class being divided into two degrees:

1. *Grand Cross*, which wears the Badge of the Order (362) on a sash and a Star of the Order identical with the Badge of the Order and in the size (361) corresponding to the Grand Cross Class.

2^1. *Commander by Number*, which wears the same Star of the Order as 1st Class, but smaller and in silver.

2^2. *Commander*, which wears the Badge of the Order (362) in silver on a necklet.

3. *Knight*, which wears the Badge of the Order (362) in silver on a chest riband.

The *Badge of the Order* is an 8-pointed star, in gold for 1st Class, in silver for 2nd and 3rd Classes, with green-enamelled rays. The motif of the centre medallion is a ploughing woman. On the Badge of the Order for 3rd Class and the Medal (see below) the motif is a ploughing man. The medallion bears the legend "Mérito Agricola" (For agricultural services) on a white background surrounded by a wreath of figures symbolizing agriculture. At the top, the wreath bears a crown symbolizing the Spanish monarchy, and at the base the Spanish State coat of arms, both in gold, which are also on the Badge of the Order for 2nd and 3rd Classes.

The *Star of the Order*, which varies in size according to class, is identical with the Badge of the Order. The Grand Cross Star is in gold and the Star for 2nd Class in silver.

The *Riband of the Order* is plain green. As a chest riband it is worn with a supporting bar.

The *"Mérito Agricola" Medal* is

The Order of Africa: Star of the Order

attached to the Order. It was instituted on 14th December 1942, and wears the Badge of the Order (362), in bronze and without enamel, on a chest riband.

363. The Order of Africa *(Orden de Africa)* was instituted on 26th October 1933 and renewed on 11th November 1950. The Order may be conferred on civilians and on the military, Spaniards and native people, for services to public interests on the African continent. It may also be conferred on foreigners. Holders of the two highest classes of the Order are given special titles. The Order ranks after the *Civilian Order of Merit* (364–365). The Spanish Head of State is the Grand Master of the Order.

The Order has five classes:

1. *Grand Officer*, which wears the Badge of the Order (363) on a sash and the Star of the Order.

2. *Commander with Star*, which wears the same Star of the Order as for 1st Class.

3. *Commander*, which wears the Badge of the Order (363) on a necklet.

4. *Officer*, which wears the Badge of the Order (363), but smaller, on a chest riband.

5. *Silver Medal*, which wears the Badge of the Order (363) in silver, without enamel and smaller, on a chest riband.

The *Badge of the Order*, which varies in size according to class, consists of a golden ring whose centre bears the Spanish State coat of arms garlanded by green palm leaves. At the base, the ring bears a crescent.

The *Star of the Order* is an 8-pointed gold star with centred plain rays. In the centre, the Star bears the Badge of the Order.

The *Riband of the Order* is green with red border stripes. As a chest riband it is worn with a supporting bar.

364–365. The Civil Order of Merit *(Orden del Mérito Civil)* was instituted by Royal Decree on 25th June 1926, renewed by the Republican Government in 1931 and by the present Government on 7th November 1942. Its present statutes date from 3rd February 1945, with amendments dated 26th July 1957. The Order may be conferred for services of an ordinary civil nature, for outstanding effort in work and for profitable initiative. It may also be conferred on foreigners. The Order ranks before the *Order of Africa* (363). The Spanish Head of State is the Grand Master of the Order.

The Order has six classes:

1. *Knight with Collar*, which wears the Badge of the Order (364), with pencils of rays behind the arms of the cross, on a collar, or on a sash of a special colour

pattern, and the Star of the Order (365), both with a laurel garland between the arms of the cross.

2. *Grand Cross*, which wears the Badge of the Order (364) on a sash and the Star of the Order (365).

3. *Commander by Number*, which wears the Star of the Order (365), but smaller and in silver.

4. *Commander*, which wears the Badge of the Order (364) on a necklet.

5. *Officer*, which wears the Badge of the Order (364) on a chest riband.

6. *Knight*, which wears the Badge of the Order (364) in silver on a chest riband (gentlemen) or on a bow (ladies).

The *Badge of the Order* is a white-edged blue-enamelled "St. Andrew's Cross" in gold, in silver for 6th Class, with faceted pencils of rays between the arms of the cross. The motif of the centre medallion is a female figure who, as a symbol of the civil virtues, tempers a sword in the holy fire, garlanded by a blue riband with the inscription "Al Mérito Civil" (For civil merit), the motto of the Order. At the top, the cross bears a crown, symbolizing the Spanish monarchy, and has a green-enamelled laurel wreath as a mounting.

The *Star of the Order*, which varies in size according to class and sex, is identical with the Badge of the Order, but without mounting wreath and with pencils of rays behind the arms of the cross. The Star for Knight with Collar and Grand Cross is in gold, and the Star for 3rd Class is in silver.

The *Collar of the Order*, which is gold, consists of five laurel wreathed medallions, with the same motif as the centre medallion of the Badge of the Order, and five white-edged, blue-enamelled "St. Andrew's Crosses" on which rest a laurel wreath and which have the Spanish State coat of arms of 1938 as a supporting link.

The *Riband of the Order* is blue with a narrow white centre stripe. As a chest riband it is worn with a supporting bar. The sash for Knight with Collar is blue with narrow white border stripes.

The *Silver Cross of Merit* is attached

to the Order. It wears the Badge of the Order (364) in silver, without enamel and without pencils of rays between the arms of the cross, on a chest riband.

366. The "Yoke and Arrows" Order *(Orden Imperial del Yugo y las Flechas)* was instituted on 1st October 1937 under the title of *The Grand Imperial Order of the Red Arrows* as the present State's highest reward. Its present title and statutes date from 27th January 1943. The Order may be conferred on Spaniards and on foreigners for outstanding services to the Nation. Holders of the three highest classes of the Order receive special titles. The Spanish Head of State is the Grand Master of the Order.

The Order has five classes:

1. *Grand Collar*, which wears a Collar of the Order, with the Spanish eagle holding the "yoke and arrows" symbol in its claws as the Badge of the Order.

2. *Grand Cross*, which wears the Badge of the Order (366) on a sash and a Star of the Order identical with the Badge of the Order and in the size of 372.

3. *Commander with Star*, which wears the Badge of the Order (366) on a necklet and the same Star of the Order as for 2nd Class, but with silver rays behind the "yoke and arrows" symbol.

4. *Commander*, which wears the Badge of the Order (366) on a necklet.

5. *Medal*, which wears a gold medallion, on which rests a Badge of the Order, on a chest riband.

The *Badge of the Order* is a black-enamelled Maltese Cross in gold with a ring between the arms of the cross. Within the ring, the cross bears the red-enamelled "yoke and arrows" symbol of the Order, five arrows penetrating a yoke, an old Spanish symbol of the Moorish yoke broken by the Spaniards and at present the emblem of the Spanish Phalangist Party. The yoke bears the inscription "Cæsaris Cæsari Dei Deo" (To Cæsar, Cæsar's – To God, God's) (St. Matthew 22 v. 21.), the motto of the Order.

The *Star of the Order* is identical

The Civil Order of Merit: Collar of the Order with Badge of the Order, Knight with Collar

with the Badge of the Order, but for 3rd Class it has silver rays behind the "yoke and arrows" symbol.

The *Collar of the Order*, which is gold, consists of 46 links with the "yoke and arrows" symbol and the House of Burgundy's red-enamelled windmill arms in a golden ring alternately. At the front, the Collar bears the Spanish eagle with the "yoke and arrows" symbol in its claws.

The *Riband of the Order* is red with a wide black centre stripe. As a chest riband it is worn with a supporting bar.

367–368. The Order of Alfonso X, the Wise *(Orden Civil de Alfonso X el Sabio)* was instituted by decree on 11th April 1939 as a successor to the *Civil Order of Alfonso X* instituted in 1902 for similar services. Its present statutes date from 14th April 1945. The Order may be conferred individually and collectively for outstanding services to scientific research and teaching or to literature and art, and also for special services in the field of education or of general cultural significance. It may also be conferred on foreigners. The number of members of the two highest classes of the Order is restricted. The Order is administered by the Ministry of Education, but the Collar and the Grand Cross are conferred by the Head of State, who is the Grand Master of the Order.

The Order has three classes, 1st and 2nd Classes each being divided into two degrees:

1. (i) *Collar*, which wears a Collar of the Order with a Badge of the Order (367), but larger.

(ii) *Grand Cross*, which wears the Badge of the Order (367) on a sash and a Star of the Order identical with the Badge of the Order and in the same size as 372, corresponding to the Grand Cross Class.

2. (i) *Commander with Star*, which wears the Badge of the Order (367) on a necklet and the same Star of the Order as for Grand Cross.

(ii) *Commander*, which wears the Badge of the Order (367) on a necklet.

3. *Cross*, which wears the Badge of the Order (367) on a chest riband.

The *Badge of the Order* is a red-enamelled fleury cross in gold with the arms of the cross in open-work. The obverse medallion bears a portrait of King Alfonso X in the centre on a blue background with the legend "Alfonso X el Sabio Rey de Castilla y de Leon" (Alfonso X, the Wise, King of Castile and Leon) in Gothic script on a white background, and the reverse medallion bears a purple-coloured eagle with spread wings and claws resting on a blue globe.

The *Star of the Order* is identical with the Badge of the Order.

The *Collar of the Order*, which is gold, consists of 11 black-enamelled eagles with spread wings, of which one serving as a mounting link is of a special size, alternately linked together with six crowned "A"s for "Alfonso" and six Roman numerals "X".

The *Riband of the Order* is plain red. As a chest riband it is worn with a supporting bar.

The Medal of Alfonso X, the Wise (368) is attached to the Order. It has one class, *gold*, and is worn on a chest riband. The medal has the same motif as the obverse medallion of the Badge of the Order.

369. The Civil Order of Health *(Orden Civil de Sanidad)* was instituted on 8th November 1943 as the then-existing State's counterpart of the *Epidemic Cross* of 1938. Its present statutes date from 3rd January 1944. The Order may be conferred individually and collectively for services of a hygenic or sanitary nature, as well as for assistance or other services in the event of epidemics. It may be conferred irrespective of sex and nationality. The Order is administered by the Ministry of State.

The Order has three classes, the 2nd Class being divided into two degrees:

1. *Grand Cross*, which wears the Badge of the Order (369), but larger, on a sash, and a Star of the Order identical with the Badge of the Order but without supporting wreath, with faceted pencils of rays between the arms of the cross, and in the size (372) corresponding to the Grand Cross Class.

2. (i) *Commander with Star*, which wears the Badge of the Order (369) on a necklet and the same Star of the Order as for Grand Cross.

(ii) *Commander*, which wears the Badge of the Order (369) on a necklet.

3. *Cross*, which wears the Badge of the Order (369) on a chest riband.

According to the Statutes, the Badge of the Order for Grand Cross must be larger than for the other classes. This, however, is not the case in practice.

The Order of Alfonso X, the Wise: Collar of the Order, 1st Class

The *Badge of the Order* is a white-enamelled Maltese Cross in gold with plain pencils of rays between the arms of the cross. The obverse medallion bears the Spanish State coat of arms in the centre with the legend "Al Mérito Sanitario" (For sanitary services) on a red background, and the reverse medallion bears the emblem of national health on a blue background. The Badge

of the Order has a wreath of oak and palm leaves as a mounting link.

The *Star of the Order* is identical with the Badge of the Order, but without supporting wreath and with faceted pencils of rays between the arms of the cross.

The *Riband of the Order* is yellow with black border stripes. As a chest riband it is worn with a supporting bar.

370–373. The Order of San Raimundo de Penafort (*Orden de la Cruz de San Raimundo de Penafort*) was instituted on 23rd January 1944. Its present statutes date from 9th January 1950. The Order is named after the Catholic author and teacher of Canon Law, Raimundo, who was born in the Castle of Penafort in Catalonia about 1180, died in 1275 and was canonized in 1601. The Order may be conferred on civil servants engaged in the administration of justice and professional lawyers for meritorious services, and also on persons who have contributed to the promotion of law and equity, to the study of Canon Law and documents, and to the legislative work of the State. It may also be conferred on authors of legal publications of fundamental importance. It is conferrable on foreigners. The Order is administered by the Ministry of Justice.

The Order has five classes:

1. *Grand Cross*, which wears the Badge of the Order (370) on a collar (371) in gold and with other ornamentation, as well as with the Badge of the Order (370) on a sash and Star of the Order (372) in gold.

2. *Cross of Honour*, which wears the Badge of the Order (370) on a collar (371) and the Star of the Order (372).

3. *Cross of Distinction, 1st Class*, which wears the Badge of the Order (373) on a necklet and a Star of the Order identical with the Badge of the Order and in the size (372) corresponding to Grand Cross Class.

4. *Cross of Distinction, 2nd Class*, which wears the Badge of the Order (373) on a necklet.

5. *Cross*, which wears the Badge of the Order (373), without loops between the arms of the cross, on a chest riband.

The *Badge of the Order* is a white-enamelled Maltese Cross, in gold for 1st and 2nd Classes and in silver for the other classes, with loops between the arms of the cross except for 5th Class. In the centre the cross bears a portrait of San Raimundo with halo,

The San Raimundo de Penafort Medal

garlanded by a blue scroll with the inscription "In Jure Merita" (Services to Law). Behind the vertical arms of the cross the sword of justice can be seen faintly. The vertical arms also bear the inscription "S. Raymundus Pennaforti" (San Raimundo de Penafort).

The *Star of the Order* is identical with the Badge of the Order, but for 1st and 2nd Classes it has palm branches between the arms of the cross instead of loops. The Grand Cross Star is in gold. The Star for 2nd and 3rd Classes is in silver.

The *Collar of the Order* consists of 11 frame-shaped links with loops, interlinked with 12 smaller blue-enamelled rectangular links, alternately with a picture of San Raimundo and with a white-enamelled shield bearing the symbol of justice, the Scales of Justitia. As a supporting link it has a palm wreath. The Grand Collar is in gold; the Collar for 2nd Class in silver. The frame-shaped links on the Grand Cross Collar are red-enamelled, and the blue-enamelled rectangular links bear golden flames at the top and base.

The *Riband of the Order* is crimson with narrow blue selvedges. As a chest riband it is worn mounted in triangular fashion.

The *San Raimundo de Penafort Medal* is attached to the Order. It has four degrees, *gold with enamel, silver with enamel, bronze with silver* and *pure bronze*, and is worn on the chest riband of the Order.

The medal is an 8-edged medallion. Within the legend "Cruz de San Raymundo de Penafort – Ministerio de Justica" (San Raimundo de Penafort's Medal) and above a horizontal scroll with the inscription "Constantia et Virtute" (Perseverance and steadiness), the obverse bears in relief a miracle ascribed to San Raimundo – his walking on the sea from Soller on Mallorca to Barcelona – and beneath the scroll are the Scales of Justitia. The reverse bears the inscription "Insigni Doctori Sancto Raymundus Pennaforti Principi in Juris Studio et Eminenti Hispaniæ Filio Honorem Redditur ac Venerationem – Victor – 23 D Enero 1944" (With the Medal of the teacher San Raimundo de Penafort, the greatest in legal pursuit and Spain's eminent son, honour and respect is given – Victor – 23rd January 1944).

374–377. The Military Order of Merit (*Orden del Mérito Militar*) was instituted on 3rd August 1864. Its present statutes date from 12th December 1942. The Order may be conferred on army officers for military services, including foreign officers. It may also be conferred with a pension, but only exceptionally to foreigners. The Order is administered by the War Ministry.

The Order has two divisions, one for *war services*, characterised by a red-enamelled Badge of the Order, and one for *military services in general*, characterised by a white-enamelled Badge of the Order.

Each division has four classes, whose order of sequence is the reverse of that generally employed for Orders.

Classes and insignia for the division of *war services* are:

1. *1st Class*, which wears the Badge of the Order (376) on a chest riband.

2. *2nd Class*, which wears the Star of the Order (374).

3. *3rd Class*, which wears the Star of the Order (375) with a red-enamelled Badge of the Order.

4. *4th Class*, or *Grand Cross*, which wears the Badge of the Order (376) on a sash and the Star of the Order (375), but larger, and a red-enamelled Badge of the Order with the name plate beneath the crown in silver.

Classes and insignia for the division of *military services in general* are:

1. *1st Class*, which wears the Badge of the Order (377) on a chest riband.

2. *2nd Class*, which wears the Star of the Order (374) with a white-enamelled Badge of the Order.

3. *3rd Class*, which wears the Star of the Order (375).

4. *4th Class*, or *Grand Cross*, which wears the Badge of the Order (377) on a sash and Star of the Order (375), but larger, with the name plate beneath the crown in silver on the Badge of the Order.

If the Order is conferred with a pension, the Badge of the Order, according to division, bears a white or red transverse stripe on the three lower arms of the cross, and the silver cross (see below) has a gold crown.

The *Badge of the Order*, according to division, is a red or white-enamelled Greek Cross in gold pendant on a crown. Beneath the crown, the cross bears a name plate on which is engraved the date of the conferment. The obverse medallion bears the escutcheon of the armed forces and the reverse medallion bears the monogram "MM" for "Mérito Militar" (Military Merit).

The *Star of the Order*, which varies in size according to class, is an 8-pointed faceted star, in silver for 2nd Class, in gold for 3rd and 4th Classes. According to division, the Star bears a red or white-enamelled Badge of the Order, but with the crown on the top arm of the cross and, for 4th Class, the name plate beneath the crown in silver. It also bears two towers and two lions symbolizing Castile and Leon, in gold for the silver Star and in silver for the gold Star.

The *Riband of the Order*, according to division, is red with a white centre stripe or white with a red centre stripe. As a chest riband it is worn with a mounting bar.

The Silver Cross is attached to the Order. It was instituted in 1868 and consists of a Badge of the Order (376 or 377), in silver without enamel, on a chest riband.

378–380. The Naval Order of Merit (*Orden del Mérito Naval*) was instituted in 1866. Its present statutes date from 1st April 1891. The Order may be conferred on naval officers, including foreign officers, for services to the Navy. It may also be conferred with a pension, but in this case only to foreigners exceptionally. The Order is administered by the War Ministry.

The Order has two divisions, one for *war services* characterised by a red-enamelled Badge of the Order, and one for *naval services in general* characterised by a white-enamelled Badge of the Order.

Each division has four classes, whose order of sequence is the reverse of that normally employed for Orders.

Classes and insignia for the division for *war services* are:

1. *1st Class*, which wears the Badge of the Order (379) on a chest riband.

2. *2nd Class*, which wears the Star of the Order (378) with a red-enamelled Badge of the Order.

3. *3rd Class*, which wears the Star of the Order (378) in gold with towers and lions in silver, and a red-enamelled Badge of the Order.

4. *4th Class* or *Grand Cross*, which wears the Badge of the Order (379) on a sash and the same Star of the Order as for 3rd Class, but larger. The name plate beneath the crown on the Badge of the Order is in silver.

Classes and insignia for the division for *naval services in general* are:

1. *1st Class*, which wears the Badge

of the Order (380) on a chest riband.

2. *2nd Class*, which wears the Star of the Order (378).

3. *3rd Class*, which wears the Star of the Order (378) in gold with towers and lions in silver.

4. *4th Class* or *Grand Cross*, which wears the Badge of the Order (380) on a sash and the same Star of the Order as for 3rd Class, but larger. The name plate beneath the crown on the Badge of the Order is in silver.

If the Order is conferred with a pension, the Badge of Order bears on the three lower arms of the cross a transverse stripe in the same colour as the anchor, and the silver cross (see below) has a gold crown.

The *Badge of the Order*, according to division, is a red or white-enamelled Latin Cross in gold pendant on a crown. Beneath the crown the cross bears a name plate on which the date of conferment is engraved. The obverse bears a gold anchor on red-enamelled Badges of the Order, and a blue anchor on white-enamelled Badges of the Order. The reverse has no ornamentation.

The *Star of the Order*, which varies in size according to class, is an 8-pointed faceted star, in silver for 2nd Class and in gold for 3rd and 4th Classes. According to division, the Star bears a red-enamelled or white-enamelled Badge of the Order, for 4th Class with the name plate beneath the crown in silver, as well as two towers and two lions symbolizing Castile and Leon, in gold for the silver Star and in silver for the gold Star.

The *Riband of the Order*, which is common to both divisions, is yellow with red border stripes, the national colours of Spain. As a chest riband it is worn with a mounting bar.

The Silver Cross is attached to the Order. It consists of the Badge of the Order (379 or 380) in silver without enamel, but if conferred for war services, on a red background, on a chest riband.

381–382. The Air Force Order of Merit (*Cruz del Mérito Aeronáutico*) was instituted on 30th November 1945. The decoration may be conferred on officers of the Air Force, including foreign officers. It may also be conferred with a pension, but in that case to foreigners only exceptionally. The decoration is administered by the War Ministry.

The decoration has two divisions, one for *war services* characterised by a red-enamelled Badge of the Order, and one for *aeronautical services in general* characterised by a white-enamelled Badge of the Order.

Each division has three classes, whose order of sequence is the reverse of that normally employed for orders and decorations.

Classes and insignia for the division of *war services* are:

1. *1st Class*, which wears a Badge of the Order (381) on a chest riband.
2. *2nd Class*, which wears the Star of the Order (374) with the red-enamelled Badge of the Order appertaining to this Order.
3. *3rd Class* or *Grand Cross*, which wears the Badge of the Order (381) on a sash and the Star of the Order (375) with the red-enamelled Badge of the Order appertaining to this Order.

Classes and insignia for the division for *aeronautical services in general* are:

1. *1st Class*, which wears the Badge of the Order (382) on a chest riband.
2. *2nd Class*, which wears the Star of the Order (374) with the white-enamelled Badge of the Order appertaining to this Order.
3. *3rd Class* or *Grand Cross*, which wears the Badge of the Order (382) on a sash and the Star of the Order (375) with the white-enamelled Badge of the Order appertaining to this Order.

If the decoration is conferred with a pension, the Badge of the Order, according to division, bears a white or red diagonal stripe on the three lower arms of the cross, and the silver cross (see below) has a gold name plate.

The *Badge of the Order*, according to division, is a red-enamelled or white-enamelled Greek Cross in gold pendant on a crown. Beneath the crown, the cross bears a name plate on which the date of conferment is engraved. The obverse bears as a centre medallion the escutcheon of the Armed Forces in a crowned pair of wings, and the reverse medallion bears the monogram "MA" for "Mérito Aeronáutica" (for aeronautical services) on a red background.

The *Star of the Order* is an 8-pointed faceted star, in silver for 2nd Class and in gold for 3rd Class. According to division, the Star bears a red-enamelled or white-enamelled Badge of the Order without crown, and also two towers and two lions symbolizing Castile and Leon, in gold for the silver Star and in silver for the gold Star.

The *Riband of the Order*, according to division, is red with a white centre stripe or white with red border stripes. As a chest riband it is worn with a mounting bar.

The *Silver Cross* is attached to the decoration. It was instituted in 1945 and it consists of a Badge of the Order (381 or 382), in silver without enamel, on a chest riband.

ITALY

383–387. The Order of Merit (*Ordine "Al Merito della Repubblica Italiana"*) was instituted on 3rd March 1951 and was provided with statutes on 31st October 1952. The Order, which replaces the two monarchial Orders, *The Order of Saint Mauritius and Saint Lazarus* and *The Order of the Crown*, may be conferred on men and on women, Italians and foreigners, for services to the nation in the fields of science, literature, art and trade, and for services in the promotion of public welfare and to social, philanthropic or humanitarian undertakings, and also for outstanding civil and military service. The Italian President is the Grand Master of the Order.

The Order has five classes:

1. *Grand Cross*, which wears the Badge of the Order (383), but larger, on a sash and the Star of the Order (385). If conferred *with collar*, the Badge of the Order (383) is worn on a collar (384).

2. *Grand Officer*, which wears the Badge of the Order (383) on a necklet (gentlemen) or on a bow (ladies), and the Star of the Order (385), but smaller.

3. *Commander*, which wears the Badge of the Order (383) on a necklet (gentlemen) or on a bow (ladies).

4. *Officer*, which wears the Badge of the Order (386) on a chest riband with rosette.

5. *Knight*, which wears the Badge of the Order (387) on a chest riband.

Grand Cross with Collar is conferred exclusively on foreign Heads of State and on Grand Cross Knights for services of outstanding importance.

The *Badge of the Order* is a white-enamelled Greek Cross in gold with the 5-pointed star of Italy in the centre and the Roman eagle in the angles of the cross. The cross is pendant on a mural crown, an old Roman symbol conferred on the first legionary to breach an enemy wall. Obverse and reverse are identical.

The *Star of the Order*, which varies in size according to class, is an 8-pointed faceted silver star with a Badge of the Order, without crown, in the centre.

The *Collar of the Order*, which is gold, consists of 22 links, eleven 5-pointed stars and ten ornamented acanthus flowers, and the ornamented monogram "RI" for "Repubblica Italiana" (The Republic of Italy) as a mounting link.

The *Riband of the Order* is green with narrow red border stripes.

388–390. The Military Order of Italy *(Ordine Militare d'Italia)* was instituted on 14th August 1815 by King Victor Emanuel I of Sardinia as the *Military Order of Savoy*, and renewed on 28th September 1855 by King Victor Emanuel II of Sardinia, later King Victor Emanuel I of Italy. The Order was reorganized by the Italian Republic on 9th January 1956, and at the same time its name was changed to *The Military Order of Italy*. The Order may be conferred on personnel of the Italian Armed Forces on land, sea and in the air, who, in war and

in peace, have given proof of responsibility, capability and bravery. It may also be conferred on military units and on foreigners. In the case of Italian citizens, a pension is attached to the Order to a limited extent. The Italian President is the Grand Master of the Order.

The Order has five classes:

1. *Grand Cross*, which wears the Badge of the Order (389), but larger on a sash and the Star of the Order (388).

2. *Grand Officer*, which wears the Badge of the Order (389) on a necklet, and the Star of the Order (388), but smaller.

3. *Commander*, which wears the Badge of the Order (389) on a necklet.

4. *Officer*, which wears the Badge of the Order (390) on a chest riband.

5. *Knight*, which wears the Badge of the Order (390), but without trophy, on a chest riband.

The *Badge of the Order* is a white-enamelled pointed Mantua Cross in gold with a garland of oak and laurel leaves between the arms of the cross. The obverse medallion bears a set of crossed swords with the dates "1855" at the top and "1947", the year of the foundation of the Republic, at the base, on a red background. The reverse medallion bears the monogram "RI" for "Repubblica Italiana" (The Republic of Italy) with the legend "Al Merito Militare" (For military services). The Badge of the Order for 1st–3rd Classes has a garland of oak and laurel leaves as a mounting link, and the Badge of the Order for 4th Class has a trophy. The Badge of the Order for 5th Class has no mounting link.

The *Star of the Order*, which varies in size according to class, is an 8-pointed faceted silver star with a Badge of the Order in the centre without mounting link.

The *Riband of the Order* is dark blue with a crimson centre stripe, the colours of the House of Savoy.

391. The War Cross *(Croce di Guerra al Valore Militare)* was instituted on 18th

January 1918 as *The War Cross of Merit*, and during the Second World War it was renewed in its present form. The decoration may be conferred for meritorious war services over a long period of time where acts of bravery have not earned a higher decoration.

The Cross is a Greek Cross in bronze. The obverse bears the 5-pointed star of Italy in the centre. The reverse bears on the upper arm of the cross the monogram "RI" for "Repubblica Italiana" (The Republic of Italy), and the lower arm of the cross bears an upright Roman sword entwined with oak branches. The transverse arms bear the inscription "Valore Militare" (Military valour). The Cross is worn on a blue and white striped chest riband.

392–394. The Order of "Stella della Solidarietà Italiana" *(Ordine della Stella Solidarietà Italiana)* was instituted on 27th January, 1947. Its present statutes date from 20th January 1949. The Order may be conferred on Italians and on foreigners who have contributed to the re-building of Italy to a special extent. The Italian President is the Grand Master of the Order.

The Order has three classes:

1. *1st Class*, which wears the Star of the Order (392).

2. *2nd Class*, which wears the Badge of the Order (393) on a chest riband designed for alteration into a necklet.

3. *3rd Class*, which wears the Badge of the Order (304) on a chest riband.

The *Badge of the Order* is the 5-pointed Star of Italy in gilt-bronze, with flame-like rays between the points for 2nd Clss. The obverse medallion bears a group of figures in relief symbolizing the Good Samaritan. The reverse medallion bears the inscription "Anno 1948" in Roman figures with the legend "Stella della Solidarietà Italiana" (The Star of Italian Unity). The Badge of the Order has an oval laurel wreath as a mounting link.

The *Star of the Order* is identical with the Badge of the Order for 2nd Class, but without mounting wreath.

The *Riband of the Order* is green with narrow red-white border stripes, the national colours of Italy.

THE VATICAN STATE

The Order of Christ *(Militia Domini Nostri Iesu Christi)* or *(Ordine Supremo del Cristo)* is a branch of the *Order of the Knights Templar*, whose origin and history is described on page 8–9. The Order of the Knights Templar, which by about 1300 had become a dangerous power factor because of its immense riches, was dissolved in 1312 by Pope Clement V on the instigation of King Philip the Fair of France. In Portugal, however, King Dionysius allowed the Order to be recreated in 1317 under its original title "The Knights of Christ", or "The Christ Order", and he made over to them the property there of the Knights Templar. This was affirmed on 14th March 1319 by Pope John XXII on condition that the Pope was also entitled to confer the Order. Thus was the foundation laid for the split in the Order of Christ into a Portuguese and a Papal branch, which still exists to-day. The Papal Order was reorganised on 7th February 1905 by Pope Pius X. The Order is the highest Papal decoration. It is conferred very rarely, and then only on Heads of State and prominent statesmen of the Roman-Catholic faith who have rendered special services to the Church or to society generally.

The Order has one class, *Knight*, which wears the Badge of the Order on a collar and the Star of the Order. On ceremonial occasions, a special uniform is also worn.

The *Badge of the Order* is a red-enamelled Latin Cross in gold with outward bent arms, with a white Latin Cross in the centre (333). The cross is pendant on a crown.

The *Collar of the Order*, which is gold, consists of enamelled medallions with alternately the Papal coat of arms and the cross of the Badge of the Order surrounded by a laurel wreath, linked

The Order of Christ: Collar of the Order with Badge of the Order and Star of the Order

together by bossed figures. The Collar has a trophy as a mounting link.

The *Star of the Order* is an 8-pointed faceted silver star with the cross of the Badge of the Order in the centre surrounded by a laurel wreath.

The German Reich Chancellor, *Count Otto von Bismarck*, received the Order in 1885, the only Protestant so far. Among holders of the Order now living is the former German Federal Chancellor *Konrad Adenauer*.

395–397. The Order of the Golden Spur *(Ordo Militia Aurata,* or *Ordine dello Speron d'Oro o Milizia Aurata)* cannot be dated for certain. The assumption that Pope Sylvester I (314–335) was the institutor is probably not valid, but the Order is referred to as being conferred in 1539 under Pope Paul III. In 1747, the Badge of the Order was described in a Papal letter as an 8-pointed cross with a spur hanging on the lower arm of the cross. The Order was changed on 31st October 1841 by Pope Gregory XVI into an "Order of Saint Sylvester" in memory of the assumed founder, but with "Militia Aurata" (Golden militia) added to the name in memory of the original intention. It was re-instituted as an independent Order on 7th February 1905 by Pope Pius X. The Order is the second highest Papal decoration, and the highest for non-Roman Catholic Christians. The number of Knights is restricted to one hundred, but there were only ten in 1954. The Order may be conferred for preferential treatment for and defence of the Roman Catholic Church, for example by the signing of concordate or the granting of freedom to Catholic missions or churches, irrespective of confession or nationality. It may therefore be conferred not only on non-Roman Catholic Christians but also on non-Christians. The Order is conferred "Motu proprio", that is to say on the instigation of the Pope himself.

The Order has one class, *Knight*, which wears the Badge of the Order

(395) on a collar (396) (before 1929, on a necklet) and the Star of the Order (397). On ceremonial occasions a special uniform is also worn.

The *Badge of the Order* is a yellow-enamelled Maltese Cross in gold with the golden spur, the symbol of the Knights of the Church, hanging on the lower arm of the cross. The obverse medallion bears a crowned "*M*" for "Mary", the Immaculate Mother of Christ, the patroness of the Order, on a white background. The reverse medallion bears the date "1905" in Roman numerals with the legend "Pinus X. Restitutor" (Pius X. The Restorer).

The *Collar of the Order*, which is in gold, consists of links with alternately the monogram of Christ "XP", Greek for "CHR", and on 8-pointed star. The Collar has a trophy as a mounting link. The Collar is identical to that employed for *The Order of Saint Sylvester* (405–408) 1841–1905.

The *Star of the Order* is an 8-pointed faceted silver star with a Badge of the Order in the centre.

The *Riband*, which was used as a necklet instead of a collar before 1929, is red with silver-white border stripes.

Among the holders of the Order now living is King Frederik IX of Denmark.

398–401. The Order of Pius. *(Ordo Pianus,* or *Ordine Piano)* was instituted on 17th June 1847 by Pope Pius IX. The Order is named after Pope Pius IV who in 1559 instituted an older "Ordo Pianus" which only existed for a few years. The Order was re-organised on 7th February 1905 by Pope Pius X. Its present construction dates from 25th December 1957, and is the work of Pope Pius XII. The Order may be conferred as a reward for personal services to the Pope and the Papacy.

The Order has four classes, 3rd Class being divided into two degrees:

1. *Grand Collar*, which wears a Collar of the Order with the Badge of the Order (398), and the Star of the Order (399), both with a different medallion inscription.

2. *Grand Cross*, which wears the Badge of the Order (398) on a sash and the Star of the Order (399).

3. (i) *Commander with Star*, which wears the Badge of the Order (398) on a necklet and the Star of the Order (400).

(ii) *Commander*, which wears the Badge of the Order (398) on a necklet.

4. *Knight*, which wears the Badge of the Order (401) on a chest riband.

The Grand Collar Class is reserved for foreign Heads of State.

The *Badge of the Order* is a blue-enamelled 8-pointed pencilled star in gold with flame-like pencils of rays between the points. The obverse medallion bears the name of the founder on a white background with the legend "Virtuti et Merito" (For distinction and merit) on a gold background, and the reverse medallion bears the date "Anno 1847" in Roman numerals. On the Badge of the Order for Grand Collar, the obverse medallion bears the inscription "Ordo Pianus – A Pio XII Avctvs" (The Order of Pius – Extended by Pius XII), and the reverse medallion bears the date "Anno 1957" in Roman numerals.

The *Star of the Order* is identical with the Badge of the Order, but with faceted silver pencils of rays between the points. The centre medallion on the Star of the Order for Grand Collar bears the same inscription as the obverse medallion of the corresponding Badge of the Order.

The *Chain of the Order*, which is in gold, consists of medallions alternating with the official Papal coat of arms and the family coat of arms of Pius XII. The mounting link of the Collar is the Papal tiara between two doves.

The *Riband of the Order* is blue with two red border stripes.

A special uniform to be worn on ceremonial occasions is part of the Order.

402–404. The Order of Saint Gregory the Great *(Ordo Sanctus Gregorius Magnus* or *Ordine di San Gregorio Magno)* was instituted on 1st September 1831 by Pope Gregory XVI as a reward to faithful citizens and Austrian troops for their support of the wordly power of the Holy See in the Papal states of that time in the politically restless period around 1830. The Order was reorganised on 7th February 1905 by Pope Pius X. The Order, which is named after Pope Gregory I, the Great (590–604), the founder of the worldly power of the Holy See, may today be conferred as an honourable reward for indisputable fidelity and zeal displayed in services to the Holy See.

The Order has a *military* and a *civil* division, whose Badges of the Order differ from one another by having as a mounting link a trophy and a laurel wreath respectively.

Each division has three classes, the 2nd Class being divided into two degrees:

1. *Grand Cross*, which wears the Badge of the Order (403–404) in Grand Cross size (231), on a sash and the Star of the Order (402).

2. (i) *Commander with Star*, which wears the Badge of the Order (403–404), in Commander Cross size (405), on a sash and the Star of the Order (402), but smaller.

(ii) *Commander*, which wears the same Badges of the Order as for 1st Degree on a necklet.

3. *Knight*, which wears the Badge of the Order (403–404) on chest riband.

The *Badge of the Order* is a red-enamelled Maltese Cross in gold, pendant on a trophy and a laurel wreath respectively, according to division. The obverse medallion bears a picture of Pope Gregory I on a blue background with the legend "S. Gregorius Magnus" (Saint Gregory the Great) and the reverse medallion bears the inscription "Pro Deo et Principi" (For God and the Prince).

The Star of the Order, which varies in size according to class, is an 8-pointed faceted silver star with a Badge of the Order without mounting link in the centre.

The *Riband of the Order* is red with wide yellow border stripes.

The Order of Pius: Collar of the Order with Badge of the Order and Star of the Order, Grand Collar

The Order includes a special uniform to be worn on ceremonial occasions.

405–408. The Order of Saint Sylvester *(Ordo Sanctus Silvestri Papae,* or *Ordine di San Silvestro Papa)* was instituted on 31st October 1841 by Pope Gregory XVI, who, in memory of the assumed founder, Pope Sylvester I (314–335), altered the *Order of the Golden Spur* (395–397) to an "Order of Saint Sylvester". In memory of the original Order, it had "Militia Aurarta" (Golden Militia) added to its name, and as such it bore on the Badge of the Order a spur hanging on the lower arm of the cross. With the re-creation of the original Order, the Order was altered on 7th February 1905 by Pope Pius X to the present Order of Merit. The Order may be conferred as a reward for both civil and military services which did not entail the conferment of the *Order of Saint Gregory the Great* (402–404).

The Order has three classes, the 2nd Class being divided into two degrees:

1. *Grand Cross*, which wears the Badge of the Order (405), but larger, on a sash (until 1905 on a collar (406)), and the Star of the Order (407).

2¹. *Commander with Star*, which wears the Badge of the Order (405) on a necklet and the Star of the Order (407), but smaller.

2². *Commander*, which wears the Badge of the Order (405) on a necklet.

3. *Knight*, which wears the Badge of the Order (408) on a chest riband.

The *Badge of the Order* is a white-enamelled Maltese Cross in gold with short pencils of rays between the arms of the cross. The obverse medallion bears a portrait of Pope Sylvester I on a blue background with the legend "Sanctus Silvestri P.M." (Saint Sylvester, Pope), "P.M." representing "Pontifex Maximus", the Pope's title. The reverse medallion bears the official Papal coat of arms with the legend "1841–1905", the dates of the re-creation and reorganisation of the Order.

The *Collar of the Order* which was used from 1841 to 1905 is the same as that used today for the *Order of the Golden Spur* (396).

The *Star of the Order*, which varies in size according to class, is an 8-pointed faceted silver star with a Badge of the Order in the centre.

The *Riband of the Order* is black with red border stripes and a red centre stripe.

A special habit of the Order is included for wear on ceremonial occasions.

409. The Papal Lateran Cross *(Crux Lateranum,* or *Croce Lateranense)* was instituted, in its present form, on 18th February 1903 by Pope Leo XIII as a reward for believers of both sexes for services to the Church in general and to the Head Church of Rome, the Basilica of *San Giovanni* in the *Lateran Palace*, to whose Head particularly is entrusted conferment.

The decoration has three degrees, *gold*, *silver* and *bronze*, which wear a Badge of the Order (409) on a chest riband.

The *Badge of the Order* is a Bisantata Cross which bears on the obverse, in medallions on the arms of the cross, portraits of the Apostles Peter, Paul and John, and John the Baptist. In the centre medallion is a portrait of Christ. All are in relief. On the reverse, the medallion bears the name of Christ and the Saints concerned. The medallions on the arms of the cross are interconnected by an ornamented ring. The cross has a laurel wreathed medallion as a mounting link with the inscription "Sacrosancta Lateranensis Ecclesia – Omnium Urbis et Orbis Ecclesiarum Mater et Caput" (The Most Reverend Lateran Church – the Mother and Head of the Church of every City and Country), distributed on the obverse and reverse.

The *Riband of the Order* is red with blue border stripes.

410. The Cross of Honour "Pro Ecclesia et Pontifice" *(Cruz* or *Croce "Pro Ecclesia et Pontifice")* was instituted on 17th July 1888 by Pope Leo XIII as a "memorial cross" for his 50 years' jubilee as a priest. It was, however, retained as a "Cross of Honour" as a reward for special devotion to the Church and the Holy See.

The Cross is a fleury cross in gold with embossed comets in the arms of the cross. Between these are Florentine fleur-de-lis symbolizing the coat of arms of the Pecci family, of which the founder was a member. The obverse medallion bears an embossed portrait of Pope Leo XIII, with the legend "Leo XIII P.M. Ann. X" (Leo XIII, Pope for 10 years) and the reverse medallion bears the official Papal coat of arms with the legend "Pro Ecclesia et Pontifice" (For Church and the Holy See). On the arms of the cross, the reverse also bears the inscription "Prid. Cal. Ian. 1888" (The Day Before January 1888 – 31st December 1887), the 50th anniversary of the founder's ordination. The Cross is worn on a red chest riband with white-edged yellow border stripes.

411–412. The Cross of Merit of the Sovereign Military Order of Malta *(Croce al Merito del Sovrano Militare Ordine di Malta)* was originally instituted in 1916 by the Grand Prior of the Grand Priorate of Austria and Bohemia, but was expanded in 1928 by the Grand Master in Rome to cover the whole Order of Malta (see No. 267). The present statutes of the decoration date from 30th June 1955. Conferment normally takes place on 24th June, the Day of John the Baptist, on 8th September, the anniversary of the termination of the Turkish siege of Malta in 1565, and on the anniversary of the election of the acting Grand Master.

The decoration has a *civil* and a *military* division. The civil division may be conferred on persons who have earned the gratitude of the Order, irrespective of sex, nationality, race or religion. The military division may only be conferred on members of the Order and – in the event of war – on military personnel of allied countries in exceptional cases.

Each division has six classes.

Classes and insignia for the *civil* division are:

1. *Collar of Merit*, which wears a Collar of the Order with a Badge of the Order (411) and the Star of the Order (412).

2. *Grand Cross of Merit with Star and Sash*, which wears the Badge of the Order (411) on a sash and the Star of the Order (412).

3. *Grand Cross of Merit with Star*, which wears the Badge of the Order (411) on a necklet, with gold-embroidered holly branches along the borders, and the Star of the Order (412).

4. *Cross of Merit 1st Class with Crown*, which wears the Badge of the Order (411), but smaller, on a necklet.

5. *Cross of Merit 1st Class*, which wears the Badge of the Order (267) on a chest riband equipped with a shield bearing the coat of arms of the Order.

6. *Cross of Merit 2nd Class*, which wears the Badge of the Order (267) on a chest riband.

Ladies, on whom the civil division of the Order only may be conferred, wear smaller insignia on ribands mounted as a bow.

The insignia are the same for both divisions, but the *military* Badges of the Order are provided with crossed swords and are worn on a special riband.

The *Badge of the Order* is a white-enamelled Greek Cross in gold with cleft arms, pendant on a crown for the four highest classes. The centre medallion bears the 8-pointed, white Maltese Cross on a red background with the legend "Mil. Ordo Equitum Melit. Bene Merenti" (The Military Knights' Order of Malta for the Well-deserving) on a white background.

The *Star of the Order* is an 8-pointed faceted silver star with a Badge of the Order in the centre.

The *Collar of the Order* for the Collar of Merit Class has not yet received its final design and is consequently not described in the statutes.

The *Riband of the Order* for the *civil* division is white with red border stripes, and for the *military* division red with white border stripes. When worn as a necklet for 3rd Class, it has gold-embroidered branches of holly along the

The Sovereign Military Order of Malta: Breast Cross, Knight of Obedience

borders. As a chest riband, it is mounted in a triangular fashion.

413–415. The Sovereign Military Order of Malta *(Sovrano Militare Ordine Ospedaliero di San Giovanni di Gerusalemme detto di Rodi e di Malta,* or simply *Sovrano Militare Ordine di Malta)*, whose origin and history was described on page 9–10, has had its headquarters in Rome since 1827. From here, the Order controls its extensive hospital and charitable work, mainly in Italy and Austria, but also in other countries. On non-Roman Catholic soil, for example England, related branches of the Order have exercised great significance.

The present constitution of the Order was published in a Papal Bull of 8th December 1956.

The Order is divided into five Grand Priorates and 14 National Associations, to which are added the Knights belonging neither to the Grand Priorate nor to an Association but who come directly under the Grand Master as "in gremio religionis".

The Members of the Order are included in three classes:

1. *Legal Knights* and *Religious Members of the Order*, who take the triple vow of chastity, obedience and poverty.

2. *Knights of Obedience*, who take a vow of obedience to their seniors with complete devotion to the Word of God and to the teaching of the Church.

3. *Honorary and Devout Knights and Dames, Religious Members "ad honorem", Magistral Religious Members, Knights of Grace and Devotion, Deserving Knights of Grace, Magistral Knights of Grace and Dames,* and *Donators* (benefactors).

Apart from the religious members and the two last degrees of the 3rd Class, the Knights, according to class and degree, must be able to prove a greater or lesser number of noble ancestors.

Legal Knights and *Knights of Obedience* as well as *Honorary Knights* and *Knights of Devotion* wear, as a Badge of the Order and on a black necklet, a white-enamelled Maltese Cross in gold with Florentine fleur-de-lis in the angles of the cross and pendant on a crown beneath a trophy with the coat of arms (413) of the Order. Legal Knights also wear, as a breast cross, the so-called "Profess Cross" (415), and Knights of Obedience wear a black enamelled silver rhomb with an inlaid white-enamelled Maltese Cross with Florentine fleur-de-lis in the angles of the cross.

The Knights of Grace and Devotion

wear the same Badge of the Order as the Honorary and Devout Knights, but with the coat of arms of the Order crowned by a helmet with a set of crossed swords above the crown (414), on a black necklet.

Deserving and *Magistral Knights of Grace* wear the same Badge of the Order as the Knights of Grace and Devotion, but, as regards the former, with the coat of arms of the Order garlanded by golden palm branches and, as regards the latter, with the coat of arms of the Order resting on a golden bow and without helmet and swords, both on a black necklet.

Donators wear the same Badge of the Order as Magistral Knights of Grace, but smaller and on a black chest riband.

The Riband of the Order, which is plain black, may be provided for holders of the highest offices of the Order, for example the offices of Grand Master and the Grand Prior, with gold-embroidered branches of holly along the borders.

Knights of every class and degree may, for quite outstanding services, be decorated with a Grand Cross, worn either on a black sash or on a black necklet with gold-embroidered branches of holly along the borders. Legal Knights, Knights of Obedience, Honorary Knights and Devout Knights decorated with the Grand Cross also receive the rank of "bali" with the title of Excellency.

Special insignia are attached to the various offices of the Order, and similarly the Order includes a special uniform.

JUGOSLAVIA
416–417. The Jugoslavian Grand Star *(Orden jugoslavenske velike zvezde)* was instituted on 1st February 1954 by Marshal Tito as a reward to foreign Heads of State for special endeavours in the development and strengthening of peaceful co-operation and friendly relations between the Federal People's Republic of Jugoslavia and other nations.

The Order has one class, which

wears the Badge of the Order (416) on a sash and the Star of the Order (417).

The *Badge of the Order* is a gold medallion with a wide ornamented border bearing five small fleur-de-lis. In the centre, the medallion bears the Jugoslav State coat of arms in stylized form on a blue background with the 5-pointed red star in rubies.

The *Star of the Order* is a 5-pointed faceted silver star with smaller ray points between the points. In the centre, the Star bears a Badge of the Order whose ornamented border is studded with ten diamonds. The ring around the State coat of arms has forty-two rubies.

The *Riband of the Order* is plain violet. It is worn as a sash with a bow mounted on the fan.

418–419. The Order of the Jugoslav Star *(Orden jugoslovenske zvezde)* was instituted on 1st February 1954 by Marshal Tito. Its present form dates from 1st March 1961. The Order may be conferred for outstanding cultural, political or scientific achievement and for service in the development and strengthening of peaceful co-operation and friendly relations between the Federal People's Republic of Jugoslavia and other nations.

The Order has three classes:

1. *1st Class*, which wears the Badge of the Order (416) on a sash and the Star of the Order (417), but both smaller and without diamonds and rubies.

2. *2nd Class*, which wears the Badge of the Order (418) on a necklet and the Star of the Order (419).

3. *3rd Class*, which wears the Badge of the Order (418) on a necklet.

The *Badge of the Order*, which varies in size according to class, is a gold medallion, round for 1st Class and oval for 2nd and 3rd Classes, with a wide ornamented border bearing five small fleur-de-lis. In the centre, the medallion bears the Jugoslav State-coat of arms in stylized form on a blue background with the 5-pointed red star in rubies. The Badge of the Order for 2nd and 3rd Classes has a wide ornamented yoke as a mounting link.

The *Star of the Order*, which varies in size according to class, is a 5-pointed faceted silver star with smaller ray points between the points. In the centre, the Star bears a Badge of the Order.

The *Riband of the Order* is plain violet. As a sash it is worn with a bow mounted on the fan.

420–423. The Order of the Jugoslav Flag *(Orden jugoslovenske zastave)* was instituted on 26th November 1947 by Marshal Tito. Its present construction dates from 1st March 1961. The Order may be conferred for outstanding contributions to the development and strengthening of peaceful co-operation and friendly relations between the Federal People's Republic of Jugoslavia and other nations.

The Order has five classes:

1. *1st Class*, which wears a sash with the flag motif of the Badge of the Order in gold (420) and the Star of the Order (421).

2. *2nd Class*, which wears the Badge of the Order (422) on a necklet and the same Badge of the Order as a breast star, but without mounting garland.

3. *3rd Class*, which wears the Badge of the Order (422) on a necklet.

4. *4th Class,* which wears the Badge of the Order (423) on a chest riband.

5. *5th Class*, which wears the Badge of the Order (423), but all in silver, on a chest riband.

The *Badge of the Order* is a 5-pointed silver star with pencils of 3-pointed rays in gold, in silver for 5th Class, between the points. The centre medallion bears the blue-white-red Jugoslav flag within a laurel garland in gold; for 4th and 5th Classes in silver and with the flag without enamel. The Badge of the Order for 2nd and 3rd Classes has a laurel wreath in gold as a mounting link.

The *Star of the Order* for *1st Class* is a 10-pointed silver star with a Badge of the Order in the centre. The *Star of the Order* for *2nd Class* is a Badge of the Order without mounting wreath.

The *Riband of the Order* is blue with red-white border stripes, the national colours of Jugoslavia. As a sash it is worn with a bow mounted on the fan, and as a chest riband it is mounted in a crossed fashion.

ALBANIA

Hero of the People *(Hero i Popullit)* is an honorary title, instituted in 1945, whose holders wear a gold star identical with the Soviet decoration for civilians and military who receive the honorary title "Hero of the Soviet Union", the *Medal of "The Golden Star"* (314), but the riband is provided with a horizontal black centre stripe.

Hero of Socialist Work *(Hero i Punës Socialiste)* is an honorary title instituted in 1945 whose holders wear a gold star identical with the Soviet decoration for civilians conferred with the corresponding Soviet honorary title, *The Gold Medal of the "Hammer and Sickle"* (315), but the riband is provided with a vertical black centre stripe.

The Order of Freedom *(Urdhëri i "Lirisë")* was instituted in 1945–1956. The Order may be conferred on civilians and on the military for notable contributions to the liberation of the country during the Italian and German occupation during the Second World War.

The Order has three classes, *1st to 3rd*

The Order of Freedom: Badge of the Order

Classes, which wear a Badge of the Order, varying in design according to class, as a breast star.

The *Badge of the Order* is a 5-pointed red-enamelled star, in gold for 1st Class, in silver for 2nd and 3rd Classes, with plain pencils of rays between the points. The centre medallion, which is silver for all classes, bears a symbolic picture of a woman bursting her chains. The laurel wreath around the centre medallion is gold for 1st and 2nd Classes and silver for 3rd Class.

When worn with uniform, a red *Riband of the Order* with one to three white stripes according to class is worn.

The Skanderbeg Order *(Urdhëri i "Skenderbeut")* was instituted in 1945–1956. The Order is named after Georg Kastriota (Skanderbeg), the son of an Albanian prince, who, in the middle of the fifteenth century, raised the flag of revolt against the Turks and drove them out of Albania. The Order may be conferred on senior officers for notable contributions during the battles for liberation against the Italian and German troops during the Second World War.

The Order has three classes, *1st to 3rd Classes*, which wear a Badge of the Order, varying in design according to class, as a breast star on the *right* side of the chest.

The Order of the Flag: Badge of the Order

The *Badge of the Order* is a 5-pointed, red-enamelled star, in gold for 1st Class, in silver for 2nd and 3rd Classes and without enamel, with plain pencils of rays between the points. The centre medallion, which is silver for all classes, bears a portrait of Georg Kastriota in profile. The laurel wreath around the centre medallion is gold for 1st and 2nd Classes and silver for 3rd Class.

When worn with uniform, a red *Riband of the Order* with one to three blue stripes according to class is worn.

The Order of the Flag *(Urdhëri i "Flamurit")* was instituted in 1945–56. The Order may be conferred on civilians and on military personnel who have distinguished themselves in the partisan war during the Second World War.

The Order has one class, which wears the Badge of the Order on a chest riband on the *right* side of the chest.

The *Badge of the Order* is a silver-gilt medallion which bears in the centre and behind marching troops a female figure symbolizing the Albanian fighting spirit. At the base, the medallion is garlanded by laurel branches, and at the

The Skanderbeg Order: Badge of the Order

top it is crowned by the 5-pointed red star of Communism.

The *Riband of the Order* is plain red. It is worn as a chest riband mounted in a crossed fashion.

The Order of the Partisan Star *(Urdhëri "Ylli Partizan")* was instituted in 1945–1956. The Order may be conferred on officers who have distinguished themselves in the partisan war during the Second World War.

The Order has three classes, *1st to 3rd Classes*, which wear a Badge of the Order, varying in design according to class, as a breast star on the *right* side of the breast.

The *Badge of the Order* is a 5-pointed red-enamelled star, in gold for 1st Class, in silver for 2nd class and in bronze for 3rd Class, resting on a garland consisting of a pair of crossed tobacco leaves.

When worn with uniform, a brown *Riband of the Order* with one to three stripes according to class is worn.

The Order of the Red Star *(Urdhëri "Ylli i Kuq")* was instituted in 1945–1956. The Order may be conferred on military personnel for special contributions in the fight for freedom during the Second World War.

The Order has one class, which wears a Badge of the Order on a chest riband.

The *Badge of the Order* is a 5-pointed red-enamelled silver whose centre medallion bears a picture of a soldier armed with a machine gun surrounded by a laurel wreath with the inscription "R.P.SH-IS". for "Republika Popullore Shqipéris" (The People's Republic of Albania) at the base.

The *Riband of the Order* is red with a silver-grey centre stripe. It is worn as a chest riband mounted in a crossed fashion.

SAN MARINO
424–426. The Order of Saint Marinus *(Ordine Equestre Civile e Militare di San Marino)* was instituted on 13th August

The Order of the Red Star: Badge of the Order

1859. The Order is named after the Holy Marinus who lived in the fourth or fifth century. According to tradition, he is said to have founded the monastry around which the present Republic was created. The Order is reserved for foreigners and may be conferred as a reward for outstanding civil or military services to the Republic, and also as a reward for humanitarian, artistic, political and scientific services which have contributed to raising the prestige of the Republic. Holders of the Order, who wear their insignia visibly, receive a military salute. The two acting Regents hold jointly the office of Grand Master of the Order.

The Order has five classes:

1. *Grand Cross*, which wears the Badge of the Order (425), but larger, on a sash and the Star of the Order (424).

2. *Grand Officer*, which wears the Badge of the Order (425) on a necklet and the Star of the Order (424), but smaller.

3. *Commander*, which wears the Badge of the Order (425) on a necklet.

4. *Officer*, which wears the Badge of the Order (426) on a chest riband with rosette.

5. *Knight*, which wears the Badge

of the Order (426) on a chest riband without rosette.

The Grand Cross Class is reserved for Sovereign Princes and Heads of State, 2nd and 3rd Classes are conferred on accredited diplomats and Embassy personnel, and 4th and 5th Classes are for other civil and military services.

The *Badge of the Order* is a white-enamelled Moline Cross in gold with golden towers in the angles of the cross and pendant on a crown symbolizing the sovereignty of the Republic. The obverse medallion bears a portrait of the Holy Marinus with the legend "San Martino Protettore" (Saint Marinus, Patron Saint) on a blue background, and the reverse medallion bears the coat of arms of the Republic on a white background with the legend "Merito Civile e Militare" (For civil and military services) on a blue background.

The *Star of the Order*, which varies in size according to class, is an 8-pointed faceted silver star bearing a white-enamelled moline cross in the centre with an oak and olive wreath between the arms of the cross. The centre medallion bears the inscription "Relinquo vos liberos ab utroque homine" (I leave you freed of any man) on a blue background.

The *Riband of the Order* is striped in blue and white, the colours of the Republic.

The Saint Marinus Medal is attached to the Order. It has three degrees, *gold*, *silver* and *bronze* and is worn on the chest riband of the Order. The Medal, which is octagonal, bears the coat of arms of the Republic on the obverse with the legend "Repubblica di San Marino" (The Republic of San Marino).The reverse bears the inscription "Marito" (Merit) surrounded by an oak wreath.

427–428. The Order of Saint Agatha *(Ordine Equestre di Saint' Agata)* was instituted on 5th June 1923 and extended in 1925. The Order, which is named after the Holy Agatha on whose feast-day, 5th February, Pope Clement XII re-established the sovereignty of the Republic in 1740 following the military occupation by Cardinal Alberoni. The Order is reserved for foreigners and may be conferred on persons who, through initiative, work or charity towards the pious foundations of the country, have earned the gratitude of the Republic. The Council of Acting Regents mutually occupy the office of Grand Master. The Order is conferred following recommendation by a twelve-man commission consisting of, *inter alia*, the two Acting Regents and the President of the pious foundations.

The Order has five classes:

1. *Grand Cross*, which wears the Badge of the Order (428), in Grand Cross size (429), on a sash and the Star of the Order (427).

2. *Grand Officer*, which wears the Badge of the Order (428), in Commander Cross size (425), on a necklet and the Star of the Order (427), but smaller.

3. *Commander*, which wear the Badge of the Order (428), in Commander Cross size (425), on a necklet.

4. *Officer*, which wears the Badge of the Order (428) on a chest riband with rosette.

5. *Knight*, which wears the Badge of the Order (428) on a chest riband.

The *Badge of the Order* is a white-enamelled Mantua Cross in gold with an oak and laurel wreath between the arms of the cross. The obverse medallion bears a portrait of the Holy Agatha with the legend "Sant' Agata Protettrice" (Saint Agatha – Patroness) on a white background. The reverse medallion bears the coat of arms of the Republic with the legend "Bene Merenti" (For the well-deserving).

The *Star of the Order*, which varies in size according to class, is an 8-pointed faceted star with gold and silver pencils of rays alternately. The Star bears a Badge of the Order in the centre.

The *Riband of the Order* is reddish-brown with yellow-white border stripes.

The Order of Saint George and Saint Constantine: Star of the Order, Military, 1st Class

GREECE

429–432. The Order of the Saviour *(Basilikon tagma toi soteros)*, which, according to the statutes, received its title in gratitude for the miraculous salvation of the nation from the Turkish yoke, was originally instituted on 31st July 1829 as a reward for distinction during the fight for freedom against the Turks in the 1820's, but it was not conferred until reinstituted in 1833 by King Otto I. At present the Order may be conferred on Greek citizens who have distinguished themselves in the fight for the Fatherland or who, in the various social fields within the country, have otherwise rendered outstanding services to Greece.

It may also be conferred on foreign personalities. The reigning Monarch is the Master of the Order.

The Order has five classes:

1. *Grand Cross*, which wears the Badge of the Order (429) on a sash and the Star of the Order (430).

2. *Grand Commander*, which wears the Badge of the Order (429) on a necklet and the Star of the Order (430), but both smaller.

3. *Commander*, which wears the Badge of the Order (429), but smaller, on a necklet.

4. *Gold Cross*, which wears the Badge of the Order (431) on a chest riband.

5. *Silver Cross*, which wears the Badge of the Order (432) on a chest riband.

Grand Cross Knights, when wearing large decorations with uniform, also wear the Badge of the Order for the lowest class on a chest riband in addition to the insignia appertaining to the class.

The *Badge of the Order* is a white-enamelled Maltese Cross in gold, for 5th Class in silver, with an oak and laurel wreath between the arms of the cross and pendant in a royal crown. The obverse medallion bears a portrait of the Saviour in enamel with the legend "E dexia sokheir, Kyrie, dedoxastai en iskyi" (In your Mighty Hand, Lord, the Power and the Glory) on a blue background. The reverse medallion bears a white Greek Cross with the legend "E en Argei dethnike ton Ellenikon synedeyses – 1829 (aoku)" (Founded at Argos by the National Assembly of the Hellenes – 1829) on a blue background.

The *Star of the Order*, which varies in

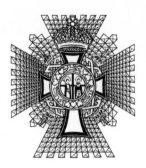

The Order of Saint George and Saint Constantine: Star of the Order, Military, 2nd Class

size according to class, is an 8-pointed faceted silver star, whose centre medallion bears the same motif as the obverse medallion of the Badge of the Order.

The *Riband of the Order* is pale blue white border stripes.

433–435. The Order of Saint George and Saint Constantine *(Basilikon oikogenaiakon tagma ton agion Georgioy kai Konstantinoi)* was instituted in 1936 by King George II. As is indicated by the Greek wording, the Order is The King's personal Order and a Royal Family Order instituted in memory of King George I and King Constantine XII, and in reverence to the Orthodox Saints whose names these kings bore. The Order is reserved for men, and its highest classes preferably for members of the Royal Family. It may be conferred as a reward for special services to the Greek Royal House. The reigning Monarch is the Master of the Order.

The Order has a *civil* and a *military* division, each with a collar and five classes of the Order:

1*. *Collar*, which wears the Badge of the Order (433) on a collar and a breast cross (435).

1. *1st Class*, which wears the Badge of the Order (433), with a crowned "G" in a back-to-back monogram in the angles of the cross, on a sash and Star of the Order.

2. *2nd Class*, which wears the same Badge of the Order as for 1st Class, but smaller and without lined crown, on a necklet and the Star of the Order.

3. *3rd Class*, which wears the same Badge of the Order as for 2nd Class on a necklet.

4. *4th Class*, which wears the same Badge of the Order as for 3rd Class, but smaller, on a chest riband.

5. *5th Class*, which wears the same Badge of the Order as for 4th Class, but in silver, on a chest riband.

The insignia are the same for both divisions, but the military Badges of the Order and the Star of the Order are provided with crossed swords.

The *Badge of the Order* is a red-rimmed white-enamelled Latin Cross in gold, in silver for 5th Class, with the crowned back-to-back monogram of the founder in the angles of the cross, except for the collar, and pendant on a royal crown. For Collar and 1st Class,

The Order of Saint George and Saint Constantine: Badge of the Order, Military, 4th and 5th Class

the crown is lined with red velvet. The centre medallion bears, resting on a blue cross on a golden background, a portrait of the Orthodox Saints Helena and Constantine garlanded with a golden border bearing three lions and nine hearts relating to the Danish origin of the Greek Royal Family.

The *Breast Cross* with Collar is identical to the Badge of the Order with Collar, but without the supporting crown and with a blue Latin Cross behind the centre medallion, which bears a crowned portrait of the Orthodox Saints Helena and Constantine garlanded by a blue scroll with the inscription "Iskhys mo e agape toy laoy" (The Love of the People, my Strength) King George I's motto.

The *Stars of the Order* for 1st and 2nd Class are respectively an 8-pointed silver star with plain rays and a faceted Maltese Cross in silver with semi-inlaid angles of the cross, both with a Badge of the Order in the centre.

The *Collar of the Order*, which is gold, consists of eight crowned lions each

garlanded by three hearts, alternately linked together with four crowned "G"s for "George" and four crowned "K"s for "Konstantine", all in back-to-back monogram. As a mounting link, it has a crowned double eagle with the crowned back-to-back monogram of the founder on their breast.

The *Riband of the Order* is dark blue with alternate red and white horizontal stripes as a border along the edges (433).

The Saint George and Saint Constantine Medal is attached to the Order. It has three degrees, *silver-gilt*, *silver* and *bronze*, and is worn on the chest riband of the Order. For the military division it is equipped with a set of crossed swords. On the obverse, the Medal bears the portrait of the founder with the legend "Georgios B basileys ton Hellenikon 1936" (George II, King of the Hellenes 1936).

436–437. The Order of Saint Olga and Saint Sophia *(Basilikon oikogeneiakon tagma ton arion Sophias kai Olgas)* was instituted in 1936 by King George II. As is indicated by the Greek wording, the Order is a Royal Family Order or the King's personal Order. It was instituted in memory of the Queens Olga and Sophia and in reverence to the Orthodox Saints whose names were borne by these Queens. The Order is reserved for women, the highest classes preferably for the Royal Family, and it may be conferred as a reward for special services to the Greek Royal House. The reigning Monarch is the Master of the Order.

The Order has four classes:

1. *1st Class*, which wears the Badge of the Order (436) on a ladies' sash and the Star of the Order (437).

2. *2nd Class*, which wears the Badge of the Order (436) on a ladies' bow and the Star of the Order (437).

3. *3rd Class*, which wears a gold medallion on a ladies' bow.

4. *4th Class*, which wears a silver medallion on a ladies' bow.

The *Badge of the Order* for 1st and 2nd Classes is a crowned gold medallion bearing, in the centre, and on the background of a red-rimmed white Mantua Cross, a portrait of the Orthodox Saints Olga and Sophia garlanded by a blue scroll with the inscription "Agia Sophia – Agia Olga" (Holy Sophia – Holy Olga).

The *Badge of the Order* for 3rd and 4th Classes is a crowned medallion, in gold for 3rd Class, in silver for 4th Class, bearing in the centre, resting on a white Greek Cross with the red contours of a Mantua Cross, a smaller medallion with portraits of the Orthodox Saints Olga and Sophia garlanded by a scroll with the inscription "Agia Sophia – Algia Olga", on a blue background in the lower rounding and with two lions and three hearts in open-work in the upper rounding.

The *Star of the Order* is an 8-pointed silver star with a Badge of the Order for 1st Class in the centre.

The *Riband of the Order* is dark blue with white horizontal stripes as a border along the edges. As a ladies' bow, it is worn below the left shoulder.

The Order of Saint Olga and Saint Sophia: Badge of the Order 3rd and 4th Class

438–442. The Order of George I *(Basilikon tagma toy Georgioy A)* was instituted on 16th January 1915 by King Constantine I in memory of his father, King George I, whose rule was so suddenly interrupted by the King's murder in 1913. The Order may be conferred on Greeks who have distinguished themselves in battle for their country or within public administration, literature and art, the national economy, politics, social activities and science, and also on Greeks overseas whose careers have increased the prestige of Greece. It may also be conferred on foreigners. The reigning Monarch is the Master of the Order.

The Order has a *civil* and a *military* division, each with five classes:

1. *Grand Cross*, which wears the Badge of the Order (438) on a sash and the Star of the Order (439).

2. *Grand Commander*, which wears the Badge of the Order (438) on a necklet and the Star of the Order (440) in silver.

3. *Commander*, which wears the Badge of the Order (438) on a necklet.

4. *Gold Cross*, which wears the Badge of the Order (441) on a chest riband.

5. *Silver Cross*, which wears the Badge of the Order (441) in silver, on a chest riband.

Grand Cross Knights, when wearing large decorations with uniform, also wear the Badge of the Order for the lowest class on a chest riband, in addition to the insignia appertaining to the class.

The insignia are the same for both divisions, except that the military Badges of the Order and Stars of the Order are provided with crossed swords (438–439).

The *Badge of the Order* is a white-enamelled Latin Cross in gold, in silver for 5th Class, with a laurel wreath between the arms of the cross and pendant on a royal crown. The obverse medallion bears the crowned back-to-back monogram of King George I on a red background, with the legend "Iskys moy e agape toy laoy" (The Love of the

People, My strength), the King's motto, on a white background. The reverse medallion bears the dates "1863–1913", the period of King George I's reign.

The *Stars of the Order* for 1st and 2nd Classes are respectively an 8-pointed and a 4-pointed silver star, both with plain rays and with a Badge of the Order in the centre.

The *Riband of the Order* is plain dark red. *George I's Memorial Medal* (442) is attached to the Order. It has three degrees, *gold*, *silver* and *bronze*, and is worn on the chest riband of the Order. The military Badge of the Order is provided with crossed swords.

443–446. The Order of the Phoenix *(Basilikon tagma toy Phoinikos)* was originally instituted on 13th May 1926 as a Republican Order of Merit reserved for foreigners in replacement of the *Order of George* (438–442). The latter Order was withdrawn during the Second Republic (1924–1935) but was altered after the re-establishment of the Monarchy on 18th January 1936 to the present Royal Order of Merit. The Order is named after the mythological Phoenix Bird, which burns itself and its nest every five hundred years and rises rejuvenated from the ashes. This is to symbolize the re-birth of Hellenism or, more concretely, the re-establishment of the First Republic (1827–1832) in the Second Republic. To-day, the Order may be conferred on Greeks who have distinguished themselves in the fight for the Fatherland or have rendered it outstanding services, whether within public administration, literature and art, the national economy or science. It may also be conferred on foreigners. The reigning Monarch is the Master of the Order.

The Order has a *civil* and a *military* division, each with five classes:

1. *Grand Cross*, which wears the Badge of the Order (443) on a sash and the Star of the Order (444).

2. *Grand Commander*, which wears the Badge of the Order (443) on a necklet and the Star of the Order (444).

3. *Commander*, which wears the Badge of the Order (443) on a necklet.

4. *Gold Cross*, which wears the Badge of the Order (445) on a chest riband.

5. *Silver Cross*, which wears the Badge of the Order (446) on a chest riband.

Grand Cross Knights, when wearing large decorations with uniform, also wear the Badge of the Order for the lowest class on a chest riband, in addition to insignia appertaining to the class.

The insignia are the same for both divisions, except that the *military* Badges of the Order and Stars of the Order are provided with crossed swords (446).

The *Badge of the Order* is a white-enamelled so-called "cross pattée" in gold, in silver for 5th Class, pendant on a royal crown. On the obverse, the cross bears a Phoenix in the centre. Since 1949 it has borne a 5-pointed star in the top arm of the cross and on the reverse the monogram of the reigning Monarch.

The *Star of the Order* is an 8-pointed silver star with plain rays. The Star bears a crowned Phoenix in the centre.

The *Riband of the Order* is yellow with black selvedges.

447–448. The Hundredth Anniversary Memorial Medal of the Greek Royal House *(Anamnestikon Sema tes Hekatontaeteridos tes Hellenikes Dynasteias)* was instituted on the occasion of the hundredth anniversary on 30th March 1963 of the accession to the throne of Greece of the Glyckburg dynasty. In addition to the guests at the hundredth anniversary festivities in Athens, it was conferred in the same year on those related to the Greek Royal House.

The Memorial Medal, which has two sizes, one for gentlemen (447) and one for ladies (448), is worn on the left side of the chest.

The Memorial Medal, which is gold, consists of an oval laurel wreath around a cross formed by four crowned Greek "P"s for "Paul I" (1947–1964), with the monograms of the four previous

The Order for Good Deeds: Star of the Order, Grand Cross

Greek Monarchs of the Glycksburg dynasty in the angles of the cross; "GI" for "George I" (1863–1913), "K" for "Konstantine I" (1913–1917 and 1920–1922), "A" for "Alexander I" (1917–1920) and "GII" for "George II" (1922–1924 and 1935–1947).

449. The War Cross 1940 (Polemikos stauros 1940) was instituted by law on 11th November 1940 as a war decoration for the Second World War conferrable on personnel of the Armed Forces for deeds of heroism on the field of battle. It was altered in 1947 to include also the subsequent internal Greek conflicts up to 1952.

The decoration has three degrees, conferred with a *gold*, *silver* and *bronze* crown respectively.

The Cross is a crowned "Cross of Saint George" in bronze with crossed swords between the arms of the cross. The centre medallion bears King George II's crowned back-to-back monogram. The cross is pendant on a red chest riband with a wide blue centre stripe. If conferred a second time, it is provided with a silver crown.

450. The Order for Good Deeds (*Basilikon tagma tes Eypoiia*) was instituted by law on 5th May 1948 in fulfilment of a wish expressed by King George II which he was unable to realize before his death in 1947. The Order is reserved for women, Greek and foreign, and may be conferred as a reward for self-sacrifice to the country, for philanthropic and social activities and for outstandingly brilliant and artistic services to literature and art.

The Order has five classes:

1. *Grand Cross*, which wears the Badge of the Order (450), but larger, on a ladies' sash and the Star of the Order.

2. *Grand Commander*, which wears the Badge of the Order (450), but larger, on a ladies' bow and the same Star of the Order as for 1st Class, but smaller.

3. *Commander*, which wears the Badge of the Order (450), but larger, on a ladies' bow.

4. *Gold Medal*, which wears the Badge of the Order (450) on a chest riband.

5. *Silver Medal*, which wears the Badge of the Order (450), in silver, on a chest riband.

The *Badge of the Order*, which varies in size according to class, is a rose-like

The Florence Nightingale Medal

flower in gold, in silver for 5th Class, formed by five blue-enamelled petals separated by five green sepals and pendant on a royal crown. In the centre, the Badge of the Order bears a medallion with a portrait of the Holy Virgin and Child surrounded by a white scroll with the inscription "Eypoiia" (Good Deed).

The *Star of the Order*, which varies in size according to class, is an 8-pointed silver star with plain profiled rays. The centre medallion is identical with the centre medallion of the Badge of the Order.

The *Riband of the Order* is corn-yellow with pale blue selvedges.

INTERNATIONAL RED CROSS

The Florence Nightingale Medal *(Medaille Florence Nightingale)* was instituted on 16th May 1912 in memory of the British philanthropist Florence Nightingale (1820–1910), whose unselfish services for the improvement of hygiene and military nursing during the Crimean War were epoch-making in relation to modern nursing and the training of nurses. The Medal may be conferred on nurses who have distinguished themselves by special devotion to and nursing of the sick and wounded in war and in peace. It may also be conferred on voluntary auxiliary nurses of the Red Cross who, in time of war or during catastrophies, have rendered outstanding services, and to sisters in management or administration. It may also be conferred posthumously. The Medal is conferred by the Committee of the International Red Cross in Geneva on the recommendation of national Red Cross Committees. Conferment takes place every second year on 12th May, Florence Nightingale's birthday, but to a maximum number of 36.

The *Medal* is an oval pointed medallion in silver gilt. The obverse bears a picture of "The Lady with the Lamp", as Florence Nightingale was called by the soldiers during the Crimean War, with the legend "Ad memoriam Florence Nightingale 1820–1910" (In memory of Florence Nightingale 1820–1910). The reverse bears the legend "Pro vera er cara humanitate perennis decor universalis" (For true and loving humanitarianism – a lasting general propriety), and has space for engraving the holder's name and the date of conferment. As a mounting link, the Medal has a Geneva Cross garlanded by a green-enamelled laurel wreath.

The *Riband of the Order* is white with

narrow yellow border stripes and wide red selvedges. It is worn as a chest riband mounted in a ladies' bow.

UNITED NATIONS

The United Nations Korea Medal was instituted on 12th December 1950 by the UN General Assembly and conferred on all members of the land, air and sea forces of the 17 participating nations for services during the UN action in Korea, 1950–1955.

The *Medal*, which is in bronze bears on the obverse the UN emblem, the polar-projected map of the world garlanded by two olive branches, the symbol of peace. The reverse bears the inscription "For Service in Defence of the Principles of the United Nations Charter".

The *Riband of the Order* consists of 17 stripes of equal width in blue and white, the UN colours. It is worn as a chest riband mounted through the bar of the medallion, and is provided with another bar with the inscription "Korea".

The United Nations Emergency Force Medal was instituted by the UN General Assembly and, according to the statutes of 30th November, 1957, it may be conferred on persons who have carried out 90 days' military patrolling under the UN for the maintenance of peace on the Israeli-Egyptian border.

The *Medal*, which is in bronze, bears on the obverse the UN emblem, the polar-projected map of the world garlanded by two olive branches, the symbol of peace, beneath the initials "UNEF" for "United Nations Emergency Force". The reverse bears the inscription "In the Service of Peace".

The *Riband of the Order* is sand-yellow with a UN-blue centre stripe and on each side a blue and green border stripe for Israel and Egypt respectively.

The United Nations Medal was instituted by the UN Secretary General as a permanent medal which, according to the statutes of 30th July, 1959, may be conferred on military personnel who, for a more specifically fixed period, have carried out satisfactory

The United Nations Korea Medal, The United Nations Emergency Force Medal, and the United Nations Medal

service under the UN in controlling an armistice or in maintaining law and order, wherever in the world this may be required.

The *Medal*, which is bronze, bears on the obverse the UN emblem, the polar-projected world map garlanded by two olive branches, the symbol of peace, beneath the initials "UN" for "United Nations". The reverse bears the inscription "In the Service of Peace".

The *Riband of the Order* varies in colour combination according to the location of service. For the UN Forces in the following countries, it is:

India and *Pakistan*; a dark green centre stripe fading into white towards each side, and with UN-blue selvedges.

Lebanon and *Palestine*; UN-blue with narrow white border stripes.

The Congo; green with white border stripes and UN-blue selvedges.

West New Guinea; UN-blue with a dark-green/white/light-green centre stripe.

The Yemen; a dark brown centre stripe fading into yellow towards each side, and with UN-blue selvedges.

Cyprus; UN-blue with a dark-blue-edged white centre stripe.

SUPPLEMENTARY SECTION OF BRITISH ORDERS, MEDALS AND DECORATIONS

The Albert Medal

In 1866 the Queen instituted the following decorations:-

1. Albert Medal in gold for Gallantry in saving life at sea.
2. Albert Medal for Gallantry in saving life at sea.

In 1877 they were extended for Gallantry on land and were called:-

3. Albert Medal in gold for Gallantry in saving life on land.
4. Albert Medal for Gallantry in saving life on land.

These decorations were known as "The Albert Medal of the First Class" and "The Albert Medal of the Second Class". The medals were inscribed "For Gallantry in Saving Life at Sea" and "For Gallantry in Saving Life on Land". King George V approved the using of the letters A.M. after recipients' names.

In January 1950 King George VI gave orders for the cessation of the Albert Medal in gold, and the restriction of the award of the Medal to post-humous cases where the standard of gallantry was not up to that for the posthumous award of the George Cross, but was nevertheless of a very high standard.

The Medal consists of a bronze, oval shaped badge, having in the centre a monogram composed of the letters V and A erect upon an enamelled background, surrounded by a Garter inscribed in raised letters "For Gallantry in Saving Life at Sea" or "For Gallantry in Saving Life on Land" and surmounted by a reproduction of the Crown

The Albert Medal

of Prince Albert. The Medal is suspended from a riband having two white longitudinal stripes. The colour of the enamel and riband is dark blue when the Medal is conferred for Gallantry at sea, and crimson when it is conferred for Gallantry on land.

Order of the British Empire – Gallantry. On 6th December 1957 a new statute was published differentiating between appointments to the order or awards of the medal made for rewarding acts of gallantry and those which were made to reward meritorious service.

Since this date awards made for Gallantry are distinguished by the wearing of an emblem consisting of two silver oak leaves on the appropriate riband.

Order of the British Empire
-Gallantry Emblem

Imperial Service Order

Imperial Service Order. The Order was instituted by King Edward VII in August 1902. It is awarded in recognition of meritorious service to members of the administration or clerical branches of the Civil Service throughout the Commonwealth. The usual qualification for Companionship is twenty-five years or sixteen years in unhealthy places abroad. The number of Companions is limited, and they are entitled to use the letters "I.S.O." after their names. Men and women are eligible for Companionship. Members of the Civil Service who are not eligible for Companionship of the order may be awarded the "Imperial Service Medal" which is granted under the same conditions as the Order.

The Badge (Men) consists of a seven-pointed star of silver, in the centre of which is a medallion of gold bearing the Royal Cypher of The Sovereign within a circle inscribed "*FOR FAITHFUL SERVICE*", the cypher and inscription in dark blue enamel, and the medallion ensigned with the Royal Crown.

The Badge (Women). This is the same as for men except that a silver laurel wreath replaces the star.

Men wear the Badge suspended from a riband on the left breast, and women wear it suspended from the riband in the form of a bow.

The *Riband* is crimson – blue – crimson of equal width.

The Imperial Service Medal is a circular medal of silver bearing the effigy of the Sovereign on the obverse, and on the reverse the words "*FOR FAITHFUL SERVICE*". It is worn by men and women in the same way, and from the same riband as the Badge of the Order. It is *not* customary to place the letters I.S.M. after the holders' name.

Imperial Service Medal

Royal Red Cross. This decoration was instituted by Queen Victoria on 27th April 1883, and is the first British decoration awarded solely to women for services not confined to a particular country. It may be conferred upon women, whether British or Foreign, who may be recommended for special devotion and efficiency in nursing duties with the forces in the field, or in Naval, Military or Air Force Hospitals or Hospital Ships. It may also be awarded to persons who have given valuable service to the Red Cross or kindred societies at home or abroad.

Recipients of the 1st Class are designated "Members" and are entitled to use the letters "R.R.C." after their names. Recipients of the 2nd Class are designated "Associates" and use the letters "A.R.R.C.".

Recipients of the 2nd Class may be promoted to the 1st Class and subsequent services are rewarded by a Bar.

Badge (1st Class) consists of a gold cross pattée, enamelled red, and edged gold having on the arms the words 'Faith', 'Hope' and 'Charity' and the date 1883. In the centre is a gold medallion on which is the head of The Sovereign, and on the reverse the Royal Cypher.

Badge (2nd Class) is the same size and shape as that for the 1st Class. It is of frosted silver and has superimposed upon it a Maltese Cross enamelled red. In the centre is the head of The Sovereign.

The Cross of both classes is suspended by a ring and is worn on the left shoulder attached to the riband in the form of a bow.

The *Riband* is dark blue with red borders.

Air Force Cross is awarded to Officers and Warrant Officers of the Air Force for an act or acts of valour, courage, in devotion to duty whilst flying, though not in active operations against the enemy. It may also be granted to

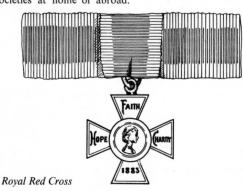

Royal Red Cross

Air Force Cross

Distinguished Conduct Medal. This medal was instituted by Queen Victoria on December 4th 1854, and is awarded to Non-Commissioned Officers and men for gallant and distinguished conduct in the field. It is of silver and is suspended from its riband by an ornamental scroll, and bears on one side the effigy of The Sovereign, and on the other side the embossed words *"FOR DISTINGUISHED CONDUCT IN THE FIELD"*. The *riband* is crimson, dark blue and crimson stripes of equal width. Recipients are entitled to use the letters "D.C.M." after their names. Further acts of gallantry may be rewarded by the award of Bars.

Conspicuous Gallantry Medal. This decoration was instituted by Queen Victoria on July 7th 1874. It is the Naval counterpart of the Army's Distinguished Conduct Medal, and is awarded to Petty Officers of the Navy and Non-Commissioned Officers and men of the Royal Marines who distinguish themselves by acts of conspicuous gallantry in action with the enemy. It may also be awarded to men of the Merchant Navy, and to members of the Women's Royal Naval Service

individuals not belonging to the Air Force (whether Naval, Military or Civil) who render distinguished service to aviation in actual flying.

The decoration is of silver, and consists of a thunderbolt in the form of a cross, the arms conjoined by the wings, and the extremity of the base arm terminating with a bomb. On the arms of the cross is another cross composed of propellor blades, the four ends enscribed with the Royal Cypher. In the centre of the cross is a roundel charged with a representation of Hermes mounted on a hawk in flight bestowing a wreath. On the top of the cross is the Imperial Crown. On the reverse is the Royal Cypher above the date 1918, and the year of award. The holder is entitled to use the letters "A.F.C." after his name, and further acts may be rewarded by the award of Bars.

The cross is worn on the left breast suspended from a riband of red and white diagonal stripes inclined at an angle of 45 degrees from left to right.

Conspicuous Gallantry Medal

for gallantry on shore during enemy action.

The Medal is of silver, and has on one side the effigy of the The Sovereign and on the other side in embossed letters the words "*FOR CONSPICUOUS GAL-LANTRY*" with a crown above, and the words encircled by laurel branches. It is suspended from its riband by a plain clasp.

The riband is white edged with narrow blue stripes. Recipients are entitled to use the letters "C.G.M." after their names. Further acts of gallantry may be rewarded by the award of Bars.

Distinguished Service Medal. This decoration was instituted by King George V, on October 14th, 1914. It is designed to be awarded for courageous service in war by Petty Officers and men of the Royal Navy, Non-Commissioned Officers and men of the Royal Marines and all other persons holding corresponding positions in the naval forces who 'may at any time show themselves to the fore in action, and set an example of bravery and resource

under fire, but without performing acts of such pre-eminent bravery as would render them eligible for the Conspicuous Gallantry Medal'.

It may also be awarded for similar service to men of the Merchant Navy, and members of the Women's Royal Naval Service for gallant and distinguished service ashore during enemy action.

The medal bears on one side the effigy of The Sovereign and on the reverse the words "*FOR DISTIN-GUISHED SERVICE*" surmounted by a crown, and encircled with laurel branches. It is suspended from its riband by a plain clasp. The riband is blue-white-blue stripes of equal width with a narrow blue strip running down the centre of the white.

Recipients are entitled to use the letters "D.S.M." after their names. Further acts of gallantry may be rewarded by the award of Bars.

Military Medal. This medal was instituted on March 25th 1916 by King George V. It is awarded to Non-Commissioned Officers and men of

Distinguished Service Medal

Military Medal

the Army for acts of bravery in the field, and is subject to the recommendation of the Commander-in-Chief. The medal is of silver and bears on the obverse the effigy of The Sovereign, and on the reverse the words "*FOR BRAVERY IN THE FIELD*" surmounted by the Royal Cypher and Crown and encircled with a laurel wreath. It may be awarded to women for devotion to duty under fire, and to personnel of the Royal Air Force for gallant service on the ground.

It is suspended from the riband which consists of three white and two crimson strips in the centre and broad navy-blue border stripes.

Recipients are entitled to use the letters "M.M." after their names. Further acts of bravery may be rewarded by the award of Bars.

Distinguished Flying Medal. This medal is awarded to Non-Commissioned Officers and men of the Royal Air Force in the same conditions as the "Distinguished Flying Cross" is awarded to officers.

The Medal is of silver and oval. On the obverse is the effigy of The Sove-

reign, and on the reverse within a laurel wreath a representation of Athena Nike, winged and helmeted seated on an aeroplane, and releasing a hawk from her right hand, with below the hawk the words "*FOR COURAGE*".

The mounting consists of two wings projecting from the top of the medal, and across the wing tips a horizontal ball-tipped bar which engages the riband. The riband consists of narrow purple and white stripes running diagonally at an angle of 45 degrees from left to right. This riband is similar to that of the Distinguished Flying Cross, but the stripes are narrower.

Recipients are entitled to use the letters "D.F.M." after their names. Further acts of bravery may be rewarded by the award of Bars.

Air Force Medal. This medal is awarded to Non-Commissioned Officers and men of the Air Forces and to others in the same conditions as the Air Force Cross is awarded to Officers.

The medal is silver and oval. The obverse is the same as the Distinguished Flying Medal. The reverse shows a representation of Hermes mounted on a

Distinguished Flying Medal

Air Force Medal

hawk in flight, bestowing a wreath.

The mount is the same as that of the Air Force Cross. The riband is similar to that of the Air Force Cross, but the red and white stripes are narrower.

Recipients may use the letters "A.F.M." after their names. Further acts may be rewarded by the award of bars.

Polar Medal. A medal for Arctic Discoveries was instituted by Queen Victoria in 1857, and it was then called the Arctic Medal. In 1904, King Edward VII instituted the Polar Medal in silver and bronze. Today there is one medal in silver. It is octagonal in shape, bearing on the obverse the effigy of The Sovereign and on the reverse a representation of the ship "Discovery" in winter quarters, with, in the foreground, a sledging party.

The medal is worn on the left breast suspended from a white riband. It is conferred on those who take an active part in an expedition which makes notable advances in the exploration of the Polar Regions, and who, in so doing, undergo the hazards and rigour set by

Polar Medal

the climatic conditions to life and movement whether by land, sea or air. Only those who have participated in an expedition sponsored by one or more Governments of member countries of the Commonwealth, or has been recognised by one or more such Governments, shall be eligible.

Every Polar Medal awarded is accompanied by a clasp worn on the riband and bearing the description of the expedition and date.

Awards of the Medal with Clasp or, as appropriate, of the Clasp only, may be made posthumously.

THE WEARING OF INSIGNIA

When a person receives the insignia of his or her Award, a Card is placed in the insignia box giving instructions as to how the insignia should be worn.

There are however rules which give guidance to those people who are holders of Orders, Decorations and Medals, as to the correct method of wearing them with uniform or civilian dress.

The Wearing of Collars
Collars are worn on "Collar Days". These are special days, such as Saints Days, and they are printed on a card which is placed in the box containing the Collar. They are also worn when The Queen opens or prorogues Parliament, and by those taking part in the introduction of a Peer in the House of Lords. They are also worn when ordered by The Sovereign and at a Religious Service of the Order concerned.

Collars are not worn after sunset.

Wearing of Insignia with Uniform
Members of the Armed Forces should wear the insignia they possess as laid down in the Dress Regulations of the Service to which they belong.

These Regulations cover the wearing

of Orders, Decorations and Medals with the different types of dress – e.g. ceremonial dress uniform, mess kit etc. Rules governing the wearing of insignia with ceremonial dress uniform are:

1. When Collars are not worn the Broad Riband and Badge of the Senior Order is worn. A Knight of the Order of the Garter and a Knight of the Order of the Thistle wears the riband over the *left* shoulder so that the Badge rests on the right hip. Broad ribands of all other Orders are worn over the *right* shoulder so that the Badge rests on the left hip.

2. *Stars* Stars of Orders are worn on the left side of the coat and a maximum of four stars may be worn.

(a) If *one* star is worn it is worn centrally over the heart.

(b) If *two* stars are worn, the star of the Senior Order may be worn immediately above that of the Junior Order, or they may be worn side by side with the star of the Senior Order nearest the centre of the coat.

(c) If *three* stars are worn they are worn in a triangular pattern with the

Wearing of Insignia with Uniform (Ceremonial Dress), with the broad riband of the Senior Order, three stars, two neck badges and medal bar

Star of the Senior Order at the top, and the other two stars in line, and below it. The Star of the Second Senior Order is placed nearest the centre of the coat.

(d) If *four* stars are worn the three senior ones are worn, as described in (c) above, and the Star of the Junior Order is placed below the two in line to form a diamond pattern.

3. *Neck Badges* Not more than three Badges may be worn, and the number depends on the type of coat.

(a) Three Badges may be worn with a high-necked coat, viz. a coat with which a collar and tie are not worn. In this case the Badge of the Senior Order hangs immediately below the top button of the coat, and the second and third Badges immediately below the second and third buttons of the coat.

If only one neck Badge is worn it should hang immediately below the top button, and if two Badges are worn they should hang immediately below the top and second buttons respectively, with the Badge of the Senior Order at the top.

(b) With coats that are worn with a collar and tie, e.g. the ceremonial dress uniform of the Royal Marines and Royal Air Force, only two neck Badges may be worn. The riband with the Badge of the Senior Order is worn around the neck under the collar in such a way that the Badge hangs immediately below the knot of the tie. The second Badge hangs immediately below the top button of the coat.

4. *Breast Decorations* Badges of the DSO., ISO and 4th and 5th Classes of Orders, together with any other Decorations and medals, are worn mounted in the correct order on a bar brooch, and pinned to the left side of the coat above the pocket.

Wearing of Insignia with Full Evening Dress

The rules governing the wearing of insignia with full evening dress are:

1. The Broad Riband of the Senior Order is worn in the correct manner, i.e. Ribands of the Orders of the Garter and

Wearing of Insignia with Full Evening Dress, with the broad riband of the Senior Order, the maximum of four stars, one neck badge and miniatures

Thistle running across the body from left to right, and the ribands of all other Orders from right to left.

The riband is worn under the tail coat but over the waist coat. With evening dress it is more convenient to have a shortened riband, i.e. one that does not pass over the shoulder and down the back of the body. Such a riband is fastened at one end to two buttons at the front of the arm-hole of the waist-coat, and the other end to a button on the bottom of the waistcoat in such a way that the bow and badge rests on the hip.

2. A maximum of four stars may be worn in the same ways as laid down for ceremonial dress uniform.

3. Only one neck badge may be worn. This should normally be the badge of the Senior Order, and should be worn on a riband of miniature width. The riband is worn under the white tie in such

a manner that the badge hangs just below the knot of the tie.

4. Miniatures of all Orders, Decorations and Medals, except those which are never worn in miniature, should be mounted on a bar brooch in the correct order and worn on the left lapel of the coat.

Wearing of Insignia with Dinner Jackets
On 1st September 1964 The Queen approved that previous rules relating to the wearing of insignia with dinner jackets should be amended. Up to that date it was correct for miniatures of Orders, Decorations and Medals to be worn with dinner jackets by those not in possession of full evening dress on those occasions when Orders, Decorations and Medals were to be worn with full evening dress.

The rules are now as follows:
1. Broad ribands of Orders will *NOT* be worn.
2. Only one star may be worn on the left side of the coat.
3. One neck Badge may be worn.
4. Miniatures of Orders, Decorations and Medals are worn in the same way as for full evening dress.

Wearing of Insignia with Formal Morning Dress
Members of the Orders of Knighthood and holders of other Orders, Decorations and Medals may wear this insignia with formal morning dress, should they wish to do so, on official occasions.

The correct way to wear these Insignia is as follows:
1. Knights of the Garter and Thistle, Knights Grand Cross and Knights Commanders should wear the Stars of Orders *only*, in the same manner as for evening dress.

2. Members of the Order of Merit and Order of Companions of Honour, Companions and Commanders of the Order of Knighthood should wear the riband to which the Badge is suspended around the neck in such

a manner that the Badge hangs about an inch below the knot of the tie.

3. Officers or members of any of the Orders of Knighthood and holders of any other Orders (e.g. D.S.O., I.S.O.) Decorations and Medals should wear the insignia mounted on a bar brooch and pinned on the left lapel of the coat.

Wearing of Insignia with Lounge Suits

It is not customary to wear any of the Insignia of a Knight Grand Cross, Knight Commander, Companion or Commander with a lounge suit. This means that broad ribands, stars and neck badges should not be worn. However, there are occasions such as Armistice Day Parades, when those attending are asked to wear medals with lounge suits. It is therefore permissible for those full size Badges of Orders, Decorations and Medals which are mounted on a bar brooch to be worn on the left side of the coat.

At an *evening* function such as a formal gathering of a Regimental Old Comrades Association, when those attending are asked to wear Decorations with lounge suits, it is quite in order for miniatures to be worn in-stead of the full size Badges of Orders, Decorations and Medals.

Wearing of Insignia by Ladies with Uniform

When wearing uniform or coats of military pattern such as are worn by Members of the Women's Services or by Members of the Women's Royal Voluntary Service, Red Cross etc., ladies should wear their insignia in exactly the same way as insignia of similar grades are worn by men in uniform.

With Day Dress and Evening Dress

In general the rules which apply to the wearing of insignia by men apply to ladies also. There is, however, one major difference. Whereas Knights, Commanders, Companions or Commanders wear the Badge of their grade around the neck, ladies wear the Badge suspended from the riband made in the form of a bow on the left side of the coat or dress. The Badge is worn above Stars of Orders and immediately below the bar brooch on which either full size or miniature Badges of Orders, Decorations and Medals are mounted.

Lady in Day Dress, wearing Star of a Dame Commander, Badge of a Companion, and medal bar with full size medals

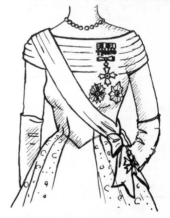

Lady in Evening Dress, wearing the broad riband of the Senior Order, two stars, one badge and miniature

Bibliography

The following list only gives the newer literature on Orders. Material of an official nature published in official Year Books, official Gazettes and Statutes of Orders have not been included.

General literature

Carmelo Arnone: *Ordini Cavallereschi e Cavalieri*. Milan 1954.

Arvid Berghman: *Nordiska Ordnar och Dekorationer*. Malmö 1949.

H. Taprell Dorling & L.F. Guille: *Ribbons and Medals*. London 1963.

Maximilian Gritzner: *Handbuch der Ritter- und Verdienstorden aller Kulturstaaten innerhalb des 19. Jahrhunderts*. Graz 1960.

Klietmann-Neubecker: *Ordens-Lexikon*, 1–3. Berlin 1951–1961.

Ernst August Prinz zur Lippe: *Orden und Auszeichnungen*. Heidelberg/Munich 1958.

Jean-Robert Schleich de Bossé: *The Orders, Decorations and Medals of the Principalities of Liechtenstein and Monaco and of the Republic of San Marino*. Luxembourg 1953.

Robert Werlich: *Orders and Decorations of all Nations*. Washington 1965.

National literature

Administration des Monnaies et Médailles: *Décorations Officielles Française*. Paris 1965.

P.J. d'Artillac Brill: *Beknopte Geschiedenis der Nederlandse Ridderorden*. The Hague 1951.

Giacomo Bascapé: *L'Ordine di Malta e gli Ordini Equestri della Chiesa*, 1–2. Milan 1940–1959.

W.F. Bax: *De Nederlandse Ridderorden en Onderscheidingen*. Rotterdam/The Hague 1951.

Ivan de la Bere: *The Queen's Orders of Chivalry*. London 1961.

R. Cornet: *Les Ordres Nationaux Belges*. Heule 1963.

G.D. Dimacopoulos: *Greek Orders and Medals*, 1–2. Athens 1962–1966.

Albert Fabritius: *Ordnernes og Ordenskapitlets Historie*. De Kgl. Danske Ridderordner og Medailler. Copenhagen 1965.

A.A. da Fonseca & J. de Macedo e Chaves: *Ordens Honorificas Portuguesas*. Lisbon 1940.

Lawrence L. Gordon: *British Orders and Awards*. Stafford 1959.

C. Baron van Heerdt: *Nederlandse en Buitenlandse Ridderorden en Onderscheidingen*. Amsterdam/Brussels 1965.

Henryk Holder: *Ordery i Odznaczenia Polskiej Rzeczypospolitej Ludowej*. Warsaw 1963.

Lauri Jäntti & Chr. Karnila: *Kunniamerkkiaapinen*. Helsingfors 1958.

P.J. Jørgensen: *Danish Orders and Medals*. Copenhagen 1964.

Kurt-Gerhard Klietmann: *Deutsche Auszeichnungen*. Berlin 1957–1965.

Hans Ulrich Krantz: *Orden und Ehrenzeichen der Bundesrepublik Deutschland*. Cologne/Herford 1958.

Vladimir Machácek: *Ceskoslovenské Rády a Vyznamenáni*. Praque 1964.

C. Neville Packett: *The Orders of Knighthood of the Most Serene Republic of San Marino*. Leeds 1959.

F.F. de la Puente y Gómez: *Condecoraciones Españolas*. Madrid 1953.

H. Quinot: *Ordres de Chevalerie et Décorations Belges de 1830 a 1963*. Brussels 1963.

Jean-Robert Schleich de Bossé: *Les Distinctions Honorifiques au Pays de Luxembourg 1430–1961*. Luxembourg 1962.

Jean-Robert Schleich de Bossé: *Les Ordres, Décorations et Médailles du Grand-Duché de Luxembourg depuis 1841*. Luxembourg 1952.

Günter E. Schmidt: *Ehrenzeichen und Medaillen der Republik Österreich und der Bundesländer*. Vienna 1960.

Carsten Svarstad: *Kong Olav V's Belønningsmedaljer*. Gullsmedkunst 12. Oslo 1960.

Carsten Svarstad: *Norges Krigsdekorasjoner*. Gullsmedkunst 3. Oslo 1947.

Joachim Theumert: *Orden und Ehrenzeichen der Deutschen Demokratischen Republik*. Dresden 1964.

P. Marian Tumler: *Der Deutsche Orden*. Vienna 1965.

P. Marian Tumler: *Der Deutsche Orden im Werden, Wachsen und Wirken bis 1400*. Montreal 1955.

James van der Veldt: *The Ecclesiastical Orders of Knighthood*. Washington 1956.

F. Walther: *Soviet Decorations – Décorations Soviétiques*. Montreal 1964.

E.F.Wrede: *Finlands Utmärkelsetecken*. Helsingfors 1946.

INDEX

The reference numbers are mainly to colour plates and correlative text. Where reference is to text or monochrome illustrations within text, the page number is given in italics.